CUBA ON THE ED(
SHORT STORIES Fₙₒₘ ₜₕₑ ₑₛₜ

Edited by Mary G. Berg, Pamela Carmell and Anne Fountain

Critical, Cultural and Communications Press
Nottingham
2007

Cuba on the Edge: Short Stories from the Island, edited by Mary G. Berg, Pamela Carmell and Anne Fountain

The rights of Mary G. Berg, Pamela Carmell and Anne Fountain to be identified as editors in this work have been asserted by them in accordance with the Copyrights, Designs and Patents Act, 1988.

Cover photograph by Richard Van Buskirk

Cover design by Macdonald Daly

First published in Great Britain by Critical, Cultural and Communications Press, Nottingham, 2007

Publisher's website: **www.cccpress.co.uk**

ISBN 978-1-905510-04-7 (UK)
ISBN 978-1-60271-000-9 (USA)
First edition

Printed by CPI Antony Rowe, Eastbourne, E. Sussex, UK.

CONTENTS

PREFACE

Cuba on the Edge presents recent short stories by twenty one of the best Cuban writers on the island. The title refers both to Cubans' awareness of living on the brink of a new future, and their edginess as they negotiate their way through current uncertainties. These twenty one very different authors, translated here by nine translators in order to better retain the remarkable diversity of voices, write primarily about current times and the challenges of survival since the collapse of the Soviet Union, when the Cuban economy slipped into the so-called "Special Period" of 1990s scarcities and ingenious coping strategies.

Twenty one different perspectives on Cuban realities are presented here, all sharp-eyed perceptions of flaws and merits, limitations and freedoms, and the tensions of living (and defining) Cubanness on this island of eleven million people, ninety miles from the Florida coast, embargoed by the U.S. for most of the past half-century yet bombarded with images of U.S. consumer culture.

These stories reflect both light and dark responses to changing times. Some are songs of despair and surrender while others show ways to circumvent shortages and adapt to changing circumstances. Some stories are set in Havana, while others depict rural or small town Cuba. The volume includes both men and women authors, features pieces of both action and description, and projects everyday detail along with abstract concepts. Some tales are leavened by humor; many are not. Some voices make reference to the past, while some suggest the future. Awareness of the present informs all of these fictions, and many address controversial topics: homosexuality, prostitution, drugs, crime, exile, disillusionment, skepticism. But the predominant tone is of celebration of survival, one of rejoicing at the warmth and strength of human commitments, and at the complex variety of Cuban experiences.

The wide variety of writing styles included in *Cuba on the Edge* offers testimony to the vibrancy of current Cuban fiction. At the same time, the mention of literary icons such as Julio Cortázar, Alfonsina Storni, Alejo Carpentier and others reminds us of the connection these works have with the wider world of Latin American writing. Most importantly, this anthology brings stories by many of the best current Cuban writers to English-speaking readers, and provides at least glimpses of Cuba in 2007, an island on the edge of change and challenge.

Mary G. Berg, Pamela Carmell and Anne Fountain

LOST PLACES
Antonio José Ponte

(Obispo Street, Old Havana)
This is my street. Obispo belongs to me, if a person can own a street without having a business or a house on it, or even the house of a lover or a friend on it. I discovered an old photograph of it in an encyclopedia from the beginning of the century: the street of shops, with striped awnings lining the two sidewalks, looks like a souk, an Arabian bazaar, seen from above. Some time ago I wrote that the street in some ways resembled a beach. Bookstores line its upper end and at the lower end the street opens onto the plaza and the port. At that time one of the bookstores sold Russian books and Soviet ships passed through the port. Obispo was contained between those two labels in cyrillic: the title of a book and the name of a ship.

Now its nature has changed a great deal. I no longer see it as a beach, but as a dry riverbed, a river of the eighties. With time even the geography of a street turns grim. Obispo is the bed of an extinct river. The water has gone and left two immense bluffs, two rows of façades.

(Paseo del Prado: empathy with a tree)
It is the first tree that faces the sea. Prado, particularly in winter, seems to me like a ship headed toward the water.

The tree must be a laurel, if the other trees of the Paseo are laurels. A laurel twisted by the wind.

When the northerlies arrive, they go along Prado, and the laurel bends before the gusts like a bony courtesan, a humpback.

At a certain time of the year, during a false autumn, the Indian almonds of the Avenida del Puerto take on fabulous beauty: greens and reds filter light just as stained glass does, and flesh seen beneath the leaves takes on splendorous colors... In Parque Central some nameless trees blossom in yellow chains, the air passing through them ignites and we are inside a colored photograph... But the first laurel of Prado, humpbacked and all, is my tree in the city. Something not yet a symbol, something confusing, never clarified, draws me to it often.

Pointing to a Greek dog, Empedocles was asked, "What makes that dog come and always sit on the same tile?"

"Empathy," Empedocles answered, "there's empathy between the dog and the tile."

7

(*Teahouse of Mercaderes, Old Havana*)
I wrote a novel there in the teahouse on Mercaderes Street.
That is, the novel had pages that happened there and I would have
liked to write the whole book at one of its tables, the way
Europeans write in a café. However, the waitresses wouldn't let
anyone write there. They were very strict about it. They would
count twenty minutes or so, bring the check and put us out. They
didn't trust us, us writers.

I had conversations there with many people: now gone, dead,
forgotten. I learned to converse at those tables. I went there every
day. When I remember the eighties, I remember myself there.

(*A park in Vedado*)
And then said it was decided, it was all over. What could I say
to that? I looked at our surroundings, I was looking with the
resignation and shock of a person who is going to die as soon as
day breaks.

"All right," I said, "better that we not go back together."

I don't know how long I stayed in that park alone. I looked at
details impossible to forget even now.

A year earlier a city had appeared where nothing had been
before. First a window lit up and after that everything began to
grow. Because the window belonged to a building, the building to
a suddenly animated street, the street to a neighborhood, and the
neighborhood to a city that emerged from that window.

And now it would disappear, Atlantis or Carthage or Guernica
or Pompeii.

(*In the old quarter of the whores*)
They must be drying their hair in the sun
the whores of back then who are still alive.
Around their necks a damp towel,
some petals in a pail of water,
their heads of vanquished queens watching a sparrow.

The sparrow is looking for rice grains scattered on the
ground.
What bird's fantasy would not hold the memory
that would save one grain and one night and one man
from so many men and nights that were.

With yellow nails like bird claws the women
lift strands so the sun will reach the skull.
How sad at this hour are the whores of back then
as they prepare their rice and fry an egg and sweet plantain
in oil.

In the old quarter of the whores weariness overwhelms.
What so many books, so many family pictures try to
awaken,
something nameable with density, depth, the essence of
human life,
is found here.
Weariness at seeing photos of groups of heads:
celebrations, rites, convictions, crowds, packed train cars.
In the quarter of repeated gestures
the air has as many layers as puff pastry.
The superpositions, the heaping up
of one generation over earlier ones,
the humus of men weighs down.
In this place one can speak of the denseness of the past as
in no other.

Translated by Cola Franzen

ONLY AFTERNOON IN GRANADA
Antonio José Ponte

I lived just one afternoon in Granada. I climbed up to the Arab quarter. Think of a labyrinth spread over a hillside.

I went into a tea house, a *tetería*. The house had wooden walls and was built as a series of cubicles, labyrinth within a labyrinth, with low ceilings and tables. The air was thick and the music Arabic. It seemed to me that these songs, unlike others, did not advance in time.

I sat down on leather cushions with gilded designs. The small flame of an oil lamp was burning on the table. It was neither hot nor cold inside although outside it was winter.

One of the proprietors (the owners were two brothers) handed me a menu. The way he was dressed reminded me of Isak Dinesen's Somalian servant in Africa. The menu was enormous; I ordered mango tea. I thought about Dinesen and about Paul Bowles. I said to myself: either this is a dream or I am in Tangiers. (My paternal grandmother is peeling a mandarine and asks if I wish a tangerine).

The utensils they brought with the tea were made of clay and I noticed the sieve was of clay also. Later I went out into the street and back down the hill. I asked what the name of that district of the city was.

They answered with an Arabic word that began with al-, like alfalfa or alcove.

The next afternoon I had already forgotten the name. No matter how hard I searched, I couldn't remember it. One night, when I'd forgotten about searching, I got on a bus. A bus in Havana. It was one that had come from Spain; some group in Andalusia had donated it. It immediately seemed very familiar to me. The route indicated by the sign was a route in Spain. I looked at a small map over the window. It had colored lines giving the names of La Alhambra and Generalife. Albaicín was what that district was called where I lived one afternoon.

The bus was traveling through a dark Havana. I could imagine myself once again in Granada.

In *À rebours*, the novel by Huysman, his protagonist in Paris decides to visit London. He prepares for the trip, and with plenty of time before taking the boat, goes into an English restaurant and orders English dishes. His meal finished, he asks his coachman to take him home, because he's already been in London. Lately I've taken Dutch, Swedish or German buses without ever moving from here. They keep their original signs but run along Havana streets. They happily undermine all directions, make Havana even more of a fable.

Translated by Cola Franzen

BEFORE THE BIRTHDAY PARTY
Adelaida Fernández de Juan

As she was going over the guest list and had gotten as far as the sixteenth child, the lights went out. She swore as usual, waited a few minutes to see if they would come back on again right away, and then since the eleven P.M. blackout continued, she grumpily began the tedious process of lighting the Chinese hurricane lamp. It was a half hour before, sweaty and irritated, she got back to the task at hand. There would be twenty-five children altogether, and if each one came with an adult, that would be fifty, but she preferred to calculate a total of one hundred, bearing in mind everyone's craving for sweets and the recently established custom of having the whole family show up for children's birthday parties. To make sure she wasn't leaving out anyone important, she double-checked her list. Her son's cousins, her own friends' children, the grandchildren of their parents' friends, and her boss's (as well as her husband's boss's) nieces and nephews: no question about it, they all had to be invited. Neighborhood kids, friends from the park, her son's classmates from school. And it would be a good idea to include the four children from the local shops: the grocer's boy, the bread distributor's two, and the new butcher's nephew. Her first estimate of around a hundred still seemed about right; it allowed some leeway for the unexpected. She went on to her second list, and she was alarmed by how little she had managed to acquire these past six months. Cardboard party boxes,* plastic glasses, spoons of some kind, a flowered tablecloth for the cake table, a lidded pail for the lemonade, little candles and paper streamers: these were all on her list, and so far she had only managed to get the tablecloth and the pail, both on loan from her cousin in San Antonio de los Baños. She adjusted the lamp as it was about to flicker out, and feeling really anxious now, she went on perusing her notebook of lists, labeled optimistically "Sonny's Birthday." Now she had to deal with the hardest part: food and drinks. The cake they were entitled to from the state, and, in case that didn't come through, a homemade cake, too, since you never know. Lemonade from the state grocery, and some instant powdered. She'd put a little arrow beside this last item, leading to a reminder

---

* At a birthday party in Cuba, food is traditionally served in individual fold-up cardboard boxes. These boxes became extremely scarce in the nineties.

note: she could sell the rice for dollars so she could get this. She'd make a cold salad with the elbow macaroni she'd put aside four months ago. I'd better check on that, and also on that twenty peso pineapple I froze so my husband wouldn't see it and be outraged by how much it cost. She was all set for the mayonnaise: the old woman on the corner who had high blood pressure had promised it, and, pleased, she crossed it off the list. As for the cakes, she'd already stood in line to place the order for the state cake, down at city hall, and she'd taken that coupon over to the other address they gave her, but she put a question mark beside it because they'd explained to her that she could come collect it the day of the party if the eggs had arrived, if there'd been enough gas for the oven, and if the power hadn't gone off, if the heat wasn't unbearable, ...and if it wasn't pouring rain because the woman who delivers them lives a long way away and travels by bicycle. No problem with the homemade cake, but I'll have to sell the unrefined sugar and the scouring powder. She wrote "Margarita" beside the cake entry, since she was always ready to buy anything. I'd better go see her tomorrow, she thought, then she focused on the drinks issue. If she couldn't get their ration quota of lemonade from the state grocery, as so often happened, then she could sell the rice to buy that powdered mix, the "Caresses" brand. At this point I couldn't care less whether it's a caress or a pinch if it tastes all right and fills up the pail. The power came back on around dawn and, relieved, she moved the lamp off the dining table. Rather than continuing to agonize over all the things she still lacked, she decided to go to her bedroom to check the box of small surprises she'd collected for the piñata and to sort out the toys she'd bought little by little for the day of the party. There aren't enough, she fretted to herself, as she wrapped them one by one. Fourteen little rubber airplanes, all of them green, twelve whistles, ten ping-pong balls, and eight little plastic boats, three of them missing their sails. It doesn't matter, I'll fill the piñata with the candies Katia the Russian lady makes, and with little wads of old newspapers. She tried to reassure herself, and then nervously opened the notebook again. But as she read the next list of things she still had to get, she felt her energy evaporate. Damn, she'd managed to forget this part. Paper hats, masks, horns and balloons: people always had them. We can use condoms for balloons, and we can get the horns made by Octavio, the crazy guy with the pushcart, but what about hats and masks? They're made out of cardboard, like the little boxes and like most party spoons. Reorganizing the various items eased her anxiety a little, and she grouped them, with a note: go out to the cardboard factory that's on the road to the airport. Talk to Jorge, who sells gasoline. The last list was labeled Entertainment. She'd have to ask the principal of Sonny's school for a tape of children's songs; she won't turn me down if I take her a bar of soap, and we can borrow a tape player from Ariel, the son of the pilot across the way, but what about the clown? She pondered a few moments, trying to think of some clown who wouldn't tell dirty jokes, who wouldn't be so old he'd scare the kids or so young they wouldn't laugh, and she remembered that neurosurgeon who brightened up the children's parties at the hospital. He was doing it for free on that occasion, we'll see what he says about this time, but it seemed like a good idea, and she looked up the number of the neurological clinic so she could call the next day. When she thought she had everything all organized and knew more or less whom she'd have to ask about each thing, she went to bed, taking care not to make a sound. She dreamed of pink paper streamers and piñatas that rained down bicycles and empty soda pop bottles. Twelve days of making deals, purchases, sales, barters, and plan changes followed, then barely twenty-four hours before the birthday party, she decided to discuss it all with her husband, just to go over everything one last time and make sure her lists were accurate.

You're worrying too much, calm down, you act like you're organizing a boot camp graduation ceremony for a huge class of cadets, he said. But she was so insistent, that he obliged and readied himself to listen. After all, what with meetings, people leaving the country with no notice, and being on call at the hospital, he really had no idea how all the preparations for the party were going.

We don't have enough cardboard boxes or spoons, she said. At the factory they said they don't sell them there, that I should go to a party outlet. And what's that? he asked. I don't know - see if you can find out, because I've looked everywhere in this neighborhood and I could only find twenty-eight boxes and nineteen spoons. Okay, tomorrow I'll track it down, said her husband. Write "pending" next to that one.

Uncle Carmelo can bring glasses on the day of the party and, since they don't make paper steamers any longer, he promised me the extra magazine pages that are left over at the print shop where he moonlights as a watchman. And what about the next item?, she asked. Yes, dear, tell me about the next disaster, answered her husband, condescendingly. No one has had new birthday candles in stock since the blackouts began. I swapped a torn towel for the bottom half of a used candle, she nearly sobbed. Calm down, calm down, I'll get four matches and that way Sonny can blow them all out. If you stick that big fat candle in, it'll look like a funeral, and it'll make a huge hole in the cake. Go on to the next item on your agenda. You're making fun of me, and I won't put up with that. We're talking about Sonny's birthday party, and none of this is his fault; you know I don't want him to suffer. Fine, that's enough, don't get all upset; tell me about the rest of it; I'm on duty all day tomorrow, and I can't stay up all night listening to your complaints. How many quarts of lemonade do we have? he asked, to make up for his impatience. Quarts, you say? At the grocery, they told me they have a nineteen-month backlog of orders, so forget about normal channels. So what are the abnormal channels? Just give me the facts quickly, without comments, sweetheart. Okay, you know I couldn't sell the rice the way I'd planned because it's the beginning of the month so it's worth less and the going price is thirty-five cents per pound instead of the fifty Lilia had quoted me. And now that bitch is saying that fifty cents is only after the twenty-fourth of the month, and she's telling me this when she knows I only have a day left before the party. I said no comments, he reminded her, you don't have to explain the commodities market to me. Stick to what you want me to do something about. Fine, if you want the short version, I'll give it to you straight out. Tomorrow night you have to go to an address I'll give you later, where there's a lemon tree whose owners are on vacation in Júcaro or Morón, I don't remember which, but somewhere over that way, because when I was told about it I remembered the famous march from Júcaro to Morón that we heard about in History class our first year at the university. Do you remember, dear? The teacher was a short woman with blue eyes and we saw her later at the Maternity Hospital having twins. They were both boys, with low birth weights. What you'd expect with such a small mother who chain smoked, and I'd warned her about that... Please, he cut in, yawning, just tell me when and where I have to steal lemons, if you would get to the point. Sorry, I just get caught up remembering. The house is really close to here, right near Leticia's – the one who sold us... Never mind, I'll give you the exact address later. Can I tell you about the next thing? Sure, let's go on, if I don't get arrested for the last item. There's a small problem with the home-made cake. I already talked to the mining engineer who is making it for us, and he's willing to make us a huge one with fifty eggs, twenty pounds of white sugar and fourteen pounds of flour if we give him a polyester guayabera shirt. I was thinking, dear, of the one in your closet, the one that you don't much like, that peach-colored one, that you were given by the patient you operated on that night we came back from the beach, remember? A really friendly guy who was selling woven sandals like the ones your Uncle Manolo likes, that have a buckle. I know the one you're talking about, sweetheart, he interrupted. It's the only dress shirt I have, but if that's the problem, it's fine with me to give it to the engineer. The problem, love, is that that's not the hard part. The thing is that we have to go pick the cake up at the engineer's house. He lives on the eighteenth floor of that building on G Street where the elevator has been out of order since the floods last year, but I think it's worth it, because with these strong, handsome legs you have, dear, you won't have any problem going up and down those stairs, if the result is a splendid cake for Sonny, topped with blue meringue like I wanted, that manly blue that he likes so much, right? What are you saying, dear? You're gone way overboard, woman! Stark, raving mad! You think I'm Mandrake the Magician?

Speaking of magicians, there won't be a clown. The neurosurgeon has gone to Miami, imagine that, he took advantage of a course he was sent to in Costa Rica, where apparently he got together with a sister who had also stayed on in San José five years ago, and from there they figured out how to make the leap. That's the last straw! You ask me to chase all over the city looking for party outlets no one has ever heard of; you want me to come up with four matches in a city of perpetual blackouts, to steal lemons, to give up my dress clothes, to climb stairways to heaven; and now I have to listen to the story of a neurosurgeon clown who took off for Miami? Don't yell, sweetheart, you might wake Sonny, and just think about him, dear, and his birthday party, love, and how pleased he'll be when he gets older and sees the photos. The photos! My lord, the photos! How could I forget about that! Do you think that Philosophy professor who was in Jalisco Park on Sunday taking pictures of children on the merry-go-round would be willing to come over here? He was whispering to all of us there, "Photos, photos, sixty cents in dollars," wasn't he? Oh, darling, first thing tomorrow could you go over to the park and ask him? It won't be more than fifteen photos, I promise you, and the money from the rice should cover it, because even if I only get thirty-five cents a pound ... sorry, I don't want to burden you with all this ... but tomorrow when you're out looking for the party outlet store, you can make a little detour and go by Jalisco Park. All right? What's next on the list?, was the answer. Right. There's an art historian who has teamed up with a plastic surgeon in a juggling act that's supposed to be spectacular. I heard about them from Olga María, the seamstress, who, incidentally, made Sonny's new shorts and shirt outfit in exchange for a bottle of shampoo you weren't using, that red-labeled one for dry hair, you just use the green-labeled one for oily hair, right? Anyway, she said she saw the act and they're terrific. They juggle balls, hoops, and torches wrapped with cotton on the ends that they light when they can get alcohol, and children love it. According to her, they charge between a hundred and fifty and two hundred pesos, but — don't have a fit — that's what a pair of corduroy pants costs, and I already talked to Margarita and she has agreed to buy the ones you gave me for Valentine's Day. You don't mind that, do you, dear? Anything else? murmured her husband through another yawn. Yes, dear, how do you think it all goes together? Just picture how it will be, and tell me if you don't think the patio looks marvelous with the table from our neighbor Cecilia covered with my cousin's flowered tablecloth, the engineer's blue cake, the pail full of lemonade, a plate of the Russian's candies left over after stuffing the piñata, and the walls all decorated with inflated condoms and pictures from magazines. In the center, imagine the team of jugglers with their hoods, balls, and flaming torches. What do you think, my love? A brothel scene right out of *Star Wars*, he pronounced. Don't tease me, darling, don't be melodramatic! If I can get some gentian violet to paint the condoms, it would brighten things up. What are you telling me now? That the circus whores had ringworm? Oh go to hell! You aren't willing to give up a thing for your son's sake! Don't you even care about making it a happy day for him? You're getting hysterical; I could tell you to go to hell too, so calm down right now. Calm down? You don't even know what you're going to give him! When are you going to get around to fixing that tricycle for him, the one that's been out in the garage since Columbus landed? When you give me time to go looking for spokes, but why bring that up now? Aren't you satisfied with how I rigged the stove to keep the gas from coming through the oven when you turn on the only burner that works? Isn't it enough for you that I fixed up that pipe in the bathroom window so you can wash your hair with rain water? Don't you like the Chinese lamp I traded for my sugarcane harvesting boots? Have you even thought to ask how I managed to seal the leaks in the living room ceiling with modeling clay? And that day in... What are you laughing about? Did I say something funny? Hey, cut that out, you look like a madwoman! Don't laugh so hard; everybody'll hear us. What are you up to, woman? Get hold of yourself, please, look what time it is.

Dawn found them in each other's arms, with just enough time for that embrace. They felt strangely joyful, as though hope, which had seemed to ebb away from them lately, were beginning to return once more.

Translated by Mary G. Berg

OPERATION DOGBITE
Adelaida Fernández de Juan

I told my mom that a dog bit me and she got furious. First of all because a dog bit me and then because I told her about it so calmly and last of all because my mom gets furious about everything. First she checked me over from top to toe looking for the bite, then she cried and shook me really hard, and last of all she hugged me real tight like she wanted to bite me. When she let go of me, I showed her the bite. It's a little scratch on my right foot. It was so tiny I didn't think it was a big deal and that's why I told my mom so calmly that a dog bit me across from the pharmacy. But when I told her that, besides checking me all over, she made me take her to exactly where it happened.

Across from the pharmacy, I said. Get dressed and take me over there right now, she said. When we were almost there, I realized that my mom was still in her bathrobe. I didn't say a single solitary word but I crossed my fingers that no one on the street would see us. My mother, all furious and in her bathrobe on her way to the pharmacy, is a scarier sight than all the dog bites on all the streets in the whole entire world. No one saw us along the way. Lucky for us.

This is the place, I said when we got to the steps of the old house across from the pharmacy. My mom grabbed my hand and we went in together. A man who watches out for furious moms in bathrobes so they don't come charging in tried to stop us, poor guy. My mom, just by looking at him, made him step back. She didn't have to say a single solitary word.

My mom climbed some stairs that went back to Spanish times, dragging me along with her. I'm not sure what times the first door we came to was from, but it must be from now because it opened when my mother touched it. When she's not furious, which is before or after she gets furious, she explains lots of stuff to me. Like how everything that was built in the old days is better. But now when we got to the top of the stairs, in the room my mom and I had gone right into, there was a bald man sitting behind a desk.

Without thinking twice about it, my mom grabbed my foot that had the scratch on it and shoved it right under that bald man's nose. The poor guy tried to pick up the phone next to him. My mom told him she demanded an immediate explanation and he should put down the phone and quickly go find the Doberman

19

that attacked me. The poor bald man said Good afternoon, Ma'am, is this some kind of joke?

Meanwhile, the man who watches by the front door had come upstairs and now he was in the room with us. My mom was yelling and calling them murderers from Hitler's times. I bet you could hear her all the way to the pharmacy and way into outer space and beyond. I closed the new door, just in case, and I managed to tell them that I got bit by a dog in the yard of this house. It's not a house, he said, it's the Union of Economic Functionaries of Cuba - my mom and me were in the offices of the prestigious UEFCU, where no one had or had ever even thought of having a dog, and so could we please just go away before they had to call the police, that's what he said.

That made my mom even furiouser than before, and she told them that first she'd shit on the UEFCU, and then on the Doberman's mother, and last of all on the police, even if they showed up on the horses they use in Canada. My son never tells lies, she said that too, and it was a sheer miracle I hadn't bled to death through my foot and she personally would strangle with her own two hands first the Doberman and then the two of them.

Let's get out of this UEFCU or whatever it's called, and you take me to the beast's yard, she said to me. We ran down the stairs. I almost got tangled up in my mom's robe and lots of people were peeking out of other rooms at the Union of Economic Functionaries of Cuba. I led her past piles of dry leaves and empty cans and wet cardboard and scraps of old soccer balls and brown newspapers that I play in once in a while. What do you think you're doing in all this shit she asked me, sticking her hands then her arms and last of all her legs into those piles of junk. She told me how there might well be squirrels, scorpions, spiders, snakes, ferrets, owls and parrots from the Isle of Youth living in there.

She said no wonder the economy of the country was in the mess it was in, if those morons in there couldn't even be bothered to notice what a garbage dump they have in their yard. When she was in up to her neck, a lady from the pharmacy who knows us crossed the street to ask us what was going on. My mother took her over to a corner of the yard where there's an old rusty metal clothesline, and explained to her. I pretended I wasn't listening, but I caught something about how if that Doberman didn't show

20

up, they'd have to give the boy twenty-one shots in the middle of his back. When she said that, my mom put her arms around the pharmacy lady and started crying.

And so did I. I went up to the side of the lady where my mom wasn't, and I cried because I was so sorry that I had ever said anything to my mom about a dog biting me. I was also crying because I wasn't going to put up with getting twenty-one shots in the middle of my back or let alone anywhere else just because of a shitty little scratch from that runt of a stray dog. And last of all, I cried because there was no way my mom wasn't going to make me get twenty-one shots in the middle of my back.

The pharmacy lady who knew us said to calm down - she was going to help us. She said the UEFCU office workers were all good people who meant well, and they got to work even before dawn, and they stayed until nighttime. And that's why they had no idea what was going on outside and they never had time to pay attention to anything. Then my mom said that I always came first for her, way far ahead of the UEFCU to begin with, ahead of all the economists in the universe second, and last, even ahead of all the Canadian Mounted Police. And that before she'd let them give me twenty-one shots in the middle of the back, she was going to find that ferocious beast. I spoke up to tell her that the dog was really tiny, pretty hairless and dirty, and it didn't look anything like a Doberman.

I don't give a damn, she said. We have to find it. Go home and get a piece of bread, she said, and we'll watch all night to see if that miserable dog shows up here.

The pharmacy lady who knows us couldn't talk her out of this and I couldn't either, so we stayed there in the UEFCU junk piles until it got light. The economists left at eleven at night, came back at five in the morning and didn't even notice that my mom was still in her bathrobe.

At seven in the morning the pharmacy lady brought over some coffee for my mom and me. She said it seemed pretty extreme to not even go home to sleep. Wouldn't it be better to just wait calmly and she'd let us know when the dog showed up? I'll give you until noon, said my mom. We'll go because the truth is that if it isn't rabies, it'll be some other damn sickness or another and then they'll have to give the boy and me eighty shots in the middle of the back, not just twenty-one.

We went home and washed up, then just before lunch the phone rang. The lady thought she had seen the dog going into the UEFCU yard. We went running out, my mom in flip-flops and me in a shirt from when I was in third grade. When we showed up there, the dog looked even more startled than the bald man that first day. My mom picked up one of the bricks from Spanish times that keep falling off the wall by the entry gate and threw it at the dog.

First because of all the junk piled up there, then because it ran faster than lightning, and last, because of my mom's bad aim, the dog got away without a scratch. It went tearing across the corner of the yard where the rusty clothesline was, and dashed into the traffic on 23rd Avenue. The pharmacy lady, the man who watches over the door of the UEFCU and me, we all tried to stop my mom, fat chance of that.

We realized what she was going to do first when she rolled her pants up to her knees, then when she stepped out of her flip-flops, and last when she took off over the piles of trash and headed for the avenue. Take care of the boy for me, she yelled, as she ran out into the lines of the trucks, taxis, bicycles and everything else that goes racing down 23rd.

I wanted to die. First because I was mortified when I saw my mom running barefoot across the most important street in my neighborhood, next because the other women from the pharmacy, the economists from the UEFCU, the neighbors and whoever else happened to be around just then all stopped to stare with their mouths hanging open at my mom running barefoot across the Avenue (which is like saying the most famous street in the world), and last because I was so sorry that I had ever said anything to my mom about that dog bite.

Since I wasn't dead, I hid behind a car that looked old enough to go back to Spanish times that was parked on the sidewalk between the pharmacy and the UEFCU. That's where I started thinking about what to tell my friends in the neighborhood when they found out. They always give me a hard time when my mom comes out to stick up for me. They don't know that nothing makes my mom furiouser than when I don't know how to stick up for myself, and that's why she comes out to yell at them. After a little while, I saw my poor mom coming back with her tongue hanging out, her hair all messed up and a scary expression on her face. The pharmacy lady who knows us handed her the flip-flops she'd been holding for her, and she gave us some big news. There's this place called AnimalWatch, which is where they keep an eye on animals who bite kids - that's what they told her when she called from the pharmacy phone. They watch them for ten days and after that a specialist decides if the kid who was bit has to have twenty-one shots in the middle of his back or not, they told her that, too.

And do the AnimalWatchers come pick up the animals?, my mom asked. No, you have to take them over there, said the pharmacy lady as she gave us the address. My mom sat down on the UEFCU wall from Spanish times that hasn't collapsed yet, thinking what to do next. The man who watches at the door came over with a glass of water for my mom and that gave me a chance to say that we should organize a commando operation like in the movies, with signals and countersigns, and all take turns watching for the dog. My mom let out a big Christmassy laugh that I didn't like one bit, but the man who watches at the door and the pharmacy lady both said that wasn't such a bad idea, that if we formed a commando unit and we all had whistles, we could communicate with each other when the dog came back, and then all together we could catch it.

My mom, without saying a single solitary word about the commando operation, decided it would be better if we went over to the place called AnimalWatch. At the door there, a nice lady greeted us. She was very nice. My mom shoved my right foot under the lady's nose so she could see that yes indeed a dog had really bitten me. The lady was really nice. She moved my foot out from under her nose while she explained that her job was to mind the door. She said a bald comrade was the specialist who observed the biting animals, but he didn't happen to be there just then. The bald comrade had gone over to the Esperanto school without saying when he'd be back. Who the hell cares about Esperanto, my mom asked, and what's the bald comrade doing at that school when he should be out picking up wild animals who attack children in the street.

The nice lady shrugged her shoulders to answer both questions at the same time. My mom looked at her furiously, like she was ready to bite her, and asked her aren't you in charge of anything? Can't you help me somehow?

She was an expert animal catcher, the lady said in a very nice way. She said she had once captured a desperately hungry bear from the Zoo who was looking for meat in a tenement courtyard in Central Havana. Another time a tourist who had brought in a crocodile in his backpack had tried to use it as a scare tactic to get out of paying his rent. It bit the landlord's daughter, she said, and so the landlord ripped off one of the tourist's ears. And another time, a woman like my mom came to AnimalWatch looking for the bald comrade because there was a nest hanging from the eaves on the roof of her building, and wasps kept flying out of it and stinging her son who was about my age. And the nice lady said that woman was tired of calling the firemen and the ambulances and the Civil Defense and having no one show up who was brave enough to deal with the wasps. Just then, the nice lady explained, the bald comrade was at the Yiddish Academy and couldn't go help anyone, so she, even though her job was to mind the door, went over with a butterfly net and knocked down the wasps' nest.

For her, a simple dog was a piece of cake. All she needed was the address of the place. And we could leave the rest of it up to her, she said. My mom wrote that down and our names and the address, and we went home. We were just sitting down to supper when the phone rang. The pharmacy lady who knows us had seen the dog go into the UEFCU yard, but when she whistled like we'd agreed, the man who watches at the front door hadn't come out. What do I do now, she asked us.

I heard my mom say that the commando operation wasn't going to work with a man in the middle of it, so please, call the nice lady at AnimalWatch and tell her to meet us at the corner of the yard where there's a rusty clothesline. Without changing our clothes my mom and I headed right over. Since the nice lady from AnimalWatch took a while to get there, the pharmacy lady and I started throwing kisses to the dog, who just stared at us looking confused from between an empty Buccaneer beer can and what used to be an egg crate from the La Puntilla store.

Meanwhile, my mom went the other way through the UEFCU yard, down past the rusty clothesline, looking for a long stick she could tie something onto the end of that would work like a rope. Luckily, she found what was left of a coconut tree that looked like it had been hit by lightning way back in Spanish times. Just like the natives from the times of the conquest, only furious, my mom broke off a big piece of the trunk and started to pull the bark into strips. By the time the nice lady who minds the door at AnimalWatch got there, me and the pharmacy lady who knows us had sore lips from all the kisses we'd been throwing at the dog

While the pharmacy lady and I almost died making sucking sounds with our mouths, my mom and the lady from AnimalWatch caught the dog, using the piece of the coconut tree and the rope made of bark strips. Then we all held the stick, with the squirming animal tied to the end of it, until the man who watches at the door got there on a rented bicycle. He said he hadn't forgotten about the commando operation but we needed some way to get the dog over to AnimalWatch, so that's why he wasn't there from the beginning of the operation.

We got into a bit of an argument at this point because according to the very nice lady we had to have her with us in order to get into AnimalWatch. The man who watches at the door said he'd rented the bicycle from the bald economist on the condition that he'd be the only one to pedal it, and we'd better keep a good hold on that dog on the way over since there was no way in the world he was going to let himself in for twenty-one shots in the middle of his back.

My mom, really furious, decided that the UEFCU man who watches at the door could pedal the bicycle to AnimalWatch with the dog tied onto the bike rack, while the pharmacy lady who knows us, and the very nice lady who minds the door, and my mom and me walked alongside it holding onto the dog. That's how we got to AnimalWatch, acting as if we'd found a treasure from the Spanish times.

After we got the animal into a cage, my mom invited all the commandos of Operation Dogbite back to our house for coffee, and they all said thank you very much but we're really exhausted from all this. When my mom and I were leaving, the nice lady who minds the door at AnimalWatch gave us their phone number again, so we could find out after ten days if the bald expert comrade decided I'd have to have twenty-one shots in the middle of my back or not.

The ten days are up today. My mom has called several times but the nice lady says the bald comrade went out to get the forms to register for Swahili. That in her opinion, there's nothing wrong with the dog and she doesn't think I'll have to have any shots, but until the expert comes back we shouldn't say a single solitary word about hearing from her.

Translated by Mary G. Berg

MY MOTHER THE WRITER
Adelaida Fernández de Juan

Today I went out with my mother.

One of her friends wrote a book and besides giving a lot of lunches and a few dinners in his honor, and listening to him (my mother, not me), today we went to the place where they presented the book. At the presentation were other friends of my mother, friends of the author of the book, and other writers. All of the friends were writers. There were only a few women there and no children besides me. The women were more or less my mother's age, and they looked alike. They looked like each other and like my mother — overall, they were a group of pretty similar-looking women. All of them, like my mother, wore those loose dresses that go from the neck to the feet, without anyone being able to guess anything about the tits or butts of these women who get together every once in a while.

It's not unusual for them to come to our house. When they come — together or separately, I don't care, I already told you what their dresses are like, as if they didn't have tits or anything worthwhile — my mother makes tea and they start saying bad things about the writers that are men.

It's not just my mother who talks. They all say things that I only half understand, but I know they are bad, really bad. After all of them say how much I look like "that sonofabitch who left the island" when my mom makes me greet them, I shut myself in my room. First I jack off trying to imagine one of their tits, and later, while I do my homework, I listen to the conversations coming from the living room where they're gathered.

"They don't have us in mind"…"those bastards who get to travel"…."they're all in that same group"…"they gave him the prize because he's a man" are some examples.

When I say I half understand, it's so that I won't seem stupid. Actually, I don't understand any of it. If "that sonofabitch" left, why do my mom and the others want to travel? What is this about a famous group anyway? What could being male or female have to do with a prize?

I always win the history and math competitions at school, and no one has ever told me that I win because I'm male. According to my mother, I am the smartest child who's ever been born and that's why I always win. She also says that being born male is a passport for life. I have no idea what that means, but I know it's good, really good.

After drinking tea and saying bad things about the men who are writers, the women talk about really boring things that no one is interested in, like lettuce soaps, aloe creams, cucumber lotions and other disgusting stuff like that. That's when I regret having jacked off thinking about one of them, but it's too late.

Anyway, if the men writers visit us (I like using the plural, as if they came to see me) they don't drink tea but instead rum, which they bring themselves.

I also have to greet them in the living room and hear that I look like "that sonofabitch". Some of the men don't say the last part, "...that left"; they just say "that sonofabitch", but it's basically the same. They always tell me how I've grown, that I should take care of my mother, that she is the most beautiful writer in Cuba, and that I should drink rum with them. Clearly I say YES to the first sentences and NO to the last one without even having to look at my mom. On days like that, all my mother's royal qualities come out, and I could imagine her as a queen.

Surrounded by them, she smiles like I think the queen bee would with the drones. I don't dare to look at her much. I'm wondering if they're from the famous group that gives prizes only to others from within its circle.

It's not good to listen in on conversations, and rum isn't good either. They drink it without knowing that later my mom calls them a "bunch of drunks" when they leave, which isn't good either, but she doesn't know I hear everything.

We are always keeping a close eye (and this time the plural is serious) on the results of the contests. If it were up to me, she would win all of them. I can't think of another house in the world that depends as much on prizes as we do. My skates, for example, were written by my mother over more than six months. It was a book called *Defended Woman*. The wicker set we have in the living room (where the writer friends come sit together) came from a novel that my mother called *Sexuality and Independence* (I should say that all her titles are complicated).

With my backpack for school we weren't so lucky. We were going to buy it with a prize my mother was going to win in a magazine. This was going to happen in August, in time for the beginning of school. A man (I assume from the famous group) won first prize. That's why my backpack isn't so good: because it's an honorable mention backpack.

Things like chickens and cleaning mops don't worry my mother and me. We can get by on the provincial prizes. It doesn't matter if the contest is about love, or owls, or the Republic.

My mother writes for her daily bread and butter (that's what she says).

These are things that I respect a lot.

When it gets near my birthday, my mom writes like crazy, day and night. My cargo pants and my shirt with the alligator on it came from a book of stories. It's called *Looking for a Lover*, and my mother made me swear I'd never read it. According to her it's a piece of shit, but the truth is, the clothes are great.

Sometimes the other women who write win, and they all get together to celebrate. I don't understand how my mother can be happy about that. I also don't understand how she stands being friends with the person who could deprive us, for example, of the lamp we need in my room. We have a list of the things we need, my mother and I. She writes the complicated title of the possible book next to each one.

The Sun that Doesn't Sleep was beside Washing Machine, *The Way We Were Then* is by Kitchen Table. Next to my Lamp is *Feminine Revindication*.

I say "is" because it's still there. That's the book we just lost with. We already got the washing machine and the table, but my lamp is still on the list. The man we went to congratulate won.

After hearing about how marvelous the winner is, how good the book is and all that, my mother hugged the two writers. First the one who talked (if he said what he said it's because he belongs to their group, I imagine) and then the one who won (he'll probably be even more famous than the group now).

I don't know why I went out with my mom today. To top it all off, I couldn't even see a single tit that was worth the trouble.

Translated by Mary G. Berg

PASSING JUDGMENT*
Nancy Alonso

The road to the airport was just about deserted at that hour, one thirty or so in the morning. All the better for Atilio who could gun his Lada and get there on time. The Cubana Airlines flight from Madrid was scheduled to arrive in Havana at two and Atilio, a punctual man, was running late. It was Claudia's fault. She had held him up with one of her endless arguments pressuring him to leave his wife, as if that were so easy.

Atilio walked into the airport and cursed his bad luck: the Madrid flight listed on the board was confirmed to land at three thirty, more than an hour late. The popular saying was right again: *Cubana Airlines: flights arrive and depart whenever.* There was nothing to do but wait. After all, was this not a waiting room? Claudia would also have to wait for him longer than anticipated.

The tourism agents in charge of hotel transportation for the Spanish delegation that Atilio was to meet were there already. Everything was under control. Everything except for the damned plane.

There were not enough seats in the lobby to accommodate the waiting crowd, so some people began a game of musical chairs ("Move your feet, lose your seat"); others paced about impatiently, looking at their watches as if that would speed up time. A few casually plunked themselves down on the floor, oblivious to the dirt, while the more gregarious ones formed groups to chat the time away.

Atilio felt the urge to smoke. He reached into his pocket but did not find his cigarettes, and remembered having left them on Claudia's nightstand. His departure had been much too dramatic to think about cigarettes. Now he would have to pay a dollar fifty for a pack of Marlboros — sheer highway robbery. Usually he got them wholesale from a friend, for just a buck.

Inhaling deeply, Atilio surveyed the surroundings. As a manager in the Department of International Relations of the Ministry of Public Health, he was an expert on airports. He knew

---

* The Spanish title "La paja en el ojo ajeno" refers to New Testament passages such as this one from Matthew, chapter 7: "Judge not, lest you be judged; for by what judgment you use, you will be judged; and by what measure you measure, it will be to you measured. And why do you see the chaff of straw in your brother's eye and do not consider the log beam in your own eye?"

the scene inside and out, and had heard or could imagine every possible story.

He was not for a moment fooled by people carrying signs: *Señor Such and Such*, or *Señora Thus and Thus*. They were only pretending to be related to *Such* and *Thus* when they really were in the business of renting out rooms in their homes to foreigners, with everything pre-arranged and for a much lower price than hotels. Trafficking in tourists, that is what Atilio called it.

Nor was he fooled by the ploys of people wearing dark glasses (at nighttime!) who strolled through the lobby, key holder in hand. These were the "gypsy" cab drivers, offering car service cheaper than state-run taxis. They have no shame, thought Atilio.

They even kept cold beer and sandwiches in the trunk to pamper their clients.

A couple of months, just a couple of months was all Atilio would need as head of a police unit to show those bums the consequences of playing with matches. If he were in charge they would all be banished in no time. It would end both unfair competition with the state, and the bad impression that tourists got as soon as they set foot on Cuban soil.

Atilio was also incensed by the lack of professionalism shown by airport personnel. The floor was filthy, there were no baggage handlers around, the PA system had so much static that announcements in English, and sometimes in Spanish, too, were unintelligible. A mess. As if all that were not bad enough, lately there had been an invasion of stray dogs, like the one lying at the feet of a girl seated on the stairs. Where else in the world — and Atilio had traveled a lot — were there dirty, scabby, flea-ridden animals traipsing around an international airport? In Cuba, only in Cuba. Atilio felt like chasing them all out, both the mangy dogs and the employees remiss in their duties. And the problem was hardly limited to the airport: the capital itself was overrun with disgusting animals. At the ministry, Atilio had repeatedly stressed the need to find some way of ridding the city of stray dogs, now that the gas shortage had all but immobilized the pound vans. He was ready to beat them to death, one by one if need be, for the sake of hygiene and public decency. Even if Claudia called him a fascist, he did not care.

The loudspeaker announced the arrival of a flight from Miami and a horde of people gathered immediately. People whose wait was over stood near the customs' exit door while those still waiting glared at them, unable to suppress their envy. Atilio observed the scene for the umpteenth time. The crowd tightened its circle around the door. Reducing the distance meant shortening the time until they could see the arriving passengers. Everyone tried to be the first to spot a friend or relative and shout: "There he is! Look, he's wearing three hats and a long coat, in this heat!" Some people jumped up and down straining to get a peek above the heads of the crowd, while others hoisted drowsy kids onto their shoulders and encouraged them to yell out the relative's name. Atilio saw right through the screams of joy and the antics of those people: they cared more about the contents of the suitcases than about the arriving passengers. No one was going to persuade him to the contrary, not even Claudia with her misguided faith in humanity.

Atilio had had enough of mingling with the riff-raff and decided to go inside the customs area where he would be in the safety of isolation. He clipped the ID authorizing him to move freely within the airport building to the outside pocket of his *guayabera* and had no problems walking into the inner lounge. Most of the customs agents knew him and he felt more comfortable there, rather than on the other side of the doors among all that scum. He struck up a conversation with one of the employees, offered her a smoke, and confirmed once more that despite his fifty years he could still play Don Juan to a beautiful young woman. He had kept himself in good shape, he thought. Too bad that there was no chance to follow through tonight. Another time, perhaps?

Fortunately, the plane from Madrid landed at the indicated time and there was no further delay at the baggage claim. He found the group leader and, after a few introductory formalities, explained the details of the visit. At ten the next morning a van would pick them up at the hotel, the Habana Libre, to take them to the Convention Center where the conference was being held. Atilio would meet them there.

He rushed back to Claudia's at ninety miles per hour. He was eager to talk to her, to beg her to be patient a little longer. Claudia had not yet gone to bed when Atilio arrived. Her face was drawn, and her glistening eyes hinted at tears she would have preferred to hide. She barely looked at Atilio when he came in, focusing her attention on her right hand that compulsively squeezed a rubber eraser. Atilio approached, took the eraser from her, and suggested another way of dealing with anxiety: making love. That way he could show her, with body language since he was no good with words, how much she meant to him. Claudia gave in once more and Atilio's ego glowed with the passions he had ignited that night. He was definitely in good shape.

They were still limp with contentment when Atilio glanced at the clock and jumped out of bed. Time had gotten away from him, and he was afraid he might not make it home before María got up. Too hurt even to complain, Claudia watched him get dressed. He picked up his cigarettes and kissed Claudia on the forehead with the promise to resolve everything much sooner than she imagined.

Again, Atilio raced wildly through the city. It was past dawn and the two-wheeled plague — that is how he referred to bikers — was already crowding the streets. Rounding a corner, he almost hit one. Atilio took a deep breath and counted to ten to contain his fury. He reflected that if he had indeed hit that black guy — if Claudia could hear him, she would surely subject him to her boring spiel about racial equality — he would have to pay as much as for a white, blond, blue-eyed victim. Not to mention the damage to his car, after all the trouble he had gone through last month getting the ministry's body shop to repair and paint it.

That episode with the car had caused an argument with Claudia since she objected to his having it done for free, and even mentioned fraud. Go figure. Atilio could not believe it. The idea of accusing him of fraud, when he put his own private car at the ministry's disposal at any and all times, for whatever reason. Claudia's notions drove him up the wall.

He stole into the house like a thief, but María was already up. Atilio told her about the plane's delay, and added a long wait for the luggage due to the simultaneous arrival of several flights, plus the fact that two of the Spaniards had lost their bags. This would almost allow him to account for the three hours devoted to making love to Claudia. María, used to her husband's endless stories, paid little attention and walked out in mid-sentence saying, "Bye, I'm off."

Atilio went to his office and checked to make sure that everything was in order for the conference. He asked Eduardo, one of his assistants, to meet some late-arriving delegations at the airport. Then he looked over the pile of requests to leave the country and felt a morbid fascination for the fertile Cuban imagination. He would bet an arm that more than half of those invitations to teach courses in foreign universities, or collaborate in medical research, were bogus, just smoke screens to mask secret intentions of escaping the country for a short time or forever. Intellectual whores, *jineteros*, that is what they were. Atilio would take a closer look at those affidavits later. In most cases, only the minister himself had the authority to grant permission. And Atilio did not want to mess up anything involving the minister.

He arrived at the Convention Center before ten and finalized a few details pertaining to the first session, including the refreshments. He made sure that his name and Eduardo's were on the list of those authorized to have snacks and lunch at El Bucán, the Convention Center's splendid restaurant. Even though they were not participating as delegates, they had to be present to make sure everything went smoothly. The food at El Bucán was terrific and they certainly deserved it after the hassle of taking care of foreigners all day. Atilio would also try to get some food to take to Claudia that evening.

While the conference was in session, Atilio took time to talk with the Convention Center managers about the next event that the ministry was hosting there. Atilio was relentless in the pursuit of excellence, so he felt morally entitled to make big demands of his subordinates. Things went like clockwork that first day and Atilio was gratified to have contributed to achieving such positive results. The foreign delegates were delighted. Their only question was why there were so few local participants, since — they all agreed — the speaker had established that Cuba was one of the world leaders on the subject. Atilio explained that the Cuban delegation was small because food services were limited due to the country's difficult financial situation.

Since Eduardo was not at the Convention Center that day, Atilio requested permission to take home his colleague's lunch. The restaurant workers did not object because there was plenty to go around and, besides, the chef had worked at the protocol section of the Ministry of Public Health and owed Atilio many favors. Atilio finished his business at the Convention Center at about six. He was tired and groggy after a sleepless night. Still, he decided to stop by Claudia's for a while and take her the lunch box: pork loin, *congrí*, fried plantains, and tomato salad. A real feast. There was a note on Claudia's door: "I'm on duty at the hospital."

On his way home Atilio wondered why he had stayed with Claudia for three years despite their many differences, their fights about his not leaving María and his hesitation about Claudia's wish to have a baby. The only explanation was that he was crazy about her. He had been from day one. Atilio was always involved in extramarital flings, but none had ever lasted this long. He would have to figure out a way to sail the rough seas ahead, since he was not about to divorce María, the mother of his two children and a good wife. Atilio was proud of his home in Miramar, one of the best areas of Havana, surrounded by a delightful garden with fruit trees. All his hard work in his native province of Guantánamo had paid off: he had been transferred to the capital and assigned to such a house. It was a lot to give up, no matter how crazy he might be about Claudia.

María was waiting with dinner and Atilio made a point of telling her how he had had to scramble to bring home the lunch box from the Convention Center. He had done it for her, he said, since he knew how much she enjoyed a good slice of pork.

The second day of the convention was much like the first, except that Eduardo had lunch at the Convention Center and, since the sessions ended early, the Spaniards invited Atilio to join them at the hotel for drinks. Atilio accepted, thinking he would kill time until six and then stop by at Claudia's. He seldom dropped by at the hospital where she worked, to avoid suspicions and to keep any rumors about their relationship from reaching María's ears.

They sat in the lobby of the Habana Libre and ordered beer to cool off. Atilio gave a detailed accounting of Cuba's remarkable advances in the spheres of public health and education despite the American blockade of the island. The Spaniards told of the difficulties in their own country and marveled at Cuba's accomplishments.

Atilio looked around, his mind wandering briefly from the discussion. There were lots of Cubans, mostly women, milling around the hotel in the company of foreigners. Atilio gazed at them contemptuously, *jineteras* no doubt, marginal people eating and drinking at tourists' expense. If it had been up to him, not one of their kind would be allowed to set foot in there again. He carefully avoided the topic of prostitution so that he would not find himself having to explain the situation to the Spaniards. The country's good image had to be preserved.

After the third round of beers, the Spaniards spoke of their desire to expand their ties of solidarity with Cuba. They were thinking of sponsoring several three-month study grants in Spain, all expenses paid. They talked it over with Atilio to get a feel for the ministry's official position on the matter, and to see if he might be able to recommend possible candidates.

Atilio stated that the ministry not only approved, but that it considered this sort of collaboration extremely favorable for the development of Cuban professionals. However, he stressed the need to use utmost care in the selection process to avoid having unworthy applicants reap the benefits of such largesse. Hoping they would not think him lacking in modesty, Atilio suggested his own name for consideration. His experience in public health administration made him an ideal choice to launch the exchange. Besides, he confessed, although he enjoyed bullfights, loved Spanish food, and was a fervent admirer of the singer Lola Flores, he had never had the chance to visit Spain. If they wanted another name he was thinking of Claudia, a wonderful orthopedic surgeon for whom he could vouch without reservations.

They asked him to submit their CVs so they could start the paper work. As a way of celebrating, they ordered more beer, which Atilio accepted on the condition that this be the last round. He did not want any more to drink because Claudia, concerned with drinking and driving, would harass him if he showed up with alcohol on his breath. For a few seconds, he turned his imagination loose and pictured himself in Madrid with Claudia on a three-month honeymoon like they had never been able to have in Cuba. What a trip, thought Atilio.

Just as he was enthusiastically arguing the advantages of having himself selected Atilio caught sight of a familiar young woman loitering around the elevators. He made a mental effort to recall her name: Dora, Flora, something like that. Maybe Nora. A pediatrician. Atilio wondered what she might be doing at the hotel. *Leeching off* a foreigner, probably maneuvering to be taken on a trip. Incredible. The things that people do for a little jaunt. His own case was different, of course. He had gone through a lot of crap for the Revolution, from the very beginning that first day of January 1959 when he was only fifteen. He had never once wavered in the struggle to make his way in life and now felt entitled to certain privileges. And, besides, he had passed the test of fire: coming back to Cuba after every trip to continue his selfless toiling.

Atilio realized that the beer was bringing out all sorts of patriotic bullshit, which signaled the need to stop drinking and find Claudia to tell her of the plans. He said good-bye to the Spaniards and avoided running into Flora, Dora or Nora, whatever her name was, who was obviously waiting for a tourist to get on with her whoring. She probably did things in bed with foreigners that she would refuse a Cuban. What a slut.

Claudia's expression when he kissed her cheek did not bode well. Atilio hastened to take the lead in the conversation, explaining the Spaniards' offer. He said that he had tentatively accepted on the condition that they both go, that he was not going anywhere without her, that this was going to be their chance to be alone together, with no worries about jobs or the Special Period.

Claudia let him talk without interrupting. She asked no questions, she voiced no opinions. Only when he wanted to know if she was excited about the news did she say: "Atilio, I'm not going anywhere with you. It's over." He paid no attention and continued describing how great it would be to discover Madrid together, away from the daily grind, not needing to hide, making love any time they wished, enjoying Spanish food and drink. He even joked about digging up some long lost rich relative and really living it up. Claudia, meanwhile, stared at the floor. Suddenly, figuring that she was upset because he had not gone to see her at the hospital the day before, Atilio tried to explain how he had been tied up at the Convention Center until very late and then had car trouble. But Claudia, shaking her head, would not budge.

Then Atilio moved to what he considered infallible emergency tactics: his voice serious, plaintive almost, he told Claudia how much he needed her, swore to get a divorce as soon as they came back from Spain and have the child Claudia so wanted. Finally, he suggested going to bed to dissipate any remaining doubts. She knew he was her man, the one who could make her really happy. And he promised to stay with her the whole night. To Atilio's bewilderment Claudia took a package from the desk and handed it to him saying: "This is what little is left of you in this house. Please take it. I don't want even the slightest memory of you."

Atilio could hardly believe his ears. No woman had ever ditched him. In all his affairs he had always managed to keep sucking the flower's nectar until he lost interest. Never, ever, had any of his lovers enjoyed the luxury of leaving him. Claudia's behavior was totally unacceptable. He insisted again, got closer to her, tried to touch her. Claudia refused him so forcefully that Atilio shrank back in astonishment. He finally realized that this time it was different, that this chapter was indeed closed.

Back home, he fretted briefly about losing Claudia and all the good times he had with her. But perhaps it was better this way, fewer hassles to distract him from work. The trip to Spain would be good, it would clear his head. When he came back, he would find himself someone he liked as much as Claudia. One thing was certain: he would never leave María, not for a woman like Claudia, a married man's lover for three years. That was something his María would never do.

Havana, 1995

Translated by Cristina de la Torre

MY LOVE AND MY SUGARCANE
José Antonio Quintana Veiga

He came by again to talk about the land. He's not quite so elegant now. The same clothes, I mean, but all ten years older now — the guayabera shirts, the cowboy pants, the riding boots, and Him. The guayaberas are faded and you can see through them, though they're not mended anywhere because his wife is an artist when it comes to washing fine clothes. He doesn't shave every day, or smell any longer of Bebito cologne. He came by on his older daughter's bike, with That Look deep down in his eyes. Beautiful eyes that reflect the loyalty of his tender soul, even though he'll be turning fifty soon. Yes, because it's twenty years since He first began to take an interest in my land. I was ten when my father died, may he rest in peace, and a few months later came that mysterious pronouncement. "What you need isn't Land, but Space to fulfill all the Promise that lurks between one eyebrow and the other. You'll have enough Time." When I demanded an explanation, He always said the same thing, just as mysterious. "When you can explain it yourself, then it will be worthwhile for you to understand."

I never had a chance to be Naive, let alone Foolish. My land, my sixty acres planted with Cane that stands before my eyes right now, he wasn't after it. Much less these days, since he's been elected President of the UBPC,* which makes him lord or co-owner of almost fifty times that much. My house ought to be His House, but he lives in El Batey with all the comforts of town — next door to the ration-book store and the other one where you can shop with Bonus Coupons. The family doctor is his neighbor too — he just has to cross the yard to get his blood pressure taken, which anyway never rises or falls. His wife, the poor thing, is Messed Up with perpetual bouts of asthma. Worse now, since medicines have gotten so scarce, and if you can Acquire them, it's from the resellers who buy in Havana at one price and sell here for a hundred times more. I couldn't wish the poor woman's death, but if she dies, let it be the Yankees' fault, not mine. He'd

---

* UBPCs (Basic Units of Cooperative Production) are the type of semi-private cooperative to which many state farms were converted in the 1990s. "He" was presumably manager of a state farm in the earlier years of the story, though in its present moment, in the '90s, he is the elected director of the UBPC. The "Bonus Coupon" store referred to in the next sentence sells goods normally sold only for hard currency, in this case to holders of coupons issued to reward high production or effort in the harvest and milling of cane.

come to live in my house then.

His visits don't have anything to do with my money, either. Those Fabulous thousands and thousands of pesos that the gossips of El Batey say I've been hiding ever since my father died, may he rest in peace — they don't exist and never did. If Don Antonio left me Four Pesos, then I ate them up in little treats before I turned fifteen, and He understands that better than anyone. When we got into the Special Period, sure, a suckling pig started to be worth two or even three thousand pesos, and I sold my share of them, but how much did a pack of cigarettes cost? Forty! And a bottle of bad rum? Two hundred! Anyway, it was thanks to my piglets that his daughter, the owner of that bicycle, had a Decent Wedding and could enjoy her Symbolic Loss of Virginity between new sheets. You know what a new bed sheet was going for in the year 1993, don't you? A Virgin Herself! That's what Yurisleidis told me, María del Carmen's daughter, who had to Sell Her Ass to the head of the warehouse for a new sheet — because that son of a b— wouldn't take money at all. I Acquired the ones I'm talking about with money, but they cost an Arm and a Leg.

In the harvest of '94 I took a loss on my cane. They paid me seventeen-thirty per hundred arrobas, while it cost me twenty per to grow and harvest it. That includes what little fertilizer I could Acquire from the ex-president of the UBPC, who comes to me now with the story that this is why they fired him. As if Everyone didn't know that happened because he conspired with every illegal cow-slaughterer in El Batey. And he sold half the gasoline that was supplied to the UBPC! It's true that the gas assigned to cane growing wasn't enough even to light the oil lamps of the thousand and one nights of blackouts, but I agree with our Representative that Shortage Doesn't Justify Theft. The next year's harvest, '95, was worse. We private growers didn't have either a mini-tractor or a single pair of oxen among us, and we couldn't take advantage of the opportunities the UBPC had, which were more fertilizer, herbicide, and fuel than it needed. Under the table, He did help out some Private Growers, but I didn't get so much as a mouthful of gas or a teaspoon of fertilizer. He was so severe with me that even his own children and friends (including the Representative) criticized him to his face and called it extremism on his part. When the new director of the Sugar Complex asked me why my cane hadn't improved its yield this year, I told him the truth. The man got mad and sent for Him, to bawl him out. But He wasn't angry at me for complaining.

When he called me Gossip and Tattletale in public, he did it with his damned Enchanting Smile, which always gives me Chills underneath my belly button. Sometimes my legs even Go Weak when that son-of-some-saint smiles at me this way. And mark one thing — He says it's My Smile that captivates him. The day I turned fourteen he wrote me a poem about my smile that gave me my First Orgasm, the very first. I'll write it down here so you can see for yourselves:

BERTICA

She's barely there
in terms of flesh and bone
until she smiles —
that quality smile!
that multiplies its surroundings
into Biblical images
brought to life by miraculous flashes
of Caribbean heresy.
Then she mounts to the pulpit
with her robe rolled high
and breaks out with a swear-word
and covers any bet
as to whether or not happiness
can be built with her smile alone.

I felt so praised. Imagine! A girl like me: very young then, a country girl, brought up by a man who was too rough and too ready with the whip. Imagine how sensitive such a girl is to the influence of words like those. Simple, I admit, but so full of flattery. Of course, I showed the little poem to Everyone: my girlfriends in Junior High, my teachers, the Representative. All of them, without exception, told me that more than a poem it seemed like a Documentary about me, because that's exactly how I was, the swear-words too. From then on, He was considered a Poet by everyone except his wife, who thought he was Something Else. I showed her the Poem, which wasn't so innocent a thing to do as you're thinking, and she looked at me over her glasses — I remember she was mending some blue socks — and said, "The poetry is pretty, and you deserve it, but If You Fuck My Husband, I'm going to Burn Your House Down." I've never spoken to her since.

So, it's not my money that brings him around here, because I still owe money to the bank. Maybe next year I'll be better off. My cane is doing well, and the yield ought to double, because I planted fifteen acres in the winter, rehabilitated another thirty, and left the other fifteen alone, meaning I didn't cut them this year, and they're looking quite fine. The rain has been Very Opportune, the fertilizer showed up Just in Time, and I didn't give the weeds a chance to seed. I think I'm going to have a good harvest, though not as good as in my father's best years, when he managed to get three hundred thousand arrobas out of this little patch of ground. Last year He brought me a new seed variety — it's called Cuba 1051 — which they gave him in Havana to try out in the UBPC. That's what I planted in the winter. Every time He comes by, he talks about that new cane. He's in love with it. He's even claimed that Cuba 1051 is the cane that's going to pull the country out of the Special Period. That's an exaggeration, of course, but I know how he feels. This variety is good, maybe even exceptional, so let's wait and see.

Anyway, don't go thinking that his interest in my cane is all that brings him around. He can go up and down my Fields without asking anyone's permission. And I'm all for it, because his Eye for pests and diseases beats any grower's around here, and he clues me in. Like the mice — an infestation of mice broke out in a little field I've got by the highway, and if not for Him, they would have ruined all the cane. That's the field I use for seed, where I've got the best varieties to come out of the Research Station. It's like a Seed Bank, and I watch to see How They Behave, to choose the ones to plant more widely. Believe me, this Man isn't satisfied to walk his three thousand acres. He's got to walk the neighboring fields, mine included, as well. That's how he spotted the mouse attack and I was able to save my Seed Bank. No farmer around here takes offense when He decides to check out their fields. And he doesn't do it in a stuck-up way, with any air of superiority. He comes to you and says, "I had to cross your property because I was In a Hurry, and so By Accident I saw that that little field is full of whip fungus. Better go take a look." And thanks to his "hurry" and his "accidents," many folks around here have had time to save their cane from some misfortune about to occur. Of course, he doesn't mention that his checking out the neighboring fields protects the fields of the UBPC, but that's the case.

That precaution isn't new. I remember when I'd just graduated from high school, in fact it was the day I turned sixteen, he appeared at my uncle's house — my father's older brother, may

he rest in peace — and gave us all a speech about How to Protect
the Jaronú 60-5 so it didn't turn susceptible to fungus. That's an
exceptional variety, very productive and resistant to almost all
diseases, besides growing well in any kind of ground. All the
growers around here fell in love with it, and in four or five years
they planted so much that it took up almost sixty per cent of the
area sown in cane. "That's dangerous," He said to us, still on his
feet and with his hat in his hand. Then he grabbed a stool and
leaned it back against the post that supports the roof of the
kitchen, since the kitchen was where they entertained guests in
my uncle's house. We all waited, me with my mouth open,
because I loved the timbre of his voice and all that he knew about
cane. With his eyes lit up by a Passion like a Revelation, avoiding
mine which were eating him up with a more Earthly Passion, he
explained that a variety like the Jaronú 60-5 had to be protected.
The first thing was to avoid extending it more than the specialists
recommended: twenty five percent of the area, at the top. He said
that there were other varieties which were Also good, which the
rest of the area could be planted with. As an example, he pointed
to one of the districts of the Sugar Complex that He administered
directly, and invited us all to come by there the Next Sunday so
we could see it *in situ* (he's always liked those Latin phrases, by
the way). We'd see how he'd distributed the varieties so that the
Jaronú would yield All That It Could Give without deteriorating
from excess use.

I went to that Demonstration as decked out as could be. When
he saw me, he took me by the arm and led me away from the
group of relatives and friends. "What are you doing here?" he
said. "Shouldn't you be in Havana starting Medical School?
Wasn't that what you promised your father you were going to do?
And why are you dressed up for a night out, to come here and
look at cane?" I couldn't help being impressed by his deep voice
and friendly tone, and I explained I didn't want to be a Doctor any
more, but an Agronomic Engineer, and there was no point
arguing about it because I'd already registered at the university
for that. As for my outfit, I was Dressed Like That because I
wanted to Impress Him, so he'd come with me when the tour of
the cane was done, to swim in the river and eat mangoes, I hoped.
I said all that with plenty of fawning and flattery, but I looked
him straight in the eye. That did the trick. Whenever I talk to him
as equal to equal, it sweeps his defenses away. He didn't give me
any more trouble, and returned to His Affairs with Madame Cane.
That was the day I realized he was making sure none of us did

anything stupid with our cane so as to protect the land under his responsibility, which in those days belonged to the state. He does the same now in the UBPC. After a while, he got the population of Jaronú 60-5 down to about 35 percent. More than that even He couldn't do.

The issue of my studies was discussed a lot within my family. I mean my living uncles and my cousins, because all the rest are dead. It's not that my relatives die young, it's that when I was born my father was Already Sixty and my mother Twenty-Five. Papa died at seventy from being kicked by a cow. My mother had left for Havana before I turned three, and then, in '80, she hooked up with some Kid from Around There and they took off for the United States through Mariel. All this I've been told, because I don't even remember her. So my change of career was an excuse to go live Permanently in the house my father left me, a big old wooden one with a zinc roof, later fixed up and extended after His wife tried to burn it down. Well, in fact she did burn it — she put it to the torch on All Four Sides — but the repair work was excellent and didn't leave any reminders of the fire. When she threatened to Burn it Again, I took the necessary precautions: I rebuilt it with concrete blocks, gave it a cement roof thirty centimeters thick, and I put four fifty-gallon water tanks on top. To burn it down now, you'd have to drop napalm on it. I've lived here with some of my cousins and their husbands for twelve years. That was the alternative my uncles gave me, if I wasn't going to satisfy their desires to have a Doctor Niece.

In truth I did have a vocation for medicine, but I was afraid that after I graduated they'd send me to work in the city and take me away from Him, so I decided to be an Agronomist and specialize in Cane. He felt very flattered by my decision, although he's never told me that right out. The Representative also took my side, when the Party Members of the Sugar Complex, in that year's annual meeting, tried to meddle in my affairs. They were put up to it by one of my uncles, who was the First Secretary of the Party in the town. Claiming I was an orphan and the Smartest Girl in the area, they declared themselves the Guarantors of my Future. I was told that in the meeting the Representative got Very Angry and said the Party couldn't meddle in this for the simple reason that they Had No Right. One of the meddlers replied that they weren't trying to Impose a Career, but to discuss with me and Make Me Think about the usefulness of my becoming a Doctor because there were more Agronomists than needed. Then the Representative looked at Him, who'd kept very quiet, as if asking for help. He stood up very slowly, they say, walked to the blackboard at the back of the room, and gave an Illustrated Lecture on the future of Agriculture in general, Sugar Cane in particular, and the real needs for Highly Qualified Experts in the next five or ten years. His speech provided a lot of grist for the mill in El Batey and for miles around. The version I heard made me so happy, it was like Coitus in the middle of the day. It went more or less like this: "Bertica is not only the Most Intelligent Woman produced by our town and twenty kilometers on every side, but also the most beautiful, pretty, daring, honorable, and frank that I've known since the Day I was Born. If she becomes a doctor, with such qualities, I doubt she'll be allowed to return to this corner of Cuba, and probably not to this province at all. As an Agronomist she also runs this risk, but less severely, taking into account that She, for some very powerful reason, Loves this place and is determined to return. Havana may need Exceptional Doctors, but Agronomists with those characteristics are needed here, and no one's going to try to take her away from us. My humble opinion is that She made the right decision of her own free will, which is How It Ought To Be."

They say that when he finished, The Silence was so thick that when the First Secretary of the Party Committee knocked his fist on the table to announce the end of the discussion, everybody jumped from fright. Of course, as always happened in those meetings, all of El Batey knew what had been discussed and decided even before the assembly was adjourned, and knew who had been on which side. One time a few years ago, this bothered the leaders so much that they ordered an Investigation because a certain very sensitive and secret Issue had leaked out. It seemed that in an argument between two women in the bodega one said to the other that her husband had been sanctioned in the Party because she'd Cheated on Him and he'd let it Go By. When she said this, the Secretary of the nucleus in the Mill happened to be standing there, and he raised a hue and cry so the Investigation was begun. They asked that first woman who had given her The Information and she said without hesitation, "It was So and So." When they asked So and So, she confessed it was Such and Such. And so on, each to the next, until they'd put together a chain of twenty-four people and reached the conclusion that The Whole Town knew — without finding out who the informant was, of course. The measure they took to counteract this kind of leaks was to warn the members that everyone who didn't want Their Shit known all around town, better just Keep Themselves Clean.

Now the Party assemblies aren't secret any more, so if anyone asks, you can tell down to the last detail what was said and what was not.

Well, so that one where they discussed my decision to study Agronomy instead of Medicine, it was secret, but I heard all about it right away. When He came to my house to explain how my cane should be cut in the harvest that was about to start, I thanked him for his praise and told him, with absolute sincerity, that I considered it underserved. That day was unforgettable for me, doubly so, because besides teaching me how to care for the root structure when harvesting my fields, he wrote his second poem, also dedicated to me, sitting at my kitchen table. I'll show it to you, to see what you think.

> BERTICA (II)
> You'll never be a memory
> filed away in my past
> not the loose end of a story
> nor one explained at last.
>
> You'll never be the breeze
> evanescent and mild
> nor the full moon in eclipse
> nor the shadow of a smile
>
> You won't be a flower's petal
> that perishes at a chill
> nor the drama that moves us
> nor a nightingale's trill
>
> You'll just be the essence
> of all that's alive
> the marrow that nourishes
> the factor that decides
>
> Poetry's true sex
> and God's only love
> the place they come together
> the orgasm of life.

Imagine that! I was just a kid, really, even though I was in college and taking care of my house and my cane. So I cried. Oh Lord how I cried that day! How beautifully! That Fabulous Man in front of me, in my kitchen, in my house, telling me those things. I read the poem two or three times without saying a word because my tears were choking me. He asked me to make him some coffee and I put the pot on the stove without even filling it. I was shaking for more than an hour. Even now, my eyes fill up when I remember that day. I feel like Running through every Canefield of the Sugar Complex till I find him and ask him to swear by his grandchildren that I'll forever be his Only Love.

It's not my cane that brings him around here so often, but his Passion for the cane is strong. Many times I've felt, and even resigned myself to accept it, that His Love for Me is a byproduct of His Love for the Cane. At first it was just a sensation, an inkling, that became a certainty when I graduated with my engineering degree and was sent to do my social service stint in the provincial Agricultural Research Station, the EPICA as everyone says. Really, I don't have a researcher's soul, and the most convincing proof is that only two men have seen me naked: my papa and Him. If the man I have seems Supreme to me, compared with what other women are Said to Have, then what would be the point of risking it in search of something the same or worse? Still I had to accept my post in the EPICA and find a way to link my solid Sense of Reality when it comes to sugar cane with the Imaginative and Meticulous tendency of the researchers. Luckily, research also needs people who know how to do things in the traditional way. They assigned me to work in the area of Genetics, whose main goal is to develop better varieties, but in the process (twelve to fifteen years) seems excessively long to me. So as not to suffer, I said to myself, "Bertica, your task is to make sure that all this cane sown around here gets taken care of the way God Desires, and produces Lots of Sugar as a result. Let the Geneticists worry about Which is Which."

Of course, I'm putting the cart before the horse, because the truth is that at first I flatly refused to work with the Researchers, for fear of getting caught up in their vice of over-specialization. But finally I had to argue it out with Him. I was staying home, determined to take care of my cane and pay the state back every last cent of what my education had cost, when the director of the EPICA, learning of my Insolence (the rector of the university told him I was Spoiled), visited me and spoke eloquently of the beauties and attractions of Research. He promised me the moon and the stars including Specialist Courses abroad. Which is to say, he tried to conquer me with counterproductive arguments.

What's worse, I compared him to my Ideal, and I didn't see that Extraordinary Love for Cane that comes out of my Loved One's pores even when he sleeps. I listened with exquisite courtesy and said goodbye with my best smile, but I confirmed my decision to say home. The director wouldn't give up, so he went to see Him, to complain about my "irrational attitude" and ask him to intervene, taking into account the Respect and the Consideration he was accorded on all sides. Before nightfall, He knocked on my door, wearing his handsomest guayabera and some Camaguey boots that I had given him the previous Valentine's Day. I was in the kitchen, working on dinner, and suddenly realized it was Him and what he had come about. I was still trying to get my hair in place when I bumped up against His Smile. My God, the smile of that Man, as Carilda says, it throws me for a loop. I forgot everything I'd planned to say to him. As usual, we started off talking about my cane and the neighbors'. Then he asked me, as if by accident, when I was supposed to report to work at the EPICA. "Last week," I told him, and put my guard up. He lowered his head, as if this bothered him a lot, and said, "Damn, what we really need is someone from around here to work for a while with those people at the EPICA. Whatever they seem like, they do know A Lot about Cane and they're very up to date about what's going in on The World in that sense. But it has to be somebody who can absorb everything within two or three years. Not some dummy who'll waste everyone's time." He looked at me sadly and added, "I know you don't want to go, but if we don't find somebody, then — if they'll let me — I'll have to do it myself."

Go figure! My eyes teared right up. He was sitting down and I was standing but I knelt down beside him and took his hands, always so warm. "Do you want me to go?" I asked him. He answered with another question. "Will it hurt you?" And he added right away: "I don't want you to do anything that will hurt you." Then I cried a little, because I like to cry when I have Such Beautiful Moments in my life, so later I can recall them and cry again. He gave me a little kiss in the forehead and asked me not to cry, because he'd find some other solution. Right away I told him no, I'd Go, because anything I could do for Him made me Happy, and in the EPICA I'd be Very Happy after all. He told me to promise — to promise him I'd be Happy — and I did. We sealed the agreement with an Unforgettable Kiss like in the movies. That night I slept in peace and satisfied I was his Only Love, after the cane. I vowed to learn so much about cane, that He'd have no other choice but to love me at least as much.

Since my high school days, many people — teachers, friends, relatives, and suitors — have told me that my Lovesick Love for a man twenty years older, and married, stemmed from the Isolation in which I lived. I was a victim of Geographic Fatalism, in short. They predicted a gradual disappointment when I matured as a Woman and came to know New Worlds and the new men who lived in them. Those Worlds. Here in El Batey, they all said, He doesn't have any competition. He's got this Aura of The Indispensable Man created by his extraordinary knowledge about the cultivation of Sugar Cane and many other subjects related to that. The fact is, few of them recognize his Exceptional Humanity, or worse still, they consider him irresponsible or unscrupulous, for maintaining Dubious Relations with a young girl, an orphan, with no relatives Man Enough to defend her from him. In parentheses, let me say that my two younger uncles and three of their sons, my cousins, fought in the war in Angola and won medals For Bravery, and if they never messed with Him, it was simply because he was Their Commander in the war and they respected him like a god. Once, when someone tried to incite them to call him to account for his relations with me, my uncle answered with words that I retain with much Love in my memory and heart. My uncle said, "That man isn't afraid of bullets, bombs, mines, hunger, cold, snakes, diseases, death, or his commanders. What am I going to threaten him with?" So, accusing my relatives of lack of Manhood was an outrage. Personally I wasn't worried that the pressure of Public Opinion would take him away from me. We talked about this on the day when, after repeated invitations on my part, He accepted being The Love of My Life, on one Condition, which was: I had to become, by applying myself to my studies and by my social and private conduct, an Exceptional Woman. He explained that only this would justify a Man of his age and social responsibility, married and with children, having such relations with a Snotnose like me. He added that if, on the contrary, I didn't turn out to be Quite a Woman, then Ipso Facto the whole thing would end. I wasn't offended. On the contrary! I liked his frankness very much and accepted the Condition in my most passionate spirit of struggle and self-improvement. Finally, when I confessed fear about pressures from other people, he told me not to worry, that He would assume the consequences whatever they might be. In no case would he leave me unprotected or Alone With the Enemy.

So, like I told you, the future of My Love for Him was threatened with death by Geographic Fatalism. Once I'd gone out in the World a little farther than the limits of my farm and those of my neighbors, all that Fabulous Love would succumb to death by simple comparison. I spent five years in the university, met hundreds of young people of all Sizes, Shapes, and Colors, and the more people I got to know well, the more I held tight to Him. Then came my work in the EPICA, where I met many intelligent and interesting people, and since such research stations exist in all the provinces, I traveled throughout the Country for events related to my work and met many more people that way. One day, after a meeting in the EPICA of Palma Soriano, when we were on our way back to the city (where those of us from other provinces were staying) we stopped for a while on the bridge over the Cauto River to watch its impressive flow. I understood then that I was a Very Fortunate Woman for having been born in an anonymous little place, without rivers like the Cauto, or mountains like the Sierra Maestra, or valleys like Viñales, but with a Man Like Him. It's true that there was just one, but that one was Mine. Such reflection led me to fully understand his enigmatic phrase, that what I need isn't Land, but Space to share all this Love that I'm overflowing with. He meant space without economic or emotional limits; an Intelligent and Sensitive Space, with qualities ranging from the Intimate Heat of bed to the Immeasurability of the universe; a Human space with a Light that illuminates me from within. And I have more than enough time to explore All of it, to enjoy it in all its Purity until its Last Breath, which I'll convert into My Essence, into the Immortal Particle that All of us carry within.

I feel I'm not being honest, because I'm Skipping Over the most difficult moments, the periods of doubt, both mine and his. His Love for the cane never slipped, not even in the worst moments of the Special Period, when there wasn't enough fuel, when there were shortages of tires and parts for the machines, of fertilizer, of chemicals to combat pests and weeds, of clothes and shoes for the canecutters and even of Food. Everyone doubted the cane would survive in such circumstances, but He sought alternative solutions to save her. He was like the Right Hand of God. He summoned oxen to replace the tractors. He gathered all the leaves and chaff he could, from our Mill and the neighboring ones, to make the lack of fertilizer less of a blow. He took a chance for the first time on a Variety that he didn't like, Cuba 323, which he considered too rough for the quality of Our Soil. He planted it with the novel method of Minimum Soil Preparation and with Straw Mulch to save the work of weeding and preserve the humidity of the ground. In sum, His Love for La Caña grew strong when She most needed it, but Apparently the same Did Not Happen with me. I've read a lot about adolescence and even have participated, here in El Batey and at the university, in conferences on the subject directed by specialists, and frankly I've arrived at the conclusion that, for better or for worse, I skipped that particular stage. Adolescents tend to be rebellious, and I was not, maybe because I didn't have anyone with whom to be that way. My uncles didn't care whether I spent three days singing or three days crying, or whether I planned to be the best student in my junior high or to drop out. They treated me like a little animal that has to be fed and cared for until it can take care of itself. That's all. That's how things were until He appeared in my life. Well, He'd been in my life since papa died; I mean to say until I decided to have a Man like Him for myself alone — and if it could be him Himself, all the better. I made my Decision a little after I turned thirteen. From then on, everything I thought or did was to the end of achieving that Goal. My conduct stabilized and I behaved like the most judicious of Adult Women. At fourteen and a half I achieved the Goal, but He imposed the condition that I had to be No Ordinary Girl, and I wasn't — and wouldn't be. Still, when I turned sixteen, something happened that shook me a lot. I was never careless about my appearance, and my relations with peers, both girls and boys, were always very good. My loquacity and my love of dancing helped me a lot. But until past fifteen-and-a-half my physical development was extremely slow and put me at a Disadvantage with respect to the other girls of my age. If I didn't get to the point of developing a complex, it was because my only Feminine Attribute, my smile, continued to be a captivating one — as He told me in his first poem, you will recall. That, and because everyone knew that in spite of my Insignificant Attractions as a female, I was the Lover of a man who was more Man than most. Even the teachers treated me with a certain deference for this cause. I shared my joy with everyone, but I didn't show off. At dances I tried to pass unnoticed, just the opposite of the girls who enjoyed showing off their new pointy breasts and their quivering behinds. Then, in a flash, Spring came to me. Generously, making me grow in Optimal Proportions everywhere. After that I threw caution to the winds. It was my period of vanity, although I showed off, above all, so that he could accurately judge My New Charms. Since I was a good dancer, they invited me to all the dances, to which I mostly went alone. That is, without Him. In those days I considered jealousy to be one of the most Genuine Displays of Love, so I started to provoke situations that would make him scold me and demand that I stop being so bold. For instance, I sewed myself the most daring blouses just in the hope the He would forbid me to wear them, as happened with my girlfriends and their boyfriends sometimes. Can you imagine how disappointing it was to have a boyfriend, or a lover in my case, who never prohibited you from doing anything at all? The most I could get out of him was a few words that, more than a reproof, seemed to me a philosophical reflection. He said, "Women anxious to show off their physical charms tend not to have any other kind."

It annoyed me so much that he didn't get annoyed with me, that one day, a Saturday afternoon, I cooked up an Arrogant Provocation designed to infuriate him. I borrowed a dress from one of my girlfriends — a dress made out of one of those filmy fabrics, cut in a way that was Very Daring for that place and time. One of those dresses that, when you wear it on the street, sometimes you feel you're dressed and sometimes you feel naked instead. I showed up in the mill, in one of the workshops where he was meeting with the machine maintenance crew, who they say (and I can confirm) are the rudest of all. When I arrived, the meeting had just ended and they were offering a toast, after which there would be food, beer, and music. The men invited me to stay, and I asked him what he thought. He arranged a lock of hair on my forehead and said, "Okay, but don't stay too late, because it's going to get cold and you're Not Wearing Much." Then he turned around and left. I stayed at the party out of pure pride, when what I really wanted to do was go home and cry. I didn't say long. I drank a beer and danced two or three numbers with my cousins. When I got home — I was still living with my uncles then — I found him sleeping in my bed with his clothes on and without a bath. My uncle said He'd fallen asleep talking, and among them all they'd gotten him into bed. One of my cousin's husbands told me He'd spent the whole night before writing a report, and that he must be exhausted because the meeting, which started at eight in the morning, had been Very Hot. I sat down ashamed of my conduct and then lay down by his side without waking him up. I cried a little to relax and fell asleep. The next morning, when I opened my eyes, he was gone. On the night table I found a little paper, kind of greasy, which I expected to be a farewell note. It was a Poem. In fact, this was really his second poem dedicated to me, which I try to forget because I didn't like it. Maybe you'll think it's more deserving of being called a Poem than the others, but I can't judge that, because I'm too involved in it. I'll show it to you, like I did the others, to see what you think. The text is completely his. The shape it took in this final form is thanks to a Collaboration of mine.

INDEFINABLE WOMAN
(This woman may be indefinable but I love her)

She is
This woman
is the holy spirit
of universal femininity
an avalanche of burning stars
in my dangerous madness of dreaming awake

Eyes as white as the tips of my own fingers
gaze at a whole lot of time to come
round like a genuine pleasure
like the lust of a fish
the first surprise of
her dark eyes

She is
This woman is
a feeling of homelessness
the sweet cause of all my sins
a good reason to be alive or be dead
the quality of my last waking nightmare

Feverish skin where the ends of my hair
brush along her libido born with teeth
butterfly saddled just as weaned
to fly in the first new moon
wings squeezed tight
against any wall

She is
This woman is
worse than indefinable
like the revenge of some god
or a tax levied on forbidden love
the erratic arrow of a drunken Cupid

bribed with the scents of virginal pubis
against the indifference of a conceited phallus
This woman is my most beautiful waking nightmare

Even at seventeen you can be aware that Indefinition is not exactly a virtue, and that nightmares, however beautiful, are bad dreams. Still I wasn't disappointed, because behind the Poem lay a person who was essentially good, a Man both defined and definable who in spite of his doubts still saw me as a Holy Spirit. I did have doubts about His Love — or, worse, I started to feel in his indifference a roughness that showed the lack of It. But I was afraid to venture very far from Him — afraid of feeling helpless, because although I thought of myself as a brave woman, my bravery depended on his protection. I would have dared Anything, I mean, if and when it would have boosted my image in His Eyes. That wasn't the bravery of a free spirit, but the Blind Faith of a Woman in Love. He replaced the Father I had lost when I needed one most; he was my best friend; he was and is my Only Man in bed, my Only Love.

That Poem hurt me, but it wasn't a mortal wound. Besides, his weapon against my loose conduct was tolerance. What came next, I'd rather not confess, but I'm afraid that my story will Lose Credibility if I don't. Because of the events related to the Poem, I made up a boyfriend — to hurt him, to avenge myself for his apparent indifference. I confessed the truth two weeks later. I Made Up the plan in school with my girlfriends of my class and dorm. The day of the weekend pass, when he came to pick me up at the place where the bus dropped me off, I acted Cold and didn't even return his kiss on my cheek. When he asked what was going on, and I told him I had Decided to end our relationship because I had Taken Up with a teacher in school. God, what a Jerk I was. How could I underestimate a Man like Him? He never answered. Only, his eyes welled up and he started to tell me that the night before, while he was welding some farming tools, the arc had hurt his eyes so much that even his voice was affected. His Story was long and detailed, so we had plenty of time to get home. While he told it, sheets of tears ran down his cheeks. Then, claiming he had to go to the doctor, he left right away. That didn't give me any time to argue, although what I wanted to do was Argue a Lot, to throw his indifference and lack of love in his face and then finally, later, to tell him that the boyfriend was all a lie. I was off balance, and puzzled, and by the time I reacted it was too late. One of my cousins, when I repeated the story of His welding accident, assured me that No Accident Had Occurred. If He was crying, it was About Something Else.

I went crazy. I took off my school uniform, asked my uncle for a horse, and went searching in the cane fields all around, but nowhere did He turn up. I went to his house and called his daughter outside, but since I was so desperate and drowning in tears, the girl got scared and made me sit down and went for water. She brought me water and a diazepam too. I took it, and later I Told Her Everything. I told her I had to find him right away because I knew he was Suffering and I was afraid something bad might happen to him. Both of us cried a while, until the pill started to take effect. Since I was the one who was supposed to be More Grown Up, I calmed down and asked her to accompany me. We both climbed onto the horse and took off at random. Almost at dusk, a peasant told us he'd seen his jeep parked alongside the Central Highway, alongside the seed bank. We went there at full speed. We found him alone, measuring the height and thickness of some stalks of Cane. I jumped from the animal, ran toward Him, hugged him tight and told him I Loved Him So Much that I was going to Die For Love. Of course, I said all this through my sobs. But that was it. Nothing happened. He didn't scold me, or even stick out his tongue. He put us both in the jeep, gave the horse a tap with the whip to send it home alone, and told us, with a Wealth of Details and his Usual Passion, the history of the Cane he was measuring. From that lamentable action of mine I got something very good: a Fast Friendship with his daughter, who is my Best Friend today.

Well, so today he came again about my land. He wants us to join in the UBPC. This presumably won't affect my rights over the land very much. Really, to me personally, keeping the land doesn't matter. With my profession and the little plot I devote to growing vegetables for the family, I get enough so as not to Leave Anyone Unprotected. My two cousins who live with me are afraid I'll leave them in the Lurch if I give over the land and go live somewhere else. The fact is that I can't go anywhere. When I accepted my post as Agricultural Subdirector of the Sugar Complex, everything was crystal clear: I met my obligations to the State but continued taking care of my own Cane. Then my baby was born and things got a little more complicated. Now I'm pregnant again, with a girl, and I wouldn't Give Her Up for anything in the world. That's his main argument for why we should integrate My Cane with the UBPC's, so I can take care of the kids, at least in their earliest years. I haven't given him a categorical answer, because there isn't any hurry. The consolidation can't take place before the end of the coming harvest, '97. Meanwhile, He's taken on all the weight of his responsibility and mine. There's nothing extraordinary in that, It Was Almost Always That Way. As far as his Family Obligations, he has to Come to My House twice a day. Once to play for a while with the boy, and the other, at night, To Play for a While With Me. So far I've got no complaints, nor have I heard Anyone in the UBPC or the Sugar Complex complain that He's neglecting his responsibilities. His children don't worry me, nor his grandchildren, who live here more than in his house, because they're Thrilled to have an Uncle who can't even talk. Not to mention that their grandmother, when she gets Fed Up with them, sends them over to me yelling "Go bother your Thirty-Year-Old Grandma a while, and play with your Newborn Uncle!" at the top of her lungs so all El Batey can hear. That's what everybody calls my baby: "The Uncle." At first it bothered me, but now, sometimes I call him Uncle myself.

Translated by Dick Cluster

UNPLUGGED
Eduardo Del Llano

I've left the country.

Spread the word. Make a big splash. Let everyone know.

Is that supposed to be a dare? No, it's more like I'm begging. Please, say it loud and clear to friend and foe; tell them Nicanor O'Donnell, the writer, is living in Europe now.

But keep this part to yourselves. The first day, Rodríguez slipped a videocasette into my hand.

"Be sure to watch it tonight, there's a line," he said, vanishing into the crowd of ice cream lovers at Coppelia.

I watched it that night. It was a revolting teleplay — Venezuelan, or Colombian, or Puerto Rican, or else some slick threeway coproduction. I was insulted that Rodríguez felt he had a right to ruin my free time with something like that, even though if it hadn't been his revolting video, I'm sure I'd have watched something just as bad on TV.

"So," he prompted at nine the next morning, "that's really something, isn't it?"

With that, an inner voice yelled out to me that my friend expected an impassioned ode to his audiovisual material. I fished around for some positive-sounding equivalent of "disgusting, pathetic piece of crap" but right then, I had a hard time finding one.

"Don't tell me you didn't realize," he said. Then he explained that the actress playing the boy's mother was the one who had left Cuba about ten years ago, and that the boy himself (before he left too) had played one of the leads in that endless detective series that's apparently supposed to prove all cops are good-looking and smart. After he explained all that, he stood there looking at me as if he had said more than enough.

"Well, whaddya know," I declared

Then he asked me to get the video to Ana, a law student and mutual friend who lives near me. I didn't say no. I almost never do. Don't ask me why. That's like asking why kids always draw houses with sloping roofs.

"Thanks," Ana said, her face all twisted out of shape. "This whole country's got a toothache." She explained to me that in the dental wing of the polyclinic she went to, the compressor (whatever that was) had broken down, so they hadn't seen any new cases for two weeks now. That morning she had gone

56

looking for other options.

"There's an epidemic of broken compressors in the polyclinics. I got the phone numbers of three private dentists, but one is out of town, the second overcharges and the third has no more openings this month.

She thanked me again for bringing the cassette; then she offered to lend me a book and said to read it in a hurry, because it belonged to her boyfriend. It was a novel by a woman writer who had emigrated some ten years earlier. That night I turned off the TV with a flourish, opting for literature instead. Ana's toothache was like a multiple orgasm compared to that novel. It was an endless succession of troubles, two hundred pages worth. Living through them all was hard enough, but even worse, they were boring.

The next morning this long-haired guy came to see me saying Ana had sent him. It was the boy friend, of course. Five or six years ago, my biotype was a lot like his.

"And look at this," he said, pulling his wallet out of his bag and a folded paper out of his wallet. He handed it to me. It was a poem by another émigré writer, a poem that was part of a novel. The guy carried it around with him like a lucky charm, and he recited a piece from memory.

"That's the best picture ever painted of Havana."

"It's pretty good," I allowed, "but not the best."

We debated the point. The guy told me that in order to see something really clearly, you had to look at it from a distance. I cracked a joke about farsightedness, and he almost punched me out.

That afternoon I spotted Rodríguez from across the street. He was coming toward me carrying two more videos, so I ducked into the first available doorway. Turns out it was the entrance to a photography studio. A cleaning lady asked me what I wanted. I said I needed some passport pictures. They made me put down five dollars, which was all the capital I'd have until the next ice age. Then they ushered me into a closed cubicle, where they had me put on a piece of striped jacket and a tie Jimi Hendrix would have detested. I slicked my hair down, blinked and naturally, that's just when the flashbulb went off. Then I left with a receipt in my pocket, and there stood my friend.

"When I saw you go in there, I waited for you so I could pass on some terrific material," he said. "And by the way, if you needed your picture taken, I could have arranged for a pal of mine to do it for free."

With that, he lent me not the videos, but a CD by a folk singer who, since leaving the island, has been doing more or less the same thing as before, only with fancier packaging.

"I can't stand the *punto guajiro*," I protested. I hate that music from out in the sticks.

"Just listen to it."

Later on that day, to the explosive accompaniment of Cuban lutes and bongoes, I gathered that God had something to tell me. So I got to thinking.

No one is a prophet in his own land. That's true enough. But in this case, something else was going on. When your average *compañero* reads the work of his fellow Cubans who have left for good, it's not so much for what they have to say — mostly, that's no news to anyone — but because the very act of reading a presumably unauthorized book makes you one of the enlightened few, a member of the sacred brotherhood of laid-back resisters. Reading that book and passing it on is an act of civil disobedience that's neither too serious nor too forbidden. That's where aesthetic battle lines blur: it's not a question of good émigré writers versus bad, but of writers who are good because they're émigrés. (And the fact that they look so sharp and pleasantly plump in those photos of theirs is one more point in their favor). There are radical readers who claim they limit their consumption to imports; they even search used book stores for whatever said writers may have left behind, then pour over old drafts looking for code words and hidden messages.

The same goes for music and audiovisuals. A trumpet solo by an émigré musician, or a documentary about insects, will always find some diehard willing to make copies and read things into them.

Anyhow, I thought all that and decided that besides giving me the chance to see how certain things are, God was hinting at a method. I had published a novel, *We, the Impotent*, two years earlier. It was well-received and even got a flattering review in one magazine. But the fact is, it only sold fifty copies.

If I wanted to be read, I had to leave.

So I did.

I've been cooped up at home for three months now. During the first month, I got five copies of my new novel into shape. Rodríguez gave me a hand with them; I had no choice but to ask him for help. He got someone to design and print a terrific cover that looks imported. He also arranged for the innards to be printed and found someone to do the binding. They turned out perfectly, with my picture on the back cover; we used that passport photo I had taken the day I ducked into the photo studio. When everything was ready, we recruited several friends for our little campaign, including Ana. Ana has turned me into an idol at the university; she also does my shopping. Her new boy friend is a dentist.

Of course, becoming a shut in—imploding that way—is a tough sacrifice. It was reassuring to discover I had a predecessor, a character of Mark Twain's who faked his own death, anticipating that he would be revered as a great painter. And for him it was worth it. That's why the important thing now is to spread the word far and wide, to convince the world that I'm living in Paris and that Gallimard has brought out my novel in a deluxe edition with several printings. According to Rodríguez, those five copies are circulating like crazy. The method works. So, please, make a big splash.

I've just left my house for the first time. Naturally, I took the necessary precautions; I have on dark glasses and an Antz cap. Nevertheless, Rodríguez spotted me on the streetcorner.

"What the fuck do you think you're doing?," he yelled. "Do you want to ruin everything?"

I was too embarrassed to say I just wanted to buy a paper, so I said something about the light and the smell of flowers.

"Stop talking like a fruitcake. You're a celebrity now. If they recognize you, you'll screw up everything."

I felt an urge to rebel. A tiny little urge.

"Who's taking the chances here, anyhow? If I'm found out, it'll be my problem, won't it?"

He opened his mouth to answer me but then, he changed his mind. He was staring over my shoulder at something.

"Turn around slowly, and take a look at that guy coming out of the snack bar."

When I did, I could hardly keep from screaming. The fellow had on a hat and a raincoat, but I recognized him right off. I had seen his photo lots of times on shiny covers.

"He only lets himself leave the house once a year," Rodríguez said.

Translated by Louise B. Popkin

DREAMS OF FLYING
Eduardo del Llano

and everything's fine until I wake up at an altitude of fifteen thousand feet. Terrified, all I can do is close my eyes and go back to sleep, but that's dangerous— preposterous, in fact. No one can actually fly while they're asleep, they just think they can. And no one can fly while they're awake either, so I begin to descend. When I'm about to crash, I discover I've been dreaming, which automatically upends all my earlier reflections. However, a few details remain murky: why is the earth still coming closer? How come I was able to soar to such heights at first, when I can't do that now? I opt for the only sensible solution—namely, falling asleep right before I land. In my dreams I finally hit the ground, but it's not the least bit painful. Then I realize that, strange as it sounds, I'm both awake and flying, and asleep, out cold. But when you come right down to it, that's not so bad. Why, you can even get used to it, as long as your arms don't get too tired.

Nicanor passed a row of empty doorways, a vacant lot and a gas station that looked like it belonged in the Sahara; but when he reached the warehouse he really needed to go, so he asked the watchman to let him in for a second, for God's sake. The watchman made him repeat his request three times and then said sure he would, except he'd have to ask his boss; with that, he went back through the huge rusty iron gate, which was still ajar. Nicanor stood there waiting with his legs crossed and his lower lip caught between his teeth. Finally the watchman came out with a guy who held out his hand and said he was Angel, the manager. Nicanor introduced himself as an art critic, saying pleased to meet you and I'm about to wet my pants.

"This is highly irregular," remarked the manager. "But I'll let you in, because I know how that can be. It's down the hall on your right, past the office and the pile of retreads."

Following the manager's directions, Nicanor came to a narrow place with an awful stench; it had a door which refused to close, sporting a huge, emblematic penis. Inside were a broken sink and two cubicles; he plunged into the nearest one, wading through lumpy liquids. Then he closed his eyes, thought simultaneously of Niagara and Vesuvius, took aim at a floating turd and in less than a second, cut it in two.

"Aah," he declared. He was engrossed in the process of returning his male organ to its customary resting place, when the swinging door to the cubicle caught his eye. (Later he could have sworn that a ray of light came to guide him, perhaps even a transfigured glow, a gentle aura, emanating from the wood.) There was an area on its surface, among all the lewd carvings and incitements to fornication, where the veneer had come off. And right there on that barren stretch, he glimpsed some smudgy patches and an all-too-familiar signature.

"Holy shit," he said, tearing out of the cubicle before he could even zip up his fly.

"Salvador Dalí? You mean to tell me there's an original Dalí on a bathroom door in Guanabacoa?"

"A version of the *Burning Giraffe*," Nicanor clarified. "It's in terrible shape, but it's recognizable. And if I may say so, it's much better than the other one."

Rodríguez—the same Rodríguez who signs his name to the most impenetrable essays ever found in scholarly journals on art history and theory; author of the book *Champions of the Ideologeme*, member of the International Association of Critics and circumstances permitting, photographer of male nudes, to boot; Rodríguez, in sum, a dwarfish polyglot and fruitcake who, when he has a headache, just picks up any volume by Lyotard or Francastel—let out a semiotically pure guffaw and shook like an asthmatic.

"Come off it," he said. "You're more likely to find a copy of Aristotle's *Poetics* in the snack bar at the Council of State."

"It's a Dalí," Nicanor insisted, "but I need for you to see it, so I can be sure. Even though I'm sure now."

"My boy, Dalí never set foot in this country. He wasn't that much of a surrealist."

Nicanor sighed. He had come straight from the site of his national treasure to Rodríguez's place, certain that waiting to see him the next morning at the University would be tantamount to high treason. And now, that big peter puffer didn't believe him. Well, OK, then, he'd give it another try. He had always suspected that those guys who witness miracles and when they go to tell about it, get all worked up and start panting and spouting nonsense, have no one but themselves to blame when other people are skeptical.

"Who's to say Dalí didn't stop off here at some point? Or maybe the doors in that bathroom are imported. Look, Rodríguez, I know it sounds weird. If you go see it and you assure me it's a forgery, I promise that'll be the end of it. You're the top specialist in twentieth century European art. But damn it, trust me, will you?"

"And you say there's shit floating around in puddles there?"

"It's a bathroom in a warehouse. What do you expect?"

"Good thing that Dalí of yours isn't on the floor. This is nuts, Nicanor," said Rodríguez pulling a pocket diary out of who knows where. "Let's see now, on Tuesday and Wednesday I'll be at that event, on Thursday I have office hours, and on Friday, I'm scheduled to meet with the curator from the Birmingham Photo Gallery. On weekends, the warehouse is probably closed. Let's say I give you a call around the middle of…"

"Lend me your camera."

"The Nikon? Over my dead body."

"Come on, lend it to me. And I'll pose for you, whenever you want."

What was on the mind of Nicanor O'Donnell, professor and third-rate critic, as he headed back to the warehouse, camera in hand and poised for action? Actually, a number of things. As he got off the bus, he said something about showing certain unspecified bastards a thing or two. And more than likely, that's what was uppermost in his mind. When you get right down to it, the primary purpose of everything we do is to teach one or more bastards a lesson.

"Don't tell me you're about to wet your pants again," the watchman commented sarcastically. "Aren't there any better bathrooms around?"

"OK, this is the last time," Nicanor begged. He had decided to keep his discovery a secret. The watchman or Angel might be self-taught art historians, or maybe they even had degrees. No one knew better than Nicanor how hard it was to find a job after you graduated.

Angel subjected the critic to a brief interrogation.

" I see you brought a camera."

"I was doing some work at the museum."

"And you couldn't take a leak there?"

"I did. But I've got a kidney problem."

"It's almost closing time."

Angel finally authorized a second trip to the toilet, on the condition that he escort Nicanor all the way to the door.

"It's not that we don't trust you," he clarified. "It's that this is no ordinary tire warehouse. It may not look like much, but there's a group of Spaniards who want to..."

Nicanor splashed his way back to the cubicle and confirmed that the Dalí was still where it belonged. He peed noisily, so that Angel would hear him. Then he focused the lens and measured the light. Click click click.

"I heard the camera clicking," the manager informed him. "You're up to something weird. I don't want to see you back here again. And close your damn fly."

No sooner was the photo paper in the developing tray, than Rodríguez started turning pale. Then, limp-wristed and ecstatic, he threw his arms around Nicanor.

"It's a Dalí, all right. If that's not a Dalí, I swear I'll sleep with a woman. Here, Nicanor, let me give you a kiss."

"Get your hands off me. I already said you could photograph me in the nude. Don't push it."

"Of course," the expert mused, a moment later, "I'd have to see it to be absolutely sure. I'd have to date it tentatively, describe its style and pictorial substance, and assign it to a period in his work. Otherwise, I can hardly write a scholarly paper and without a paper, nobody will believe me."

"Believe *you*?" Nicanor said. "I'm the one who found it. Look, we can both announce its discovery, but it has to be clear that I'm the one who found it. This is my big chance."

"OK, fine," Rodríguez conceded. "Don't get upset. We'll put both our names on the paper. Now, let's go over to the warehouse."

"It's probably closed by now. We can go tomorrow. Of course, you have that event..."

"They can take their event and shove it. Oh, Nicanor, come closer, let's celebrate. I'm so happy..."

"Enough is enough," Angel roared. He had a crowbar in his hand, and he was wielding it like a sword. "Beat it, or I'm calling the police."

"But my friend and I have the same kidney problem..."

"Yeah, I bet you two have the same problem. Damn it, it doesn't pay to be nice. First you show up here by yourself, next you bring a camera to take pictures of your gross weirdo stuff and now, you bring a friend. What do you think this is, anyhow?"

"Angel," said Nicanor, putting his hand in his pocket, "if you want, we'd be happy to show our appreciation...Come on, it's really urgent."

The crowbar shook menacingly.

"If it's all that urgent, go do it under some bushes. I don't want to discuss it any further. We're expecting an important visit from a group of Spaniards. So, take your hand out of there and get moving before I bust your brains out!"

Rodríguez pulled on Nicanor's arm.

"Drop it. Come on, let's go."

Angel watched them leave, still brandishing his cautionary crowbar.

The watchman chuckled.

"Artists do the damndest things."

Two days later, Nicanor walked into the National Library and headed straight for the table where Rodríguez was sitting.

"I've found an old man who was a custodian at the warehouse back in the fifties, when the place was part of the Sánchez pharmacy chain. I showed him a picture of Dalí, and it rang a bell. He let him use the bathroom once. Dalí had problems with diarrhea..."

"That guy must be at least eighty by now. I'm not sure he's a reliable witness."

"The old man is perfectly fine. I taped him and took a few snapshots. He says Dalí had a little satchel with him. I bet he kept some tubes of paint in there. You know how it is with diarrhea. He was stuck in that bathroom, he saw the door, and he figured he might as well paint a little doodad... I can just picture him."

Rodríguez nodded slowly.

"Well, there is a period of a few weeks in Dalí's biography, precisely during those years, when he's unaccounted for...so that may be. From what I can see in the photos, it was painted in a hurry; the brushstrokes are very fluid. And it does anticipate the new figuration of the sixties. Oh, Nicanor, that lousy giraffe is worth its weight in gold. The tough part is, I can't stick my neck out unless I actually see the door. We'll have to go back to…"

"Look, I already told you," Nicanor replied, "don't even think about it. If we talk to the manager of the warehouse, he'll see to it we get screwed; or even worse, he'll try to take all the credit himself. Which is exactly what will happen if we go through the Ministry of Culture. The only thing we can do is what we discussed."

"But that's nuts. We'll be asking for trouble."

"No, we'll be safeguarding a national treasure. Either we steal that door or any day now, someone's going to carve a bare-assed lady right over the giraffe. Come on, Rodríguez, make up your mind or I'll have to do it by myself."

Rodríguez made his mind up the next day, when he read in the paper that a Spanish firm had signed an agreement with the government to create a mixed venture for the production of tires. The Spaniards would supply startup capital for the renovation and reopening of the company's run down facilities, and they would make use of abandoned buildings, especially old warehouses, as the sites for additional new ones. Our first job is to clean up, decorate and repaint, declared the head of the company earnestly; you can't expect to motivate people without a genuine work aesthetic.

"If they don't toss that door and put up a new one, we'll know they're on to the giraffe," whimpered the expert. "Remember, Dalí was Spanish. One spic with a belly ache and we could lose everything. You were right, Nicanor. We've got to beat them to it."

To throw them off track, Nicanor went straight to a show by a small-town artist and published a review about it the following day, three paragraphs on the next to last page of the paper. In his classes, he avoided glowing references to surrealism or twentieth century art in general. Rodríguez met with the English curator and made a point of dismissing the vanguard movements out of hand. My thing is postmodern iconic resemantization, he commented. That should be obvious from my published work.

On Friday night, Nicanor called Rodríguez to say that Picasso had always been a creep. That was their signal.

"There's a way in through the back," Nicanor explained. "And we can use this iron to jimmy the lock. The watchman will never know the difference."

They had parked the car on the corner, about fifty yards from there. It was Rodríguez's car, of course. On the way over, they put on some black gloves.

"We should have brought along a door that's in decent shape to replace the one on the cubicle," the expert remarked. "Angel or the watchman is bound to suspect us, when they realize someone took it."

"They have no idea why we care about that bathroom. Or, to be more precise, they have the wrong idea. I don't think they'll notice anything missing tomorrow. What on earth could be more natural than a cannibalized toilet? Besides, we'll be lucky to get out of there with a door. Let's not push our luck by trying to get one in."

Forcing the back entrance wasn't hard. Rodríguez kept an eye out, while Nicanor pried open the lock. One average click and they discovered that the night outside wasn't all that dark.

"Get out the flashlight."

"It's on already. Thing is, I had to use the batteries from the radio."

Making it down the hallway, which reeked of burnt plastic, was like walking a tightrope. They inched their way carefully past piles of tires, wooden boxes and cartons, old machines and puddles of grease. Even so, Rodríguez tripped over something and fell; he sounded like a piano coming down on a heap of saws.

"Maybe I didn't make myself clear," said Nicanor. "The whole idea is that the watchman shouldn't hear us."

"Sorry," Rodríguez stammered. "Mother of God, are we ever nuts."

One way or another, Nicanor managed to find his way to the bathroom. He heaved a sigh of relief as first his nose, then the flashlight, informed him he was wading through familiar puddles of filth. He located the cubicle, opened the door and tried his best to sound ceremonious:

"Rodríguez, look at this."

The painting looked pretty beat up, but the giraffe and the signature were still there. For a brief moment, the glow from the flashlight took on the golden hue of Fra Angelico's halos.

"My God," the expert murmured. "What a treasure. It really is Dalí."

"What did I tell you. Now, hang on to the door, will you? Steady, like a man."

Nicanor pried off the first hinge. And the second. Then they heard a noise that wasn't theirs.

"It's the watchman. Hurry up, there's only one to go."

"Hold on."

There were footsteps out in the hall. Wary, anxious footsteps belonging to one person. A voice asked who was in there.

"There's still another hinge," whispered Nicanor. "Pay attention. Now is no time for cold feet."

"Don't forget I'm a faggot," said Rodríguez.

A dark silhouette appeared at the entrance to the bathroom. Nicanor barked an order and with a single tug, they tore the swinging door off the cubicle; then they rushed at the watchman, surrealist shield in hand.

Bam.

They were barely out of there when the first shot rang out. The watchman must not have appreciated being stepped on and poked in the eye with a corner of the door. He fired another shot. Nicanor and Rodríguez made it to the back entrance, now an exit, and escaped into the darkness.

A passerby, or someone with just enough time to look out the window, would have seen a wooden rectangle with two pairs of legs running into the wind and climbing into a Lada 1600, while some guy chased after them with a hand over one eye, carrying on and firing a gun. That's all. It wasn't much, and the police officer who showed up twenty-five minutes later had a pretty hard time finding witnesses.

Rodríguez burst into tears, cried for about half an hour and was still crying when Nicanor put his arm around him and gave him a little peck on the ear.

"If he had...hit me...damn it, I wouldn't care. But this...just breaks...my...heart."

The door lay on top of a table, in the middle of the room.

There were two holes in it: one had beheaded the giraffe and the other had left the painting without a signature. What's more, a tiny crack that had appeared when the last hinge came off now extended over fully half of its museum-quality surface.

"It's not too late to do something," said Nicanor half-heartedly.

"There's...nothing we can...do. A famous painting can be restored, but first you have to prove...it's...famous. If we show up at the National Museum with this, they'll just laugh at us, same as if we try to sell it...to a...foreign...collector. Our national treasure is kaput. And we'll be...going to...jail..., for sure. God, we really are nuts..."

But Nicanor wasn't about to give in.

"It's not fair. We didn't go risking our necks over a shitty old broken down door. If they don't come after us in a few days, go ahead and write that paper. This is still our big chance. Let's try and convince the bastards we've got a Dalí."

"You don't get it, do you? We'll just be wasting our time and asking for trouble. God, why didn't I run off with that German? By now I'd have gotten a sex change and a new name. I'd be... Ana. I've dreamed about being Ana since I was a kid."

"You still can be. You're famous, and you're always going off on trips. I'm the one who's really screwed."

"I'm too old for that, Nicanor. Too old and too tied down here. That German was the love of my life."

"Oh, you're just in a snit. Are you going to write that paper or aren't you?"

Rodríguez burst into tears again and shook his head no. Nicanor felt like hugging him, smashing his head against the floor, crying with him and then committing suicide. What he did instead, was start taking his clothes off.

"If you write that paper and hang in with me while we give it a shot..."

Rodríguez looked at him, still sniveling.

"I said I'd pose for you, didn't I? Well, here I am. Take my picture....Ana."

The police hardly investigated, since they couldn't get terribly worked up over two burglars breaking into a warehouse to make off with nothing but the door from a bathroom cubicle. They found no fingerprints, and the witnesses couldn't even agree on the color of the getaway car. Moreover, with his memory affected by the attack, the watchman's account was none too coherent. From what he said, it wasn't clear if the object in question had been stolen, or it had decided to leave on its own after poking him in the eye. The new heads of the company promptly replaced both the watchman and the door.

Nicanor and Rodriguez waited a week, then tried, cagily and unsuccessfully, to establish the authenticity of the Dalí. All they got for their efforts was a reputation as a couple of lunatics. The "lunatics" part wasn't true; the "couple" part eventually was. One day, in a fit of rage, the two of them went at the painting, scratching and defacing it to carve phalluses and slogans on top. After that, everything returned to normal and to this day, all those bastards can read reviews by one and the other in scholarly journals and the press.

Nicanor is now Rodríguez's only model. Mostly, he poses as a bird, or as Icarus. When you come right down to it, that's not so bad; why, you can even get used to it, as long as your arms don't get too tired.

October 8, 1995

Translated by Louise B. Popkin

THE MAN FROM NOWHERE
Miguel Mejides

For my father

Some people always go against the grain, but I don't go against anything. That may stem from the great handicap that's marked my life: I'm cross-eyed. Ever since I could think, since the first time I studied myself in the mirror and saw my eyes, I told myself I was a man destined for silence and meditation, for smiling and long walks through the city I'd one day choose for my solitary life.

My mother, thank God, always understood I was the quiet type, like a mute songbird. Likewise, she came to accept my decision to head out of our little town and make something of myself in Havana. I've never been able to shake the image of her seeing me off at the train station, waving a linen hankie in farewell, the train smoke all around her and the saintly smile she never lost, not even in death.

Havana affects me the same way. See how it's rained these last few years. Until not long ago I enjoyed surveying Havana with the same gaze I had when I first arrived, back in January, 1990, when the city still retained a haze of lights and mysteries. The bus entered by way of the old main highway, continued toward the statue of the Virgin of the Road and straight down Luyano Street. At the end of my journey, I was awe-struck by the statue of our poet-hero, José Martí, in Revolution Square and by the twinkling Ferris wheel in the amusement park across from the bus terminal.

I'll never forget the taxi that took me to Infanta 234, a bright orange DeSoto, the coat-of-arms of some age-old Spanish province and the number 13 painted on the door. The driver was a short geezer with an Andalusian accent, wearing a colorful hat.

"That's the place," he said, flashing his stained teeth.

When I paid him, he got a good look at me and his eyes widened in alarm. "Buy yourself some specs," he told me.

My Aunt Buza greeted me half-solicitous, half-surprised. She gave me the same look the taxi driver had and spoke of charms that cured eye diseases. Her husband was in a bad mood when he greeted me and asked if I knew how to drive. When I said no, he talked about modern times, how a man at the turn of this century

70

has to know how to get around by car. Then he discussed in detail the interview I'd undergo the next morning.

"Just talk about the basics, don't blow your nose, and lie: say you know how to drive."

I still have no idea what that had to do with the job I was applying for. That night they settled me in a small room next to the kitchen. Its only charm was a large window looking out on Havana. Everything was so different from my home town. I was struck by the city's traffic and the sea which I guessed was on the horizon of the night sky, and the Progreso Radio Building across the street, where soap operas were born, the love stories that made Mom sigh. I'm in Havana, I said, and I'll never turn my back on its flame. This town could shower you with pleasure one minute and turn into hell the next.

But since I was in that grieving phase (I don't know if I'll ever come out of it), the interview was a disaster. At eight in the morning, we planted ourselves by the manager's office at the Hotel Nacional. I was so nervous, I told my aunt's husband I needed to go the bathroom. He pointed out the way and when I glanced in the mirror, I saw that my eyes'd never crossed so hard. I was afraid my pupils would fall out of their sockets and into the sink.

When I got back, they were waiting for me. The manager ushered us into his office. He was about 30 and had a mole on his nose. He said something about Greek beauty, about the Greek ideal of beauty, and that hotels were the palaces of kings.

"I'm sure you understand, Jeronimo," he said abruptly.

"Maybe if he wore dark glasses no one'd notice," my aunt's husband said.

"But he can't wear them at night. A hotel is a living organism," he said with conviction. "If just one body is out of sync, that beauty is spoiled."

On the way back, I recalled what the taxi driver had said. I decided that, first chance I got, I'd buy a pair of glasses. My mother had convinced her sister that Jeronimo could come up with a job for me at the Hotel Nacional where he'd worked since he was a teenager. My mother had failed to mention my crossed eyes. She'd sent many photos of me, just my profile, as if I were the best looking guy in the world. My eyes would force me to go back home. They'd force me to grow old in that little piece of the world where a cemetery marks the turn-off to the only road connecting it to Camaguey.

"Stay a week, if you like, and then buy a ticket back," Aunt Buza said.

"There're no opportunities back home," I said.

"In those tiny towns, people get used to diseases like yours," she pronounced.

That very afternoon, I bought glasses from a street vendor in Galiano. They weren't high quality, but you had to look hard to detect my eyes. With my new look, I spent all my time walking around Havana. By seven a.m. sharp, I'd already hit the streets. First I walked around El Cerro; then Marianao. By the time I started my trek down Carlos III, more than a week had gone by. I wasn't much trouble to my aunt and uncle. I didn't turn on the lamp at night, I rarely relieved myself in their bathroom, and in the morning I just had coffee. When I returned in the dead of night, I ate whatever leftovers were on the stove. I sincerely hoped to find work so I could stay in Havana. But everywhere people looked at me funny and told me they had no openings. A month went by like that and my aunt's patience wore thin. I recall the night I tiptoed in and didn't find any food. In place of the usual pan, there was a no nonsense note saying they'd bought me a train ticket for the next morning. That's when I realized I was on my own in Havana.

Without any fuss, I picked up my suitcase and set off. I went to Prado Park and stretched out on a marble bench in front of the Hotel Seville. The laurel trees were the best cover for my derelict state. I set my suitcase at my feet and settled down to sleep, my hands crossed behind my neck. I was just drifting off when I heard voices coming from the roots of the laurel trees. It was a diatribe on the last Christmas, about the curse the city was having to come to terms with.

"Who's there?" I managed to say.

I thought about how hunger can make you hallucinate. Yet that seemingly endless conversation soothed me. The voices were coming from a sonorous cone. The conversation was drowned out by a snicker that went on and on.

"Hey! Are you fish, angels, or what?" I shouted.

And I flopped down next to a laurel, put my ear to its roots, and heard the Glenn Miller band playing "String of Pearls." I lay there for a long time, my face resting on the ground. Next I half-way made out a devilish laugh and a dialogue that seemed otherworldly.

"That hive of humanity that lives up top, that Havana that's slave to the light will raise a monument to our catechistic labor some day, a monument to our galleys that sail the furrows of the earth, a monument to our warehouses crammed with salt and coffee, cured meat and garlic, our galleys brimming with the priesthood of commerce and good service, full of the lively noise of the world..."

Just then I clearly made out the scraping sound of my suitcase being snatched from the Prado bench. I saw two people running off into the distant night on the street next to the Hotel Seville, then laughter echoed from under the earth. I said one of those words you only utter when you're miserable. My voice was drowned out by the thunderous blare of the jazz band...

I didn't sleep that night. I spent the night walking around the Prado and Central Park. Many believe that being cross-eyed makes you see objects in a different dimension. But I saw the city the way it really looks. I'd observed Havana for a month and now detected the danger. There was no public lighting. All I could make out was the marquee of the Hotel Inglaterra. The García Lorca Theater looked like a sylph's castle. The Payret Theater billboard lifted Catherine Deneuve high overhead. The Capitol building was the ultimate mirror of the city. Central Park mimicked an ordinary day when people come out to talk on and on about scandals. Blacks in guarachera shirts looked ready for Carnival. Women in dresses cut by pious seamstresses on Monte Street strolled down shadowy trails. Sodomites tattooed trees with men's hearts and night owls lost extravagant bets on the illegal Chinese lottery.

And there I was, walking around the forbidden city, my hunger following the aromas, aware of the chiromancy of my somersaulting gut. Up walked a mulatto man pushing his sweets.

"Come on, big shot, buy yourself a nice piece of rum cake."

I mumbled like a fool, "Pains and misfortunes."

I was thinking about what I'd just said, how I'd heard my mother use that saying about mankind's luck. About how Havana was so different from my town, how foreign the night sounds were. My town didn't have night owls, just early birds taking the train to Camaguey. And the great city was a shop window for people who rejected the law of daylight hours, people living in tenements dark as a cave, in shacks where fathers discovered their daughters' young beauty early on, shacks where you never saw the sky, where the sun was a curse to the laws of the switchblade and blood, the laws of Old Havana, a Havana designed for carriages and slaves, for lights from bitter firewood, a city that still had to come to grips with the workings of the modern era.

And in the farthest corner of the park, a dingy little kiosk, with little or no signs of life, where a little old man bought and sold old magazines. Nat King Cole singing at the Tropicana; Che Guevara with his visionary eyes; Camilio Cienfuegos, a revolutionary hero astride a horse of one hundred waters; the 1962 missile crisis; Khrushchev pointing out a black star... People buying magazines that were the biographies of their souls. And me, fleeing from that experience, from the photos that at once had no connection to my life and yet did. Wandering past the doorways of the tobacco factories with the rustling of fine Pinar del Rio tobacco leaves, the murmuring of binnacles that housed Romeo and Juliet, Partaga, and Montecristo cigars. Searching for Prado Park again, down sleepy, crumbling paths, and now in the park, passing the time until morning, then taking my train to the vegetal world of the province, returning to my mother, to the routine of taking a piss, then going to bed at ten. To the oppression of obedience and pretense.

Finally I came back to the marble bench where they had stolen my suitcase, the laurel tree humbled now by the absence of Glenn Miller's music.

"Get your peanut brittle here!" shouted a dwarf on the same corner of the Hotel Seville. Repeating his patter like someone about to slit his wrists. "Hey, kid, peanut brittle!" he shouted at me from over there. I wanting to tell him I didn't have a cent, I felt like the biggest lowlife, nothing could save me, especially the train taking me far from Havana. Then the dwarf crossed the street and planted himself right in front of me, smiling, wearing a corduroy cap, huge shoes and muslin trousers.

"Here," he held out a peanut bar and told me he was headed home. "Come on, come on, eat it." I dug into it, as he watched me and I watched him too.

"Who buys your wares at night?" I asked him.

"No one. Nighttime amuses me."

And off he went, hawking his wares. "Everybody's crazy around here," I muttered and looked down the deserted streets. All you could hear was a far off voice coming from the top of the

Hotel Seville, the voice of a woman wailing, out of the loneliness boleros tell of and someone, also a woman I think, trying to calm her in a low voice. I fell asleep for a little while, more than a little while.

I awoke with crow shit splattered like a corn tortilla next to me. I looked at the critter and thought, how ironic. The sun was coming up and the crow looked like burnished tar. Sparrows were flying out of their hideaways, too, to start their nameless battles in the laurels. I felt around in my pocket and found my ticket to Camaguey, the ticket that would take me away from my hope. I started to walk to the station and saw that the Prado had suddenly come to life. Crowds of people scurried from one side of the park to the other, not heading anywhere in particular, lined up at bus stops to board nonexistent buses. There wasn't one restaurant, no smell of coffee along the way. As day broke that morning, the city was just a point on the map with no aromas, only a fresh breeze blowing from the sea. Just the smell of that sea waking up.

"God exists," said a woman in her fifties as she passed by me, very close to the station.

"So does the devil," I said, not giving her another thought.

In rapid succession, I showed my ticket to the guard at the door to the station lobby, then stood at the ticket window, holding out my ID card, my laminated photo, the one with my eyes crossed, so they could verify the ticket was mine. The woman looked at my eyes, then at the eyes in the photo, checking my ID number, like the brand on some tame bull, my height in inches, my mouth's nervous tick, my travel permit.

"The train leaves early," the woman said. "Go to platform three, coach 52, seat 81. If you're traveling with food, it may be confiscated, no animals allowed, all travelers must..."

I quit listening and walked to the entrance to platform three where someone asked for my ticket and demanded to see my ID card again. This time it was a short, fat man with a gray mustache. Finally, with a little shove, he let me pass, and I ran down the platform, with that fear I have of arriving late to places. What about coach 52? All the others were there, not mine. I started to yell. A crowd of about 30 people grouped around me. The locomotive whistled its final warning. Coach 52?!!!!!!!!, I demanded. The fat man came up and said that because of an unpardonable error they hadn't hooked up coach 52. In a wheezy voice, he informed us that the price of the ticket would be

refunded and we'd leave the next morning. I drew up to my full
height and said I wanted to see the administrator, someone, to
demand coach 52. The man pulled on his mustache and said that
given the imperialistic blockade, one must have a conscience, a
spirit of sacrifice. Travel tomorrow, folks.

I decided not to pursue it. No one would pay attention to me. I
returned to the ticket window where the same woman read me the
handbook on travelers' responsibilities and refunded the price of
my ticket. Barely twenty pesos. I made a decision — I would stay
in Havana. Perhaps my destiny was here with two million souls
facing the Gulf of Mexico. What's the difference if I died in
hock? Who cares about a cross-eyed guy? Who'd cry for a cross-
eyed guy? Only my mother would suffer, but she'd get over it.
Just like when Papa died. Days of grieving, of mourning, and then
Christian resignation.

I left the station, headed nowhere in particular. I was
convinced — I've always suffered from fantasies—that someone
would feel sorry for me. In the meantime, where should I go?
Hunger kept on pummeling my stomach. With my twenty pesos I
figured I'd eat one of those fish fritters they sell on Puerto
Avenue. I just had to go down a couple of winding alleys and I'd
be there in no time. As I was about to set off, I saw on the same
corner where they parked the rental cars, on the sewer culvert that
jutted out into the street like a metallic helmet, the dwarf who had
given me the peanut brittle at dawn. He recognized me and waved
his corduroy cap. I went over to him and was really surprised
when I saw him muttering angrily. He said something about kids,
how you couldn't recruit today's youth, that the hidden people
will dwindle in number, that the Grail would have to import
creatures from another planet.

"What're you talking about?" I asked him.

"Nothing," he answered. "An old dwarf's crazy ideas."

Like before, he handed me a peanut bar. I admit I was grateful
for it, but I craved something else. Still I gobbled it down with the
same savage appetite and he asked me where I was headed. I told
him what had happened to me and about my resolve to stay in
Havana.

He suddenly asked, "Do you have the guts to work for a
dwarf?"

"Tell me what to do and I'll start right this minute," I said.

"I'll take a chance on you," he added.

I was going to tell him I was an honest man, when the dwarf squatted down, slid down the culvert and, somehow, maybe by magic, the dwarf reappeared dragging a package, looking every direction, carefully selecting his words.

"Someone we thought was reliable was supposed to take this package to 111 Aramburu Street. I can't budge from this corner, maybe one day you'll understand. I'm confident you can carry out this mission, your future depends on it."

He paused, took off his cap, scratched his head, and spoke about the forces that rule the underground, the palaces King Solomon built in the interior of the cities after his death, populated cities or in the ones not yet unveiled.

"Take it or leave it."

I hoisted up the package and felt it rattle like a box filled with treasure. I was about to say something but the dwarf interrupted me.

"Sausages! Harmless sausages!" he repeated, overcome by a strange giddiness. "Be very careful. At the first sign of trouble, toss the package at the police's feet, that way they won't follow you."

And so the dwarf launched me on my first shady venture. Of course, my nerves were on edge as I went down the street. Each time I saw a policeman, I was ready to ditch the blessed sausages at his feet. But I got to Aramburu Street without a hitch. I rang the bell at number 111 and an old couple opened the door. They grilled me about a password I knew nothing about. I explained it was my first day as a delivery boy. They said when I visited them I should say, "Pontius Pilate!" Then, they led me to the living room and opened the package. It was thirty-odd cans of frankfurters.

"Here," the old lady said to me. I saw two twenty dollar bills and two ones. Pleased with myself, I returned to the train station but found no trace of the dwarf. One of the taxi drivers told me he'd seen the dwarf get into a blue car. I didn't know what to do with the money. It was way past noon by then and I all wanted to do was eat, sit down at a table and gorge myself, something I hadn't done since I left home. With that in mind, I went down to Puerto Avenue, by way of Central Park and the Prado, not taking the short cuts through Old Havana, which at that hour were covered by a fiery heat that consumed the street corners.

After bargaining with a woman in the shadows of a colonial

doorway on Park Avenue, I bought a fritter and a tamarind drink at black market prices. Next I walked around the souvenir shops by the Cathedral. I was fascinated by cigarette lighters with scenes of Havana, American cigarettes, ball point pens that showed naked woman when you shook them, racks of fashion magazines from all over the world... All the while I asked myself why we were so isolated from the world. The archipelago, the island, was like a ship adrift that fled from commercial kitsch, explaining itself in a retro rhetoric, a rhetoric that's also kitsch. Next, I went to the Bodeguita de Medio and walked through it; in the bathroom I wrote my name in fancy Persian calligraphy and left. I went back to Central Park and watched the Catherine Deneuve movie in the Payret Theater.

When I came out, it was late afternoon so I went down to the port again. In the Dos Hermanos Bar, I ordered a double shot of rum with the little money I had left. From the bar I could see the ferries to Regla and Casa Blanca transporting passengers. In the Dos Hermanos people did some serious drinking. The longshoremen were knocking back a bottle of that infernal rum as if it were water, the bartender shouted the orders in a lingo I didn't understand, and the women who came in looked like they'd walked right out of some Japanese comic book, wearing dresses so tight they looked like badly rolled cigars.

"Take off those specs," one of them said provocatively, fawning on me. She was must have been close to 35, a half Chinese mulatta, pleasant to look at. She'd gotten fat and her hips were too round. Tourists no longer sought her out, passed her over in the game of international flags of love.

"I'm cross-eyed," I told her bravely. I lowered my glasses and she looked at my eyes, examined them, and talked about how cross — eyed people bring luck. She touched my head as if to exorcise her bad luck. In a very loud voice, she said something like, "Hey, this guy's cross-eyed!" Two more women came over and touched my head, too. The bartender was generous and filled my glass. A black longshoreman came over and talked about the blind virgin, how there's a church in Guanabacoa, on the outskirts of the village, in the mountain, on the edge of the jungle, there's a hermitage where a virgin lives, they say she's from Toledo and can cure eye diseases. When he left, the Chinese mulatta said the black guy's a big windbag. She ordered a drink and got the bartender to fill my glass again.

"So, does the virgin exist?" I asked.

"God knows if she does, God only knows..." she said to me.

To make a long story short, I have to confess I tied on the biggest bitch of a drunk in my life. At ten I left with port dwellers and that riot of women in between tricks, everyone hugging me, touching my head. With so much alcohol everywhere I turned, I barely managed to hang onto those forty-two dollars that weren't mine, and since the dwarf hadn't showed up, they would be my only lifesaver. In that condition, we walked down Puerto Avenue and left the port authority behind. In front of the Commercial Market, one of the longshoremen, the shortest one, a cocky guy from the Canaries, started to shout the name of Obdulio Miraverde, bookkeeper at the warehouse. He was telling me, breathing into my eyes, how the guy threw himself off the golden cupola on account of some lousy five hundred pesos that they'd stolen from the cash box, afraid they'd blame him for the theft.

"You don't understand, you cross-eyed piece of shit! He killed himself for 500 little pieces of paper with Martí's face on them!" He was shouting now. "He was my friend! Look, there's his ghost," he took me by the chin. "Look, there's Obdulio, reenacting his leap every night at midnight."

And the Chinese mulatta at my side, sticking her tongue in my eyes, like a windshield wiper, her tongue in my ear, between my teeth, my tongue and hers, the party, the mulatta's tongue, the suicide, the alcohol. And now out on the Point, with the fortress El Morro and its lighthouse in front of us, her hand down my pants, shaking me like a flask of elixir, me overflowing, in plain view of Havana, the coral horizon of lights, the chimerical city, and me with my traitorous barb. "Come on, soak me, fill my hand with your suds," she repeated and me, thinking about that dame, about Havana, about the jolt that left a stain on my pants like a map of the jungle.

Suddenly into my head popped the idea to leave, go to the Prado and get over my hangover. Without warning I started to run, I left the Malecon boardwalk behind, that barrier between the sea and the souls of the city. Not stopping till I was in front of the Hotel Seville, taking refuge in its doorway, next to the dwarf with his corduroy cap, his table loaded down with peanut brittle. And he, seeing the strange trance that had come over me, said to me, "Kid! Hey, kid!" And me, talking about the virgin who cures bad eyes, that virgin in Guanabacoa, the virgin from Toledo.

Demanding to know if she exists, repeating, almost rudely, since I didn't know or remember his name: "Hey, dwarf. You. Dwarf. Over there. Come over here, dwarf..." Until he held out the third peanut bar in less than a day and I took a bite, and he brought up the money I'd been paid, and I dug around in my pocket and gave him the 42 dollars. He took the bills and held them up in the moonlight, looked them over, inspected them, and handed me back two dollars, your pay, hee, hee, hee, hee, hee, your first pay as a man. And I started to vomit, splattered the dwarf's muslin pants, the life went out of me and in the midst of all that, the dwarf kept saying: "They call me Pascualito. Don't drink any more, you can't do that in our business." At that, I went over to my bench, rolled around on the marble and stretched out like a snake. The dwarf shouted from the corner, "Meet me at the station tomorrow. Don't let me down." Once again I spewed a bilious, black, lumpy soup onto the laurel roots, listening to the dialog coming from under the earth, someone belting out a psalm about vegetables and grains, and Glenn Miller. And I fell asleep thinking about the crow shit that would wake me up at daybreak.

The next day I met the dwarf at the station. He told me he expected my approval any minute. "The Grail gets together in the mornings and hands out permits," he told me solemnly. We passed the time discussing my future. Pascualito insisted I should buy myself some new clothes, get rid of that shirt only a hick going nowhere would wear. From under the culvert, they said something, I guess it was OK. Pascualito patted me on the back and said, I'm never wrong about people, I don't get mixed up with riffraff. He handed me a chit for the shop in the Hotel Seville. Ask for Carmen Rosa, she'll fix you up with some clothes. Then he handed me a letter of introduction so they'd lease me a room in the crumbling building that had been a hotel and a Packard dealership in the forties.

"You'll live like a Christian there. I'll come by tonight and we can talk over your future."

This was the most radical change in my life. I bought clothes at the shop in the Hotel Seville and then went to the Packard dealership where a sad woman in a lacy, monogrammed blouse met me. She told me I'd share a room with Jeremias Batista. He's downright crazy, she warned me; furthermore, the city housing authority was not responsible for lost articles. No women after 11 PM.

"Here's your key."

The room was no great shakes. It had two beds, a couple of night stands, a tall armoire, and a bathroom with a very large bathtub, sitting on steel beams and a towel rack decorated with the goddess Minerva, or so they said. The fact that the rain and the noise from the busy street below came in through cracks in the walls worried me. "But what more can I ask for? Just two days ago I was sleeping in the park and today I have clean clothes and a bed. I can even take a shower," I thought. Happiness is never complete, as you'll see. The water had to rise six floors to get to my room. But it was better than the park and the crow that shat at dawn.

At seven that evening, Pascualito came to the door and called out, "Five lights for Pontius Pilate." When I opened the door, he gave me a heart-felt "Hurrah!" He praised my good taste in clothes and told me I'd start work the very next morning. From his back pants pocket he took out a map of Havana and unrolled it on one of the beds. Cheerfully he said the city was divided up into business districts, where the sewer culverts were located. With a pen he marked the corner of 23rd and 12th, the Colon Cemetery and the Falla Bonet Mausoleum, the corner the Hotel Seville was on, the corner of Tejas, the rental car parking lot at the train station, the Virgin of the Road Statue, the League for the Prevention of Blindness, the Rumba Palace on Playa Street, 70th Street in Miramar. After marking a couple dozen points on the map, he leaned back and said he was happy I had been approved as a messenger for the Congregation. He apologetically informed me I'd been thoroughly investigated and that they knew about my mother, my Aunt Buza and her husband and my school days. Everything suggested I was trustworthy.

"From now on you're one of us. You'll be paid punctually, with bonuses for extra effort. You'll regulate the city and its needs. You'll have Havana at your feet because you'll be the link between the promises of the underground and the humans above."

"And who are you all?" I asked.

"Don't worry about that, it's not important..." he evaded me. "Tomorrow you'll start your trips under Jeremias Batista's orders. Your password is five lights for Pontius Pilate. Every time you knock at a door or talk to me, say: "Five lights for Pontius Pilate!"

I walked him to the door, he shook my hand and, as he was

leaving, turned back to me and said, "The Virgin of the Eyes does exist, one day I'll take you to her sanctuary in Guanabacoa."

At eight I was in the dining room. The food was bad, but I ate it gratefully. I considered seeing a movie at the America Theater in Galiano. Then I gave up and decided to head off to bed. I thought about how this vast city gave me a better welcome than I'd foreseen. True, my new path was illegal. But who could live an honest life? I was a humble supplier of merchandise. Surely God would grace me with His pardon.

In the room, I met Jeremias Batista. He was in his skivvies, muttering, cutting his toenails. I introduced myself and he said he knew who I was. I was going to ask how but he interrupted me, asserting that the dwarves knew a lot. He declared the following:

"All that glitters is not gold. I can't tell you more than that, the rest you'll learn for yourself. I carry my orders out to the tee. Tomorrow we'll start by passing out the beef. I'll get straight to the point about being roommates — l like to sneak street walkers in here. When I do, you take a hike. I don't like farting. I don't like people who snore or have long toenails. One more thing. Learn everything you can about this fucking city or you won't be any use to the business. I'll wake you up at 3 AM."

And he really did get me up at that hour and we quickly headed for the Virgin of the Road Statue. There we took our positions, barely speaking a word. At nearly dawn a truck pulled up loaded with cattle. Jeremias Batista chatted with the driver then suddenly Pascualito materialized through a culvert, along with half a dozen dwarves. Without raising his voice once, Pascualito ordered them to open the back of the truck. Then they prodded the cows that jumped into the void of the culvert. In a while all that was left was the unmistakable odor of animal fear on the pavement.

"It's like there's a relic down there you have to offer sacrifices to," Jeremias commented.

That day, till nightfall, we went back and forth as messengers. So it went every Friday, slaughter day. Saturdays and Wednesdays you parceled out canned meats. There was hardly any work to do on Sundays. Mondays started the work week with orders for clothes. Tuesdays were catch-all days and you could be loaded down with anything from an elephant to a package of needles. Thursdays were medical days; we circulated around Havana medications that came from the pantheon of the Falla

Bonet Mausoleum in Colon. You carried a lot of money around and soon Jeremias taught me to make the most of that. We sold the dollars we'd just been paid in the afternoon, and bought them back cheaper in Trillo Park at night. You added these riches to the bonuses Pascualito handed out on the corner of the Hotel Seville.

I was getting rich so I bought myself a walkman, some cowboy boots, flowered shirts and a new pair of glasses. I started sending my mother an allowance and it looked like I'd go on like that forever. Late at night I went dancing in the discos and there I had my first love affair with a little mulatta, who was a fine piece of work, Jeremias left me the room and I discovered what making love was all about. Then I lost interest. About that time, Pascualito took me to the sanctuary in Guanabacoa to see the virgin. She was a very pretty virgin, surrounded by flowers. I asked her blessing half-heartedly. I wasn't convinced that a blind girl could cure a cross-eyed guy. Pascualito argued that the painter who did her portrait was drunk and drew her with no eyes. She was really the Virgin of Toledo. When she discovered her condition, she decided to make miracles.

Let me pause to say a few words about Jeremias. He was a tricky fox when it came to women. There wasn't a pretty woman along the Prado Jeremias didn't get into his bed. He was a flashy dresser: flannel hat, loud pants, and two-toned shoes he never parted with. His gruff character was just a front. He also took me to see the city skyline that constantly changed as buildings crumbled. "Behold Havana, the transvestite," he'd say. "One city today, another city tomorrow. Just like the god, Changó..."

With Pascualito the Good, we kept up a familiar dialogue. The dwarf never expressed his opinion about that world of waste water. Only by letting things unfold did I grasp his secrets. He was not at all willing to describe the changes in the Congregation's hierarchy, even less willing to describe the Supreme Boss's misfortunes. I also learned that no dwarf could be buried in the underground. They had ruled out having a cemetery in the cave's vaults and so the dwarves had taken one over in Guanabacoa, abandoned by the Jews who'd fled to New York in the sixties. There I got lucky when Pascualito bestowed upon us the job of digging a grave.

"Tomorrow you and Jeremias will dig the final resting place of a brother who's died," he said.

Cemeteries had always terrified me. We entered the cemetery

seized with fear, Jeremias muttering angrily. It was on a small hill, covered with ceiba trees, surrounded by crumbling walls. The Jewish graves were lost among the fallen leaves and you could only identify them by the columns with Hebrew characters. At last we came to the small mounds, next to the adobe wall in the back, where dwarves were buried. That's where we dug and by noon we'd made a small hole. Then, Pascualito appeared alongside the wall and offered us a swallow of a concoction made from some roots. He said he'd give the order to begin the mourners' send-off. When that started he said we'd have to leave since the ceremony was only for residents of the underground. We took our time gathering up our tools and glimpsed the court of the Grail enter, with a great chalice in front held high by a boy dwarf. For the first and only time, I saw the Supreme Boss — "art among arts, guide and splendor, sovereign of the sun," the boy proclaimed. The Supreme Boss was fat, pot-bellied and bare-chested, with a belly button like a tomato. That's as much as we saw because Pascualito shooed us away.

The next week I was promoted to a special delivery service for the sale of household goods. Tulle, flowers, good champagne — the underground had it all. That's when Rosendo Gil came into my life. He ran a laundromat he'd set up in his home on Murral Street. There was a sign at the entrance "Lightning Laundry: Washed and Dried in a Flash." Every day Rosendo handed me a list of deliveries. I don't think I'll ever work that hard again. He handed me deliveries packed with lace outfits and there I was, traveling by bus all the way to the ritzy neighborhoods of Miramar and New Vedado. I saw so many pretty girls undeterred by the bad weather! What I didn't like was those grand homes with gardens and dogs. People there looked at me like I was a criminal. I didn't wear my glasses just to fuck with them. When I rang one of those doorbells in Avon Llama, just like the homes in the commercials, I made myself more cross-eyed.

"You're weird," Rosendo Gil would say to me.

So that's how things went for me in this part of Havana, cut off from my friend Jeremias. Although we shared the room in the Packard, our jobs were so different we hardly ever saw each other. Until my fairy godmother — or bad luck — came along. It was a Wednesday, the 25th of December, my second Christmas in Havana. My delivery was bound for Mason and San Miguel, TV Cubana, ask for Reinita Principe. I got there and asked for her and they brought her right over. She was the actress who played the maid on the popular soap opera. I had taken off my glasses and my eyes had crossed really hard. At that moment I longed for my eyes to be aligned. The woman said we'll have to wait, Lucecita's taping. You know, my daughter, Lucecita, she clarified.

"I want her to try the outfit on. Then we'll settle up."

Next she invited me to the studio and I saw a TV show for the first time. They were filming Snow White. Lucecita was playing the main role. I'd never, ever seen a girl like her. I've never seen such pretty eyes since. Flung there on a rock, Lucecita was radiant, happiness personified. It was the scene where the Prince saves Snow White, when he arrives and kisses her and she comes back to life. Then, the dwarves dance and run around the studio. The end of the story made me break out in tears.

"This's the guy who brought the ball gown," Lucecita's mother introduced me. I held the box out to her and she smiled with that happy glow and went to try on the outfit. I waited there in limbo, watching the cameras that memorized dreams.

"Doesn't she look lovely!" Reinita Principe said when her daughter returned. The dwarves sang her praises, touching the tulle. All the studio admired her. "Let's go home," her mother urged.

Right now I don't know, I can't figure out if they hoodwinked me into loving her or if I got on board all on my own. They didn't invite me in that day and left me standing outside the door. As we turned the corner at Mason and San Miguel, next to the Napoleonic Museum, across from the university, Reinita Principe said, in the maid's voice she uses in the soap opera that she had only half the money. She talked on about how the television station was a hell hole, how they weren't doing any shows now that her beauty was fading. And in that situation I wasn't going to back down. I never say too much. I was a businessman, but I didn't know if the dwarves dreamed up everything that went on in Havana. I reasoned to myself, if they were already in TV, they could be anywhere.

"I can give you credit," it occurred to me to say.

"Hey, he's my kind of guy!" said Lucecita.

From that moment on, I believed a woman can change your life with a single word. I became Lucecita's biggest fan. Not an afternoon went by when I wasn't in the studios. I finagled a special pass and sat in the front row, watching the shows. "Is this love?!" I asked myself.

I was hurt when they didn't invite me to Lucecita's birthday party. That night I walked along the University walls. When I saw the fuss they were making over her, I lost the nerve to go in. I remember I went into the Napoleon Museum and stood in front of the Great Corsican's bed for an hour. I was so smitten by Josephine's portrait, I longed to take it home, just to have a girlfriend. But imagination is one thing, life is another.

"Put the squeeze on the mother," Rosendo Gil told me, who'd become my confessor. "Either she gives you her daughter or she pays," he smiled salaciously.

So I approached Reinita Principe. I told her my boss demanded payment from me and, if I didn't get it, they'd retaliate. Her smile dimmed. She mentioned the money owed her and that she'd been chosen for a leading part. I turned a deaf ear and spoke of the terrible band of thieves that lurk around houses at night. She promised she'd take care of the debt that very week. Transformed from then on, she scolded me for not coming to the party. I looked at her with such scorn she changed the subject and invited me over for coffee.

"I want you to meet my husband," she said.

It was a typical Havana apartment that had seen better days: furniture missing its upholstery, crumbling walls, broken windows. Reinita tiptoed in and said, "Nicanor Jose". All we heard was a rasping cough. Reinita said, "Follow me," and we entered a bedroom where a man in his seventies was smoking a cigar. Behind him, tacked to the wall, were photos, posters, diplomas, and a map of Havana. The main photo—for some reason l guessed the caption was in German — must have said something banned. It showed a crane setting a concrete block down in the middle of a street. At the street's end, there was a trolley that had come to a stop. Lucecita's old man was barefoot, wearing a sweater that hung down over his wool pants. He looked me over and, seeing my interest in the photo, said it was the all-powerful Berlin Wall.

"It was the wall that saved us," he said. Then he showed me his diplomas, describing them like in a newsreel at the movie theater. "Ah, this one! From the KGB, a year-long course in Moscow. Oh, this one, from that second rate Czech security agency! Yes, that one, from the highly trained German police force!" He coughed again and spit out the window, then pointed to the map of Havana. "See those circles? See them?" he asked, forcing me to answer yes quickly. "That's where the sewers empty out. I was the one who discovered the scourge, I was the first to say the city was being taken over by the Jews who disappeared from the synagogues in Havana just as the Berlin Wall was being built. They hid underground and became predators, draining the people dry."

From then on, I became a regular visitor. Reinita Principe told me her husband had been an officer and had traveled all over the world taking courses in espionage. They'd discharged him when he raised a ruckus at a meeting with the generals, insisting, to no avail, that there were dwarves in the sewers of Havana.

"Then came the fall of the Wall," Reinita explained. "And he hasn't gotten over it. Every waking moment, he has cursed Vaclav Havel. He once met him in Prague, you know."

Lucecita didn't like the fact that I visited every day, loaded down with cans of sausages. Her mother pressured her to be polite but Lucecita took great pains to sour my life. For the whole month I stayed for supper, she sat at the table and stared at me or made comments about people who thought they could buy love. I doted on her, tried to flatter her more each day and spent my savings generously. But she didn't repay my generosity. She persuaded her father to declare war on me. The old man began his campaign against me and threatened to have his old comrades arrest me as a Jewish spy.

"Make yourself scarce," my friend Jeremias advised me.

That's what I did. I didn't set foot in the studio or the house. Such sadness came over me! I had no desire to spite her by sleeping with one of those girls for hire. I started to hate Havana and my memories. In the afternoons I went to the Dos Hermanos Bar and got really drunk. There were the same longshoremen, the Chinese mulatta who squeezed me dry that night by the light of El Morro. Everyone kept touching my head.

A month later, my life took a new turn. One afternoon I ran across Pascualito at the entrance to the Packard. The little guy beckoned to me to follow him. He talked about the Great Grail, the Supreme Boss and the difficulties they had picking up the TV signal underground. He asked me if I was still catting around in the studios at Mason and San Miguel. When I explained my amorous setbacks, he insisted I go back to the studio and focus all my time on spying.

"They'll pay you well."

"Why me? What about those mountebank dwarves?"

"Oh, no, they're artists."

I went back to Mason and San Miguel and got in Reinita Principe's good graces. I made friends with producers, set designers, cameramen. In two weeks I managed to make off with building plans and a list of guards. I had a clear picture of how the studio was run. Because her mother forced her to, Lucecita began to flirt with me and insisted I visit their home again.

In the blink of an eye, I resumed my visits, loaded down with provisions. They locked the old man up in his room and Reina lit incense and we got drunk. Lucecita drank too much and was toasting the birdies circling her head, like in the cartoons. At exactly midnight, we uncorked some hard cider and Reina pushed me toward her daughter's bedroom. Lucecita was still talking to the birdies and I stammered in fear as if I'd smoked pot. She asked me never to take off my glasses. "You're cuter that way." And I fell asleep by her side, peaceful, barely touching her.

"It's our secret," she conspired with me.

That morning, in a spectacular raid that took Havana by surprise, the studio at Mason and San Miguel was dismantled. From Reina herself I learned they'd caught the night guards sleeping on the job. She also told me there'd be an investigation and they'd dredge up Havana as if it were a mined field.

"There's a lot of hatred," she said.

And me? They simply forgot about me. They even interviewed the street sweepers and no one remembered me. I didn't exist.

"I'm invisible," I told Lucecita.

"Cheer up," she answered. "That may be the very thing I'll love about you some day."

Pascualito met up with me at Rosendo Gil's home and said that the Great Grail sent their congratulations. The Supreme Boss would give me a medal and I could ask for anything I wanted. I didn't know what to say. It was Pascualito who suggested a restaurant.

"What do I have to do?" I asked.

"Nothing. Live and look after the Grail's share."

It was easy to convince Lucecita to set up the restaurant in her home. People worked hard in those days. From out of the sewers came the tables, tablecloths, food, everything. My good friend

Jeremias was the supplier for our new business. That was the only condition I'd set. He became someone who handed out happiness. The same sort of thing happened to Reinita Principe and I ask myself if Jeremias had won the heart of that pitiful actress who'd seen better days. What's more, Lucecita came to love me. I don't know if she loved me out of pity or because of the money we were making. But I swear, one night, she told me I should stop acting like a silly fool. I made such love to her that the sun found us still in bed. For a short time after that, I was the hardest working guy in town.

My restaurant was always full, open 24 hours, decorated with posters from the country's heroic days. There's nothing a foreigner likes more than bygone heroism. You should see how they went crazy over a worker's fist held high or the gears of a machine flattening bureaucracy. Lucecita's father got in on the act, too. Tourists gathered in his room and he recreated the story of his travels through KGB headquarters and the afternoon he saw Vaclav Havel in the middle of a Prague snow storm. The old man recounted his biography with pride, donning his old military jacket and displaying the map of Havana and repeating his story about the conspiracy. Although he never thought to charge, each day Reinita left a five dollar bill in a silver ashtray to give the visitors the idea.

About that same time, my mother died. I had her frozen and brought from our town and gave her a Christian burial with bundles of aspirin and cough syrup alongside her in one of the niches at the Falla Bonet Cemetery. My mother never dreamed she'd be laid to rest on Carrara marble. During that time, Lucecita and I got married in the church. It was a sumptuous wedding. I was decked out in a black suit and a turquoise tie. Five months later Pascual Jeremias was born, named for my two friends.

"You're a winner!" my mother told me in a letter shortly before her death. I felt so proud I forgot I was cross-eyed, I forgot all about my suffering, the injustices. I was starting to see life as one endless spending spree. There was no one at the door of my heart to give me a wake up call. About that time laziness caught up with me. Little by little Lucecita took over the reins of the business. She knew how to juggle the day's sales figures and she carefully divided the Grail's money, money for the inspectors, bribes to keep them quiet and of course some money for us.

"That extra money will make us rich," she said one night.

"What if they find out?" I said fearfully.

"How will they know?" she said kissing my waist and taking off my glasses for the first time. "Who's going to talk? You? Me? Jeremias?"

Now I know that part of life's adventure is taking big risks. Good fortune went out with the old man and the toilet bowl. See, we made sure he didn't talk. But the old guy still found a way to communicate, to get the word out. He scrounged every mayonnaise jar, every mustard jar, filled them with letters telling all about our evil deeds and put them in circulation with every flush of the toilet.

The first fateful sign came the Monday Jeremias disappeared. I tried in vain to find him. I went to the Packard, searched his room, peered into every corner of the Prado where he made his conquests. No one had seen him since Friday. Then I visited Pascualito at his spot in front of the train station. I tried to hug him and he pulled away from me. He spoke of the cruel moon that poisons the human heart. He told of the waters that wash you clean of shame.

"Something funny's going on," I told Lucecita when I got back.

"Jeremias is in love and Pascualito's a neurotic dwarf," she tried to calm me down.

"The dark age is coming," I said.

"No! Our son won't be subjected to the jobs you and I did," Lucecita answered.

"The dark age is coming," I said.

And I was right. At dawn a horde of dwarves attacked us. In minutes they cleaned out everything. A big-breasted female dwarf snatched Pascual Jeremias from his cradle. Then they carried off Lucecita and Reinita Principe. The old man disappeared, wrapped up in his map of Havana. I stood there without the strength or will to act. At that moment, Pascualito walked in and repeated that line about the cruel moon and signaled for them to carry me off. He kissed me on the cheek and I don't remember anything after that.

I awoke in an ice storeroom in a cavern. My body was trembling. Good Jeremias came toward me. Oh, my God! He was a despicable dwarf! Short legs, an old double-breasted coat over his small body, his ears mangled, wearing felt boots, not his two-toned shoes. He had an air of resignation that horrified me.

"I don't exist any more," he told me, helping me to my feet. That was when my cry froze the cavern even more. I was a dwarf, too, a dwarf with lips tangled up by confusion, a dwarf with no eyelashes.

"You'll get used to it," he declared like a priest who'd talked on and on about Christ's commandments, about punishment and absolution. He spoke Pontius Pilate's name as if he were a patron saint of that winter. "How long will I be like this?" I sobbed.

"For eternity," was his reply.

Today there was a slaughter. The slaughterhouse is next to this freezer and, since dawn, all throughout the day's work, the cows' moos have tormented me. I wonder if the cows ponder life and death. But those subtleties are moot. My tragedy is double: I've stopped breathing the air of Havana and I'm despised. Dwarves — I talk as if I weren't one — have a definite standard of beauty. They're delighted with their short bodies and beautiful eyes, a trait of their brotherhood. For that reason I have to do the worst jobs. Tote boxes, cut out the cows' livers, cremate their bones, slice off the bulls' tongues.

"The Big Show's about to start," Jeremias tells me, still my faithful friend. Now I'll end my story. Now I'll sit in front of the TV — the only pastime allowed — and come face to face with Lucecita. Artists always manage to weasel out of their punishment. It's a program made for her on underground TV. They'll introduce her as the World Famous Vedette from the Follies Bergere. She'll come on with the under-appreciated sensuality she's capable of displaying. Lucecita, not small, but human size for the lonely nights of my torment. Every time I see her, I forget about that normal-sized woman, the lover I adored. All I care about is whether my Pascual Jeremias was saved like his mother. Now Jeremias calls to me that the show's starting. I'd give the world to stop hearing that Glenn Miller tune broadcast over and over on the loud speakers. I want to have wings and fly, take my son with me like the jaguars from the legends and climb that mountain that is Havana and, there, be a man. My Lucecita sings the show's theme song and I travel across that space of light and fantasy on the screen to love her.

Translated by Pamela Carmell

THE HAPPY DEATH OF ALBORADA ALMANZA
Leonardo Padura Fuentes

Alborada Almanza woke up gently but completely, with the keen sensation that something extraordinary was going to happen to her that day. She had barely opened her eyes when she felt the sharp prick of a premonition, and she tried to figure out the cause. It was a seizure of joy, after another bad night plagued, like always, with intense nightmares in colors that she couldn't even remember now. From her bed she observed the calendar, the one she had made herself, and although today was the saint's day of her beloved Saint Raphael the Archangel, the date did not appear to suggest anything special because it wasn't her birthday, or any other birthday she could remember, and it wasn't the long awaited day on which groceries would be sent from the corner *bodega*.

Slowly, so as not to aggravate the stiffness of her arthritis, Alborada slipped her feet out of the bed and into a pair of threadbare slippers. Summoning all of her strength, she got out of bed and stood up all at once, perfectly upright. That was when she began to fear that the beautiful beginning of the day was just another dirty trick of her nightmares: the very thing that made her endure hunger, heat and old age. But for the moment, everything was light and pleasing very much like a vigil. I must be sure to enjoy a dream like this, she thought. She felt a surge of confidence that the day might bring something unexpected, even if it weren't her birthday or the day when groceries would arrive. She walked to the kitchen with a determined air and checked the jar where she kept coffee, searching for the incontrovertible evidence that she was in a dream. The smell of rich dark coffee that filled the receptacle made her happy. How different from the customary and tormenting absence of coffee; the allotment of a meager two ounces of coffee every two weeks barely lasted for three breakfasts and for the remaining twelve days the morning grumbling of her intestines had to be satisfied with concoctions of anise, orange leaves, or bits of soursop, prepared with a plentiful dose of sugar to stir up energy and fortify her for another day.

While the water for coffee was heating, Alborada searched the cupboard for the packet of powdered cereal, the kind with a soil aftertaste and astringent qualities, that served as breakfast on many a morning. To her delight, she saw, intact and triumphant, a can of condensed milk with two cows on the label and the familiar Russian letters. It had been ten years since that thick and creamy milk had disappeared from the Island's markets, yet there it was. And that milk would have been the best gift possible except that on the stove top, near where the water and coffee were coming to a boil, Alborada discovered two flaky pastries filled with guava paste, the kind that her husband, Tobias, used to bring her every morning from 1933 to 1967. The pastries stopped when the neighborhood bakery was shut down by a committee of the Revolution. And along with them, gone forever, were the chocolate *montecristos*, the coconut *masarreales* and the petite Morón cakes.

It's worthwhile to dream after all, mused Alborada as she strained the coffee. Its rich and invigorating aroma — strong enough to awaken the dead — filled the air. What if it wakes me up, she thought with alarm, and decided to devour the two pastries first and then drink the condensed milk, and leave until last the slow savoring of the perfectly measured coffee that tasted just a little more bitter than usual since it followed the pastries and the sweet milk. Fearfully, Alborada sipped the coffee and waited for the dreadful awakening, the eternal aching in her bones and the rumbling dissatisfaction of her bowels. She even closed her eyes to make everything seem more natural, but when she discovered that the taste of coffee lingered in her mouth, she understood wondrously that it would not be easy to take leave of such an exotic and absurd dream.

Following the command of her skin, Alborada took off her clothes in the kitchen. She let the worn nightgown that had lost all its lace fall on a chair; she undid the string that held up her drooping underpants — a loose fit over the bones of her hips — and allowed them to drop to the floor. Although she was having the best dream of her life, everything seemed so real that Alborada preferred not to run the risk of seeing her body wasted by the privations and hunger of the last few years. She walked toward the shower, head held high, with the anticipation of bathing with Palmolive soap, brushing her false teeth with her favorite brand of toothpaste, and applying a perfumed Avon lotion that she had seen for the last time when it was a gift for her forty-eighth birthday in 1962.

As the water purified her and the Palmolive soap caressed her body, Alborada had the feeling that she was not alone. It was a remote sensation, like all those she was recovering on this

93

morning, because not since the death of Tobias, twenty-two years ago, had anyone shared the bathroom with her.

"How nice it is not to be alone," she said out loud, because the sensation that someone was with her was as palpable as each of the small pleasures rescued from forgotten times, like the agility that was returning to her flaccid muscles, like the desire to never wake up and to live forever in that world where guava pastries, condensed milk, Palmolive soap, and above all the coffee — pure coffee, without horrifying extenders — were as likely as was their absence in the other world where she had been living. There, in the harsh contours of her real life, she'd gone to bed hungry at night more than once and when she looked up through the cracks in the roof at the star-filled sky, she had asked God and Saint Raphael the Archangel to grant her a quick and painless death that would free her from the nightmares, the heat, and the morning infusions doused with sugar.

"That's why I'm here," said the presence, and Alborada thought about covering up but then something stopped her. "I'm glad you smell so good…"

"Is it you?" asked the elderly woman.

"Who else could it be? I am Raphael, one of the seven archangels in the Lord's service, one of those allowed to abide in his glorious presence. You asked for me to come and the Lord has granted your request."

"Then…?"

"Yes, Alborada, you are dead just as you wished, and I have come for you. Put on your perfume because we are going to heaven."

"Oh my goodness," murmured the woman, contemplating the loss of what she had only very recently recovered.

"What's the matter? Why do you doubt?"

Alborada pushed back the shower curtain and saw before her a tall, strong, luminous mulatto completely nude and without the wings he was supposed to have. But between his legs shone a brilliant penis furrowed with purple veins and with the glans red and polished, like the apples that in previous times Alborada used to offer to her beloved Saint Barbara.

"You don't look like him…" she said, unable to take her eyes off the magnificent attribute of the recent arrival and pointing toward the rosy sphinx that she had in the room.

"You should really say that he doesn't look like me. Is it that you don't like me the way I am?"

"No, it's not that. It's that you're so human. And, well, to have to leave right now, like this..."

"That's what you asked for. On my day, the Lord allows me to choose the person I want to take with me and the way in which the person is taken. Since you are practically a saint, I decided to grant your wish."

"But when I wanted to die I didn't have coffee, or pastries, or milk... and now that I have tasted them again..."

"You want to stay for things like that? Not go to heaven and be condemned to hell?"

Alborada began to tremble. Now she knew she was dead and it didn't matter because the suffering and depravations of her life would never return. The terrible part was that the ritual coffee mixture — a sorry excuse for the real thing — that she drank six times a month, the scent of sweet basil with which she seasoned her meals, and the expectation of finding out who the heroine of the soap opera would marry, would not return either. Life could be terrible, but it was life.

"Yes, Alborada, you are dead and you are going to heaven."

"And, if I don't want to?" she dared to ask. Nothing worse could befall her now. Suddenly she realized that the entire bizarre dialogue carried out while she was totally nude, made her feel uninhibited and freed from the sense of fear she had known her entire life. It is really awful that this is happening to me when I'm dead, she thought.

"I'm sorry," said the Archangel, smiling for the first time. "That's the way life is. Some go to heaven for being brave others for being cowards. There's no turning back now. I am the reward for your fear...."

"Thanks for your sincerity..." murmured the elderly woman who had recently died.

At last she dared to look at her body: it was old, wrinkled, with bones right near the surface of the skin: a bad reminder of her other existence, a malignant proof that there are miracles that never occur. Then she understood that it was best to simply obey, like she'd always done. After all, she already knew what hell was like and perhaps in heaven there would be guava pastries and coffee: the coffee that she remembered longing for when she was still alive and used to cast forlorn glances at the gloomy and almost-bare pantry.

"Are there pastries in heaven?"

"Always, and freshly baked. That's why it's called Glory."

"All right... Can I do something else before we leave?"

"That depends, Alborada," whispered the Archangel.

"It's very simple: I want to see the ocean, I want to pet a dog, and I want to hear a *danzón*."

The celestial mulatto smiled again and Alborada felt her cheeks blush.

"Granted," he said. "On the condition that you let me dance the *danzón* with you. It's been centuries since I danced."

"It will be an honor," said Alborada looking at the spectacular attribute of the mulatto sent from heaven. She thought for a moment and concluded that her cowardice had been worth the price: at long last she was going to a place where they served warm guava pastries, God had given her the best of all possible deaths, and she was going to heaven to the rhythm of "Almendra," her favorite *danzón*.

Mantilla, May 1999

Translated by Anne Fountain

JONI MITCHELL WAS SINGING *BLUE*
Karla Suárez

Blue, here is a shell for you
Inside you'll hear a sigh
A foggy lullaby
There is your song from me
 - Joni Mitchell, *Blue*

Joni was singing the blues in the room on the other side of the wall. On this side, I was humming along. There was a long corridor between Joni's room and mine. You were in the hallway, pacing back and forth, over and over. You were muttering words choked with fury. You were sputtering anger you could barely put into words. I don't know what was going on, but something was sure happening to you, as it did every night. Meanwhile, I was all ears (for Joni). You stomped along that way, as if you were kicking out a deep rut that would cut down into the floors below and sink you down into the earth's center, and once you got to the earth's core maybe you could find something that you couldn't manage to find up here.

Joni was singing and I closed my eyes. Closing my eyes I can travel to another place. A place where I'm perfectly set up to watch myself from the outside and figure things out. You kept pacing and tossing your cigarette butts onto the floor for who knows who to have to clean up later. Meanwhile, the downstairs neighbor began to bang gently on his ceiling because your continuous tromping steps kept him from sleeping. Sleeping is another way to travel to somewhere else. Not being able to sleep brings on irritability. Then the downstairs neighbor bangs even harder to protest the thundering steps right above his head.

We didn't notice the noise. Joni Mitchell strummed her guitar and I felt my ability to concentrate was at its peak. There's a moment in every day when one needs to break free of daily stuff to keep from dying of stress. My astral body began to levitate. You stamped out your cigarette butt with the heel of your shoe. The heel banged so hard over the neighbor's head that he had to go out onto his balcony and yell for silence. His lungs were so full of air that he woke his next door neighbor's child, who started to cry. The neighbor turned on her light and went to calm the baby, while her husband came out on the balcony in a fury to shut up his neighbor who was keeping them all awake at this hour of night.

Joni kept on singing and her voice was so mellow that I hardly heard you cursing when you nearly burned yourself with the new cigarette you'd lit. You leaned your full weight on terrestrial crutches, without realizing it's easier to achieve equilibrium by working out a harmony with yourself. The downstairs neighbor was arguing with his neighbor on the adjoining balcony, until the woman upstairs woke up. The woman next to us, the one who's got all those illnesses. She opened her eyes in the middle of the night and when she heard the baby crying and the men yelling at each other, she thought the building must be on fire and she screamed in terror and fainted. Her granddaughter hit the ground running when she heard the scream, and when she found her grandmother on the floor, she went out onto her balcony to ask for help.

I smiled because Joni does whatever she wants with her voice. She lets me wander far away, far from the others and closer to me. To a distant place where a singing voice is all there is, and everything falls into place. You coughed the way you do when you've been smoking too much. The neighbor below us began threatening to beat up the guy next door to him. The baby cried inconsolably, but his mother heard the granddaughter of the lady upstairs crying for help and she went out onto the balcony, too. Her husband was inviting the next door neighbor to go down to the street and slug it out. The granddaughter upstairs asked them to call an ambulance and then lights began to go on in the building across the street. The twins' father came out into the street to ask what was going on. The twins took advantage of this to slip out through the front door.

Every time Joni sings I feel as if the world were something else. And in fact, it is something else, a little bit simpler, a little bit more human. Only we've got too many bad habits. Too many unanswered questions. Too much materialism and too much fear of uncertainty. You kept smoking and pacing as if nothing were going on, always anxious with no access to that peaceful state I can summon up. Where I don't even hear the twins' fat mother cursing at them to make them come back inside at the exact moment when the neighbor next door hurled a plant at the downstairs neighbor's balcony. The baby cried louder, because his mother was jostling him around as she tried to hang onto her husband, while the granddaughter upstairs wailed sadly for an ambulance and the twins' father, in his resonant bass voice, pleaded with the neighborhood to telephone. By then, of course, after the angry shouts from the twins' mother, the entire building across the street was waking up. Some took the side of the neighbor below us. Others sided with the baby's father. Others with the granddaughter of the old lady who passed out. And other people were speaking out against the fat mother of the most obnoxious twins in the whole building.

I don't know why so many people forget that poets exist, but Joni doesn't. She makes poetry and I lean my head back. On the day the world ends, there will be a poet who will tell that story. Then everything will have to start all over again. Gestures and emotions will begin again. Then you'll go back to pacing and smoking, but maybe you'll find solutions or at least hopes. Today you're only pacing while the guy who lives below us goes out to the street with his next door neighbor just as the first wail of the ambulance siren can be heard, still far away, and the entire block is out and about. The guys who live on the corner are betting on the neighbor from below us or on the husband of the baby's mother. And the baby's mother is out on the street, too, in a see-through robe, holding her baby, who is still crying, while the twins' mother goes over to try to calm her. The twins take advantage and slip out again and their father rounds up some other strong men to carry out the unconscious woman. The strong men's wives all try to console the poor granddaughter who is yelling now, because she's discovered that her grandmother has gotten up and in the middle of all this confusion, she's called the firemen. There's their siren now.

It's all so simple with Joni. Everything is so straightforward, but understanding it takes a lot of effort. As long as you keep singing for me, it will keep me safe and sound. The most complicated things tend to have the simplest explanations. Getting across an emotion can turn out to be the most natural thing in the world, so natural that we can even envision emotions we've never felt ourselves. Difficult things like the silence and discomfort of the guy pacing the hallway, grinding his cigarette butts down onto the ceiling of the neighbor below us. But the downstairs neighbor doesn't get annoyed, because he's just been slugged in the middle of his stomach by the father of the baby who is being held right now by the twins' mother. And the twins are having a good time peering at the bodies of the women milling around in the street wearing see-through robes. One of the women's husbands says things can't keep going on this way and he calls the police, while the granddaughter of the lady who lives above the neighbors who are next door to the neighbor who lives under us tries to apologize to the strong men who went up to help out her grandmother. Her grandmother hears the siren and nobody can tell her whether it's the ambulance, the firemen, or the police.

It's the last song. When I know the record's coming to an end, a trace of it stays within me. Something that is mine and is me. When I open my eyes, the world will be different, Joni. Each primary image is a different image and it has to be a better one. You light up the last cigarette and toss the empty pack on the floor to join the heap of butts that who knows who will have to clean up tomorrow. Tomorrow will be different. The neighbor below us will surely be breathing air back into his lungs in the hospital where the ambulance is taking him. The neighbor next door to the neighbor below us will pay the fine the police are giving him for being a public nuisance. The firemen will be telling each other the story of their rescue of two twins who had climbed a post to try to see the underpants of a girl on the second floor of the building on the corner. The granddaughter of the lady next door, who lives just above the mother of the child next door to the neighbor who lives below us, will give pills to her grandmother so she'll sleep well. The twins' father will fight with his wife accusing her of being irresponsible and in addition to that, of going out into the street to show off her body to everyone. The strong men will say good morning to each other and will smile thinking about how they saw the others' wives out there in their underwear. The women will go shopping to buy themselves some new underwear that's better than their neighbors'. I'll listen again to Joni Mitchell's record, *Blue*. You'll keep smoking. Surely tomorrow will be different. Now the record has ended and I lift up my head.

"Something wrong?"

"I'm a little worried. Every day that goes by, I feel things are getting worse. I don't know, I feel as though this city is smothering me, the whole world is smothering me, and on top of that, I've run out of cigarettes."

"Don't worry, my love, tomorrow will be another day. Let's go to sleep now."

Translated by Mary G. Berg

THE COLLECTOR
Karla Suárez

He was a famous salsa singer. She collected things and did occasional tattoos. He was married to a rich Japanese businesswoman. She had a French lover.

They met by chance. She was trying to convince a cafeteria clerk that five cents didn't make any difference in the price of a pack of cigarettes. The clerk, for his part, responded with a big smile and a resounding "no." A hand reached over her shoulder and gave her the five cents. She looked back, smiled when She recognized the face and said "Thanks" as She quickly put the pack of Marlboros away. He smiled and invited her for a beer. She preferred to walk, so they walked.

"I don't like salsa much, but I recognize you. Everyone in the world knows you."

Everyone in the world knew him because He was a famous star with an attractive smile and expressive eyes. She wasn't famous. Her favorite pastime was collecting. She collected wineglasses stolen from different bars, corks of bottles opened on memorable occasions, sand from beaches, candles brought from churches around the world and some She had made, using medicines as dyes and eggshells as molds. She collected all sorts of things and did tattoos once in a while, when She was in the mood.

"I have a French lover who comes by every month and we drink wine, he gives me books and candles. He's a writer."

He wanted to know his name, in case He knew him, you never know, but She refused to tell him.

"Never tell anyone who your lovers are. Besides...he's married, like you."

Famous people don't have private lives. The whole world knew about his Japanese wife and He sighed, thinking how liberating anonymity would be. To walk along the street without anyone staring at you and admiring your new car, a recent gift from your wife, who's a few years older than you — a woman who no longer interests you and spends almost all her time traveling, like you, but in different latitudes.

"Dubadubdub," She said, thumping her heart. "You've been so quiet, throb throb, sad little heart, I thought all salsa players were a lot of fun."

He wanted to be a lot of fun, so He invited her to a concert, but She detested salsa concerts and the whole rigmarole of glitzy high fashion outfits and stepping out of a car almost no one else could afford, and feeling everyone staring at her as she sat at the table.

"Tell me one thing: which do you like better, night or morning?"

"I'm a musician, a nocturnal animal."

"Winter or summer?"

"We've got summer all year round, I like winter better and that's enough questions, I'm fed up with journalists."

"One more question, just one more, cats or dogs?"

He smiled.

"I have two cats at my mother's house, Ochún and Changó."

She smiled, biting her lips.

"OK, I won't go to your concerts, but we could get together, just the two of us…"

So they kept seeing each other. She'd wait for his call after his concerts, and they would go to the beach, far from the city. He brought her wineglasses and wrote the date on the corks of the bottles they drank together. Then and during and before and after they made love. He'd sing ballads in her ear while She kissed the pores of his skin one by one.

The first month her French lover came, She warned him she'd be gone a week.

"Do you love him?" He asked. She smiled and didn't say anything. "If you don't love him, why don't you leave him and stay with me?"

"Throb throb, egotistic little heart, my writer is coming to see me. When your Japanese wife shows up, you'll take a vacation, too."

He wanted to say something, but He kept his mouth shut. The next day He wrote a song for her and waited an entire week. The months that followed were made up of segments, a week for the Frenchman, a few days for the Japanese wife, concert tours, and the rest of the time was left for being together.

One time they crossed paths at a marina far from the city. She was drinking a tonic water with lots of ice, next to the pool. The French writer was reading, sunning himself by her side. He got out of his car and walked by with his wife on his arm. The Japanese businesswoman recognized the writer and stopped. He gazed at Her. His wife leaned over to him and whispered the name of the gray-haired man with the magazine. He nodded without comment, He didn't recognize the name. The couple walked on and as they went past the other couple, the Japanese wife bobbed her head in greeting to the writer, who had just lifted his eyes. He lowered his gaze. She continued drinking her tonic water. The writer smiled, annoyed that he had been recognized.

They never talked about that encounter. He had no wish to bring it up. She kissed the pores of his skin and made love to him in Spanish.

"Throb throb," He said, patting his chest. "You know what? I love you."

She gave him a candle in the shape of a snail.

One night She showed up very happy. She had a book that her writer had just dedicated to her. It was on sale all over Europe and her name was on the first page. The book was about her and for her.

"He did it to please you," He said. "I'd be glad to dedicate a recording to you, but my wife would want to know who you are and as you said, 'never tell anyone who your lovers are'..."

She smiled in pleasure, kissed the book and then kissed her salsa singer on the mouth. Her lover started phoning her when he was on tour and talking to her about the cold and the nights and the bottles of wine that He was buying to drink with her. When He came back, he'd bring the newspapers and magazines where his photo appeared, press reviews, ads for his records and odd pencils He'd sought out for her collection. On one of these returns, He found her a little out of sorts, preoccupied.

"It's nothing," She said. "I need colors. I should do a tattoo but I don't have the right ink colors. It's really important, you know."

He helped her find them and made her sadness go away. She was happy. Tattooing was something She only did on special occasions. Someday, if He wanted her to, She could do one for him. She didn't have any on herself, but She did them really well. She liked doing it.

A week later his Japanese wife came back and He stopped seeing Her. His wife stayed around for more than a month. He only managed a few phone calls and one short visit, a real juggling act. His marriage had become a real bore; they barely managed to be civil when they discussed the next tours and contracts. The Japanese wife felt he was being too distant, and He blamed the heat. She noticed that most of his new songs were ballads and He alluded to "a creative spurt." She found some strange candles on top of the wardrobe and He explained that they were in case of a power outage. At the airport, He embraced her, He kissed her forehead and wished her a good trip. Two seconds after He watched her disappear behind the glass, He jumped in his car and went looking for Her.

But She wasn't home. They met the next night and were happy to touch each other's bodies. She didn't know that the Japanese wife had left and told him She wasn't home because she'd met a Spanish filmmaker, an interesting guy She'd talked to for hours. He wanted to stay with her as long as possible and asked her when the Frenchman was coming.

"He isn't coming again. It's all over, " She said. "He's crazy. Last week he said his wife knew all about it. He told her himself because he wanted to leave his family and take me to Paris so we could live together, but I don't want to. I don't love him, so we broke it off completely."

He sighed with a certain undisguised relief and hugged her tight.

"Throb throb, crazy little heart, now you'll stay with me."

She smiled and licked his nose with the tip of her tongue. She said She wanted to drink tonic water and make love on the Japanese wife's sheets. It was the first time they'd made love in that room. He didn't want her to leave the next day. He wanted her to stay and wait for him to finish that night's concert. And so She did. She waited for him naked, with incense burning in every corner. He got back very late and splashed rum onto her body and got drunk licking it up. In the morning, still naked and tired, he wrote another song to her and didn't want her to leave. She didn't leave. She watched the concert on TV at his house, as He premiered the music written for the most marvelous woman He'd ever met. She was happy and He came home full of love for her.

Next there was a short tour in Japan where his wife met him with a possible contract for six months in Europe to promote the recording he was just beginning to make. He was eager to do this, but He didn't love the Japanese businesswoman, He loved Her. She, who greeted him with a bottle of Spanish wine and desire for his body, didn't want to stay at his house this time. He began to record and spent long days at the studio. They agreed to meet when He had breaks in his schedule. He put all his energy into each song. With Her in mind, He'd make the whole world dance. He'd shake up old Europe.

The day he finished recording He went looking for her, flowers in hand. He bought a case of rum, two of tonic water and proposed a huge celebration. They holed up in his room. He switched the phone to the answering machine and turned the ringer all the way down. She lit incense and took her clothes off. When they'd almost finished the first bottle, He said He had a surprise.

"You're driving me crazy. I'm crazy," he said. "You changed my life, you spun me around in the opposite direction, and it's not fair to hide how I feel...the recording is dedicated to you, and it's about to hit the market. Your name will be blazed on the cover of a recording sold all over the world." He smiled and patted Her heart. "Throb throb, I'm in love, crazy little heart, sweetheart..."

She hugged his neck and licked his ears. She shivered as his hands ran down her spine again and enveloped her. Their lips met.

"I'm happy," she said drawing back a little. "I want to give you something very important. I want to give you something that will keep us united forever. I want to be part of you forever...let me give you a tattoo."

He felt a strange emotion and bit his lips. He drank from the bottle, almost bursting with joy, and He accepted. The drawing was on the nape of his neck, a strange little drawing, very distinctive. When She finished, He was drunk and exhausted from holding his head in the same position and from so many hours without sleep. She caressed his face and stood up to drink tonic water, while She watched him fall asleep.

The six month tour through Europe was set to begin the next month. The record was about to be released. The Japanese wife came to deal with last minute details and left again, with his promise that they'd have a long talk, when things calmed down a little, about her husband's recent strange behavior.

"This record will be a success, I know it will," He said, stretched out on the sand watching the sunset.

"It will change your life, I can predict that," She said, stretched out beside him.

"Change..." He said and turned his body to look at her. "Throb throb, little heart of mine...I was thinking, what if you come with me? We'd be together. The devil with my marriage: you're the one I love."

She sat up, and stretched out her back. She smiled.

"It's over. I don't love you."

He closed his eyes and opened them again. He said something, but She interrupted him adding that, besides, She had another lover, She wouldn't say who, just that he was a Spanish filmmaker. Plus She didn't think it was a good idea to leave the Japanese businesswoman in the middle of such an important tour. He rubbed his chin. He couldn't believe it.

"But, what about..? All this...everything we had together..."

She caressed his face and stood up, brushing off the sand. She said He shouldn't bother to come with her, it wasn't late, and her Spanish lover would pick her up very close to there. He stood up to say something but couldn't get the words out.

"Throb throb, silly little heart," She said, patting him on the heart. "Did I ever tell you I loved you?" She kissed his sweaty cheek and took a few steps. "You know what? It's just...I collect people, I enjoy it, it's really my favorite pastime...as you travel around the world, you'll recognize my mark. There are many out there with that drawing on the napes of their necks." She smiled. "And they're all famous...."

He was a famous salsa singer and his tour of Europe was a great success. She collected people and tattooed her mark on them. He was divorced from a rich Japanese businesswoman. She had a lover.

Translated by Mary G. Berg

WATERS
Alejandro Aguilar

The last trip from the gas station had left him thoroughly exhausted. The distance, the weight, the climb up the steep staircase, all had conspired to crush him. Now before his eyes, defying his famished body, is the rusty container with the hostile red ink letters, TREATED WATER, written in a thick scrawl, the leg of the A extending like a mocking tongue. He lowers himself to the floor, barely keeping his balance. Crouching barefoot, he flinches at the contrast in temperature between his overheated muscles, his sweaty skin, and his testicles grazing the cold and grimy floor tiles. He attempts to stand up but fatigue overwhelms him. He ponders the hours spent without a single bite of food, the greenish mildew staining the bathroom walls with whimsical splotches. He watches the sunlight filter in through crooked blinds and spread around the room until there is scarcely enough light to make out the letters on the container. His legs twitch and he needs to piss. He tries to get back on his feet again, succeeds this time, and starts to move around. The faded piece of shirt he uses for soap is all too familiar. Months ago the harshness of the fabric and the seams bruised his skin, but now he rubs vigorously, even happily. The treated water gets him to imagining that he's a luxury automobile in an automatic carwash. Such thoughts use up the last bit of humor he had deliberately saved for Sunday.

In the kitchen, still standing, he gulps down two spoonfuls of soggy rice and peas, those same *petit pois* that could be so good when mixed with a little cream à la St. Germain. But with neither electricity nor spices, there is no way to dress up these basic, cold little green balls, salt-free to boot. He feels a stab of pain in his stomach and the fine mesh protecting his brain begins to unravel. There's a universal remedy for headache –aspirin– but he will have to make do with a sea breeze. His neighbor systematically refuses to give him any medicine, driven by a mean habit of hoarding or, more accurately, by her fanatical guarding of strategic reserves.

Immersed in his worries, he steps out onto the street. Crossing a cave-dark intersection, he is almost run over by a barely visible bicycle. The scream, "Are you blind, you sonofabitch?" sounds too metallic to be coming from a human being. He is overwhelmed by the suspicion that the machine has somehow managed to go riderless, and talk.

At length the sea breeze on his face wipes away the bad mood and those absurd thoughts as if they were dust. His headache subsides with the sound of the waves prancing over the reefs, oblivious to the dangers of being ripped apart by the coral's sharp edges. Hordes of people walk by him going in the opposite direction: youngsters bent on weird exploits; adults chasing after the unknown even as they hawk the most exotic items; resplendent half-naked young women showing off their bodies and offering their company to anyone who looks foreign. Other gray silhouettes, seemingly lost in their muteness, sway in the soft evening wind. And, occasionally, the dull motor of some ancient car or the hiss of a tourist minivan alludes to a witches' Sabbath, a gathering of early-rising predators and lewd black women. The rest is shadows and the ceaseless splashing of waves.

He searches for a suitable place on the seawall, away from noisy groups and necking couples. On a concrete jetty, a man hunches silently, alone and folded into himself. This is not really the kind of atmosphere he is looking for but, out of respect for the other man, he asks if it is OK for him to sit there and if he can help. A shrug is the only answer. He settles down with some difficulty, trying to find the serenity he craves. But it is not easy. The day loaded with incidents, the humidity seeping through the worn fabric of his pants, and the ever-present sea, dark and brooding... water everywhere, barely penetrated by dirt-covered roads pulsating with chaotic lives. That is all, an island and the certainty of the city with its random sounds. Far away, closer to the horizon than to the tips of his toes, a swarm of colored lights signals the garish passage of a cruise ship. The distance deepens its otherworldliness. The shape to his right clings to the edge of the seawall and leans over the water, vomiting with spasms and noises that make him fear the body will just spill out, abandon the wrinkled skin, and float up above the city, like scraps of paper in a gathering storm. Minutes later, and somewhat recovered, the figure casts out an orphaned question, seemingly as preamble to a suicide. The little man stares at him for the first time and, unable to keep his balance, waivers between looking at the intruder and out to sea, where his glance finally comes to rest. "Can I help you?" He tries to gain time, to get ready to assist, but the other man's broken voice takes up a litany, a mixture of curses with bits and pieces of an unintelligible story, speaking to the whole city and to no one in particular. Who would answer?

His attempt to get out of himself has failed. He decides to amble toward the big hotels but something catches his eye. A dark woman, tall yet fragile, and another very pale and blonde are exchanging a black baby, very black, while splitting some wrinkled bills they were carrying in their bosom. He catches the drift and concludes that imagination knows no bounds. Looking at the occasional mothers with their rented baby, he is convinced he was not delirious when he thought the bicycle was riderless and could speak.

He decides to return home with every intention of lying down to rest. But he is still not used to sleeping alone. His wife left him a few days ago without a word of explanation -not that he demanded any- just when he was about to admit to himself that he had become indifferent to her presence. She had turned into a shadow hovering over his daily concerns, a noise that distracted him from the tricks he had developed to make it alive to the end of every day. Actually, it was lucky that she had made such a quiet exit, like the French are known to do.

The power is out and God treats him to a long and particularly scorching sleepless night. Shortly before dawn, a divine perk. A few feet away from his eyes, in the room across the street, a woman walks around naked and vulnerable in front of an open window in shimmering candlelight. Her body glistens with sweat and the most beautiful insomnia he has ever witnessed. Lust turns him into a hormone-crazed adolescent who lets up only when his legs are about to buckle. Is it hunger or pleasure? He will never know. No matter. It is one fine way to start the day.

Elbows resting on the remains of a park bench, he becomes absorbed in the unfolding morning. The splendid sun in the usual flawlessly blue sky. The day premiering with the bustle of people going places, of kids waiting for their school friends, of shriveled old people straining to be at the head of the endless shortage lines. How beautiful the city is as it awakens! Some young dude from the barrio walks by and, sensing his moroseness, offers him a swig to gladden his day. And also to challenge the old ladies who, out of sheer inertia, adamantly try to control everything that goes on around them. As he walks away the youngster yells, Yeah, a swig feels good this time of day. Hey, it's already night in Europe and those bars and discotheques are really hopping, so long live geography! That next to the last swig hits him squarely in the neck, the eyes, and especially the stomach. His eyes mist over, setting aquiver the monument to the last mayor of the city to be freely elected, sometime around the beginning of the century. The statue, in the middle of the park, dims and seems to lower an arm weary from holding up the steel saber. He gets up to clear his head knowing that, in the absence of a cold shower, walking is a possible cure. Besides, that way he can discover new corners of this withered city each day. A crack here, a collapsed wall there, foul-smelling puddles, hydrants oozing blackened waters.

He strolls aimlessly around and, unwittingly, makes his way back to the gas station. The guard recognizes him. We're really in bad shape today, citizen. Citizen. How long had it been since he had heard that word? Got any gas? he tries to fake it. No gas, no oil, no air. Plus the treated

water ran out last night. People even carried off the tank, so go ahead and keep the can I lent you yesterday since I won't be needing it anytime soon. The guard, all his years heavy with silence, tips back his stool, and stares at him wondering what will become of the old man in that gutted building.

He has almost finished the third bottle of homemade rum that tastes like sheer heaven to him. The image of the empty can breaks through his mind's fog. It sits uselessly on the grimy bathroom tiles, those red letters dancing mockingly in the twilight.

TREATED WATER TREATED WATER TREATED WATER

By now it is close to six, and he has wandered back to the same piece of bench. Fatigued and nauseous he lies down on the grass, all the while staring at the clouds, at the stubbornly blue sky that denies the gift of a shower. There is no hint of rain, no threat of storm. Up there, in the distance, there is a tiny silver speck. He asks himself for the umpteenth time where airplanes go, what one feels inside that bird-like machine, what he would do if he ever got to board one. And then he thinks he might just pass the time looking down trying to spot, between one body of water and the next, those guys who lie down in parks to watch the clouds and the planes.

Havana 1994
Translated by Cristina de la Torre

THE COLONEL'S ALLEGRO
Alejandro Aguilar

David has a colonel for a neighbor, a very nice man. Every morning the colonel greets him as he leaves for work in his spotless uniform and sunglasses; always admiring the shine of his own shoes that move with surprising ease despite his age. It is unusual to see a person nearing sixty come down the stairs so nimbly. Even more unusual is to hear him say "Buenos días" without so much as looking at the other. That is one of the colonel's unusual habits, David has noticed, but so what, he still greets him faithfully as he leaves for work just when David is returning from his nightly jaunts. David answers with a somewhat tentative "Buenos días" uttered sideways so as to reach its mark on the rebound, in the hope that his alcoholic breath will cling to the walls and avoid the range of the colonel's nose above his thick mustache and under his dark glasses. It never quite works, and when their paths cross, as David is on the way up and the colonel's going down to his car where the chauffeur is waiting (or whatever the military term is for the person who drives the colonel's car, who is the same person who lugs the shopping bags of the colonel's wife, who comes in and out carrying either empty or full gasoline cans, bottles of rum and cases of beer, who shines the car, and stops by with his wife occasionally to pay a social call on Mr. & Mrs. Colonel), David has noticed that the colonel turns his torso ever so slightly to continue looking him up and down so accusingly that he feels a weight on his back that makes it hard for him to climb the steps. But if the colonel is thinking something horrible, it must not be that horrible because he keeps it to himself. Or he used to.

A few days ago the nice colonel neighbor crossed paths with David, like most mornings, on the stairs. David and Tom. David greeted him with the almost usual "Buenos días," only this time it was projected towards the ceiling to avoid seeing himself reflected on the colonel's dark glasses. And the colonel started to reciprocate with his almost usual greeting with his eyes fixed, as usual, on the shine of his own shoes. The routine was unfolding in its usual awkward way when, suddenly, everything froze and not just due to silence. It was Tom, who uttered a "Hello" which changed the peaceful course of the encounter, sustained with difficulty until then, so that in one second or perhaps even less, the sparkle of the colonel's dark glasses abandoned the usual shine of the colonel's shoes, climbed diagonally up the wall and came to a standstill on the limpid eyes and the unmistakably American face of the youth. Tom's presence loomed. And never before had the silence of a withheld greeting sounded so much like the cannon shots that always signal the opening of hostilities in war. David's nice colonel neighbor halted the passage of time, the motion of air and sound in one single look and, from that moment on, nothing would ever be the same, not even the sober greetings exchanged each morning as they met on the stairs when the colonel left for his duties and David returned from his nightly forays. What was it that altered the precarious balance, the subdued tension, the violence so far suppressed thanks to the wholesome habit of the reticent greeting? It was Tom's American accent. That "Hello" that should never have been uttered. The enemy's flagrant presence was seeping into zones already threatened by David's existence; someone much too effeminate for the taste of the colonel's other neighbors, much too cool, wild, and irresponsible, for the colonel's own. But David was a homegrown product. How to put it? A sicko, a pervert, yes, but still someone perfectly controllable, limitable, repressible, disappearable even, in the closed circuit of the building, the neighborhood, the country, the nation. The homeland! But how to accept, admit, tolerate, apprehend, reduce, oppress, destroy, erase, an alien arrived precisely from there, from that region of the planet whose image had been, for the colonel, nothing less than the bull's eye of the target on which all his regiment's weapons had been trained, on which all the efforts of the men who obeyed the slightest sparkle of his dark glasses were focused? MEN, yes, straight, hard men, tempered by the ennobling endeavor of bearing arms in the service of their country... Men. Single-minded, inscrutable men, untarnished, imperturbable. Everything around David's nice colonel neighbor had to be an extension of the untainted quality of his regiment; everything except for David, that inconsequential, insignificant pervert, yet nevertheless still tolerable as a neighbor. How long had his licentious ways been allowed, his coming home to sleep off the damage done by his shameless orgies just at the moment when the colonel, and all the other upright neighbors, were leaving for work? Much too long. And the proof was right there. In that muscled, rosy cheeked, insolent, aggressively handsome boy whose apparition tore through the dark surface of the colonel's glasses thanks to a strategy that he knew only too well: surprise. Just as it had been conceived in order to compensate for an enemy's numerical superiority, used to wrench away the initiative and control him, the strategy of surprise played a role in this encounter. The colonel blinked under the dark cover of his impenetrable glasses; he stumbled slightly, briefly lost his balance and, for the first time ever, had to reach for the railing in order to turn his torso and admire that boy escaped from enemy lines, that flawless gringo, as flawless as the majority of his men who, when standing erect swelled their chests out, tightened their buttocks and, as a result, the bulge between their legs became more evident than ever. And, as the colonel reviewed his troops one by one, his face before each of theirs, his eyes, hidden behind the dark curtain of his glasses, would plunge straight down to those succulent bulges that now accompanied the gallant stance, the aggressive, charging stance of his soldiers, untainted, unpolluted, invincible, untouchable... Once David's nice colonel neighbor reached the street and the curving stairs blocked the vision of the two gorgeous guys cheerfully climbing, he let out a sigh. The rays of the morning sun blinded him momentarily, intensifying the arousal that still unnerved him. Once again he breathed deeply regaining his composure, and headed for the car where the person who drives, carries things in and out, comes and goes, where that who-knows-what-he-is-called-in-military-speak person was waiting. The colonel settled stiffly into his seat and, staring straight ahead, gave orders to proceed to headquarters. While he went over in his mind the things on that day's agenda, his imagination fluttered toward those bodies just admired on the stairs, and, like every morning, the colonel let his hand rest languidly on the inviting and well-padded bulge on the soldier's crotch, the same one who drives, carries things in and out, comes and goes, and no-one-knows-what-to-call-him when things like these go on between David's nice colonel neighbor and one of his own regiment's unpolluted soldiers. Just then, David opened the door to his place and, softly pressing his hand on Tom's hip, invited him in.

Translated by Cristina de la Torre

A NUDE IN THE RAIN
Ena Lucía Portela

For Evelyn Hatch, should she ever come back to life

One rainy afternoon, E settles down in front of the camera. A powder flash (so to speak) in the studio's shadows and, *voilà*: for the umpteenth time, Bruno captures her smile.

E's smile. I'll repeat that phrase many times, in many ways; that look on her face, imprecise, not in time or space, but in the vast number of things you can read into it — an unclear, ironic expression, you might say. Stubbornly natural. You could even polish it up and keep it in a little ivory or marble box, on a whatnot shelf along with other curios from bygone eras. But that wouldn't do any good.

The enclosed space and time of day have no bearing on the deep twilight in Bruno's studio. He set it up, it's artificial, to duplicate an intimate atmosphere, late afternoon, so sultry it makes your head swim, but you stay on your feet thanks to a small dose of amphetamines. In it (the twilight), the soft box mutes the colors and the thin rays of light the lamp casts. The lattice on the window diffuses the outside light into ghostly leopard spots in a ghostly jungle over E's body and the soft surfaces outlining it. The umbrella casts a golden light on an even wider area: E's ambivalent smile, the rain inside...

Sounds pretty good: rain inside, her ambivalent smile, the leopard... an excellent stage set. A guy could get all romantic and sing along with the victrola-era songs till he's convinced he's the greatest sorcerer in the world, crafter of beautiful phrases for some patient reader to pour over and paradoxes to unravel while stretched out in an easy chair. And that's where things go haywire, where the true message gets sidetracked, fades and takes on the deceitful tint of a phony bleached blond.

Because, Bruno admits, it looks dreadful. Despite all the manifestos and all the scholarly writing and all the semiotic theories about how Botticelli painted his Birth of Venus, his Spring and other noteworthy canvases culled from the catalog of some long lost art gallery. Despite all that — which wouldn't fit on these few pages and would take volumes and volumes and some prestigious endorsement to give it its proper due — let's don't overlook the fact that no description can do a visual image justice. An image either speaks for itself or it's shit.

Bruno has told E that that look won't do, smiling that way spoils everything. He repeated those same words yesterday and Friday, more proof there's a region, a vast region, where the futility of words reigns. If she needs to know why (some girls are really quite smart and Bruno has concluded that E's one of them), he explains that last night he developed some shots from a previous shoot. So, doubting woman, you can go look at them if you like. They're hanging in the basement. Maybe somebody'll like them, some reader in his armchair or E herself, who'd rather see herself as at least spiritual, ethereal, soulful, but they're a real disaster. They're more romantic — or experimental, like photos from the era when photography was an avant guard art form — than what he's after. They piss him off, make him want to pull his hair out. If the great sorcerer showed them under the title, "How to de-erotify the erotic object", they would be the epitome of what not to do.

What's the problem? Nothing, no matter how much he retouched them, moving shadows and lights from one place to another, toning down the leopard spots, your eye still doesn't go to her nipples, the main thing he wanted to highlight. Inconceivable, since her nipples are big and very erect, as if they were aimed at an invisible enemy lurking on the roof or in the corners of the studio. They embody the desire to pinch them, suck them, bite them...

This and this alone is what Bruno's going for: a provocative, playful image, the urge to attack them and caress them at the same time. No airbrushing — he doesn't use any type of filter— or technological innovations. Most of all he wants the essence, what's already invented, the everyday. The eternal. Not an excuse for reflection or pondering. No poetry. Nothing to come between E and the observer's most urgent fantasies. Unfortunately her smile devours all of that. With a force he doesn't quite get, her smile becomes the central focus that devours his objectives.

She shrugs and says well, let's try again. She never questions, never argues, never resists him. She doesn't seem resigned, uncomfortable, tired or even annoyed. She seems to feel absolutely nothing, not even indifference. Aponia, ataraxia, blood thick as a milkshake, the very stereotype of a person who becomes an English aristocrat or a Tibetan monk. Bruno isn't sure she's listening to him. Yet between bursts of light, he senses she's not lying, she's willing to cooperate. Still he's wary of her image on the film.

But sometimes his thoughts get fuzzy, he lets his guard down and a complacent, cheerful demon takes over and he coochie coos her stomach with a feather and makes funny faces — the same thing happens to writers, musicians, artists and other sorcerers — and then, still caught in the vicious cycle, in the *ritornelle*, his critic's eye eludes him and he sees only what he wants to see. A little puppet who puts on a cape to dance, then takes it off again, a whirling griffin, a serpent biting its own tail. To escape that, he would have to quit the game, knock down his king well protected after the *fianchetto* and take a walk, witness a traffic accident, someone's arms and legs twitching under a double-long bus, a landslide, a fist fight, have a beer. This woman confuses him.

Like a beginner, he writes it all down: the type of camera (the same kind as always, but no one's hired me to do an ad), the brand and speed of the film (*ibid*), exposure time and lens aperture. All fine. Brazenly fine. The only problem is her smile. But no one can overpower E's smile. If you can, we'll give you an extra large shrimp pizza or a South Seas cruise, absolutely free! Forget Utopias! It (her smile) can win out over any high-tech gadgets, no matter how expensive, and who knows how many photography classes, not counting years of experience. What do I do? Bruno asks himself when a wave of futility washes over him, whenever he feels he's repeating himself.

Thunder rumbles, the rain falls harder, pinging against the windows.

E stretches out on the rug again, surrounded by big cushions, like in a Titian painting. Or in a Manet that, perhaps unconsciously, parodies a Titian: where there was a splay-legged puppy, here there's a muscular cat, its hair standing on end; where there was the Venus of Urbino, here there's Olympia; the backdrop and servant girl are duplicates in the end. Yet neither Venus' majesty nor Olympia's brazenness of the second satisfies our artist. Neither of these women arouses him, God forgive him. Maybe the pose is the problem, he thinks, it's so contrived, like the Duchess of Alba and so many other women painted in oil, water colors or pastels. He motions for E to spread her legs.

He'd wanted to leave that for last. The usual routine: the model covers herself with one hand, reveals more and more, and finally shows with feigned carelessness more than she hides —

you know it's fake, you're no dummy. But it's like in the theater: the audience has no qualms about taking part in the fantasy. Her index finger points to a vortex that comes into sharper and sharper focus, as if whispering in your ear "See? See this? How do you like it?", and then a close-up, then another and another, with no fingers and no tricks. Ah, the index finger must be like E's! Long and tapered, suggesting skill. The nail trimmed short so as not to get in the way or scratch or disturb the perfect image of the scene. At times, Bruno wonders how women with such long nails manage, in one respect so un-aesthetic, not good for ...well. not exactly good for typing.

The girl raises her knees and separates her legs. There's a tiny mole on the inside of her left thigh which looks painted on by some jokester or by a minor French master of the 18th century. An eye-catching detail, like a grain of salt on a guava tart. It would be a crime to cover it with makeup, so the great sorcerer forgives life.

E moves slowly, she knows that right now all Bruno's time — and a healthy check to deposit in the bank — are hers. Besides it's not in her nature to hurry. Run? What for? Hurry? Where's the fire?

E crawls along, delighted. She's slinky, a true whore, she's perfect.

She abruptly raises up to her elbows, looks around, grabs a velvet cushion and places it under her butt.

"Spread your hands," Bruno says. "Let's see what happens."

She poses again and now displays her rosy, slightly moist, bubbly vulva, surrounded by her sumptuous copper down that matches her unshaved armpits. Her little oval — pursed for no apparent reason, there's nothing to be scared of in the studio just like there's no invisible enemy to defy her "no trespassing" sign — her erect lobe, poking out between minute folds. Delicious, firm, visible. You feel the urge to lick it for a long time, to sink your mouth and nose in it.

Bruno thinks nobody ever painted women like that, the way they looked their best. Didn't dare dream of it. They stone artists and destroy their paintings for less. Or hurl it all, artists and paintings, into the bonfire of the vanities. He's always been naive, maybe that explains why he never understands people who think the vanities are bad.

"We photographers have been luckier in our struggle than

most artists." He enunciates each word, like an orator, "if you can call it luck. Considering we are the newest artists and we often inhabit the margins of what's holy, we're given some leeway. Pornography and art, there's a fine line between them, each in its place, a label pinned to your back. If nothing's ambiguous, you're safe... Why do I think about these things now? Why do I care? I can't stop being who I am — and I don't want to! And I don't want to change anyone else either. There's something immature, something pathetic, and fun in whining like this. Don't think I don't know that."

Getting back to the body on the rug, to the cushion, the fringe on a shawl, her vortex. God, she's beautiful! The whole scene makes him ache to discard his camera. Words almost fail Bruno.

As he studies her, he slowly comes to believe that E would make a great lesbian, celebrated like those at Helen of Troy's fan clubs or budding young girls who rub their breasts against each other's as they dance or Djuna Barnes' almanac of women. Or maybe she's already a lesbian, he hasn't asked her. Surrounded by foam, gauzy see-through clothes and lace, the Sapphic point of view. Bruno would be a happy man if he could somehow slip into those clubs. He'd dress up like a woman if that's what it took. He's a simple man, the kind who thinks the more women, the better. If this pose turns out well... Hope springs eternal, like what flies out of the bottom of Pandora's box of evils, spins through the air across the studio, lights on his forehead. Maybe he should suggest to E a couple of sessions with...

For the moment, she (E) looks great, wearing her vertical smile... an improvement over that other smile. Her ineffable, persistent, almost mystical. mystifying smile. The one that dares to take the leading role smack dab in the center of the flash.

"That's not it. E, that's just not it." Something is wearing him out. "I don't have to develop it to know that's just not it."

The girl gets into a full lotus and looks at him. Sad? Who knows. That sheer makeup suits her, it accentuates her skin color. They're no marks on her skin. Not a blemish, not even a wrinkle or a scar, nothing. Anyone would think she was a virgin, and not the enemy, but more encompassing in a way.

Suddenly he feels the urge to slap her, to wipe that look off her face, the look he doesn't understand, that ruins his work. He counts to ten, breathes. Eleven. It's not enough. He goes back to his thirty five millimeter single lens, his SLR, a mental "Look at the birdie," eighty-five millimeter lens, the lens, another mental birdie, F5.6, F...

"You're driving me crazy, y'know that?"

He lights two cigarettes at once and hands her one. He's never seen her smoke, but the little witch takes it docilely.

"Come on, honey, can't you give me some other expression?"

She cocks her head the way a dog does when it sees something strange, as if three very shocking transvestites crossed the desert with their music, high heels and sequins. She watches him through the smoke she barely inhales, she protects herself. Bruno thinks that if he got too close to her, she might bolt, run into the street and get lost in the rain, naked to boot. He thinks he might not be able to catch up with her. Who knows when he'd see her again.

He describes the expression he wants from her, although at this point any grimace would do so long as it doesn't look like the fucking little smile that not even a cigarette can extinguish. It's not easy to describe an expression, even harder when you're dealing with something so subtle, but Bruno gives it a shot. And it makes no sense to show her the other girls' photographs, she shouldn't imitate them, every little witch should let her personality shine through. But isn't that what she's doing? Here our artist gets tangled up again, bites his tongue not to fall back on a beginner's copybook with his mental "birdie."

Outside there's a downpour, thunder here, thunder there, till it forms one magnificent, singular thunder clap overhead. The modest hills of the Vedado neighborhood loom as stormy summits.

"I never claimed I'd stripped a virgin on the rocks, understand? Never!" He didn't mean to shout, but he's shouting. "I've told you a hundred times. I go to Barcelona, to an erotic film festival! The Mostra d'Art is about art. That's right, erotic *art*! Not spiritualistic art, not psychoanalytic art. Erotic art. E-ro-tic art. And that look of yours! Beats the hell out of me what that's all about. You'd make any guy impotent. It's a fucking bucket of cold water! Hold your mouth like this! Look at me!"

She hasn't taken her eyes off him for a second. "Like this!"

He makes a face. She cocks her head again. And she lets out a great big belly laugh. Like a little Christmas tree covered with bells, shaken by the wind blowing on the other side of the wall. She laughs so hard she nearly bursts into tears. Her breasts rise and fall in time with her laughter. Then the little smart aleck nearly chokes on the smoke. OK, OK. let her laugh. What can Bruno do? Talking gets him nowhere. He shuts up. He has no choice.

He could drape her red hair over her face. A subtle candle, a landscape you can barely make out behind the flame. That is not ideal but, if there's no alternative... Because he's not about to look for another model. No way. Even if he has to wring her neck. She's his, he found her, he picked her out in the street among thousands of flashier women. E: common, brazen, free, he brought her to his studio.

Aside from her thin, but very pretty legs (in the other shoot she's wearing black stockings in several photos, too bad they didn't turn out) what he'd liked most about her, Bruno recalls, was, strangely enough, her smile.

I can't find a way to describe E's smile, to make you see it so you'll understand poor Bruno and not think he's weird. It's not a matter of just pressing the shutter and *presto*. Not everything is photogenic. You could say, perhaps, that it's the smile of a someone who's lived through a frightening and wonderful time in her life, a very special adventure, the kind that happens once in a lifetime. The smile of a person who recalls a unique, irreplaceable lover, with sarcastic kindness, happy rancor and who knows how many more contradictions.

When Bruno saw her for the first time, how could he have guessed that that smile was clamped on its owner like Monseigneur Louis's iron mask? In the end, does she own the smile or does it own her? It (the smile) didn't attract him so much as what was hidden behind it. How foolish. How could he have guessed it would bother him so much? Because it bothers him a lot: not even the coppery curtain of her hair has had an effect. Another failure. Always the same mistake. Her ghostly smile persists even behind the fire. What's worse: the observer's eye is compelled to intuit, tune out, decipher. He goes no further than her chin.

What if he always photographed her with her back turned? Something interesting might turn out if you don't see her face. That might work. Mystery girl or something like that. Who is she? A famous actress? A neighbor? His assistant? His wife? You decide! To stay calm, Bruno lies to himself. He continues with that train of thought. His mystery girl won't resemble

Valpincon's bather, or Velazquez's Venus, the one with the mirror, the best ass of all time. Those women are too famous, too recognizable. Bruno loves mirrors, they fascinate him, their multiple possibilities stimulate his imagination. But he doesn't try them out with E. Why duplicate what annoys him?

The mystery girl, propped up on her elbows on the rug: her round, slightly flabby buttocks, shockingly flawless, shaped like an upside down heart, an apple or a pear, like the buttocks that chorus girls in the Moulin Rouge bared, the one the dwarf drew. A ring even more pursed than her little oval, warning the invisible enemy: "don't even think about it." Pink like all the pink on her, maybe a bit darker. Her copper-colored down, her vertical smile now backwards, but equally spongy and tempting between two chubby little lips that droop a bit toward the back of the composition, taking advantage of the favorable angle. Her breasts droop, too, like ripe mangos, pointed, the real thing. pre-dating the silicon culture that doesn't do a thing for the great sorcerer.

How slowly she moves, cat-like, her whole body undulating. What Bruno wants now is to kneel behind her, cradle the weight of her breasts in his hands — her hard nipples tickling his palms, squeeze them, pull them, make them hurt — and penetrate her with a hard thrust. Her little oval or ring, either one. Pursed like that, he imagines how they'd squeeze him. How she'd moan, cry out, writhe...

He comes back to reality: his studio, his camera and all its attachments, the storm in the street; not to high art, like he should, but back to E's smile. He can't make out her face, but he can't focus either because, he's surprised to admit, he knows she's smiling. They call that paranoia, don't they? I think so.

I never thought about E as a lover. His, I mean. The model is the observer's lover, what Bruno feels for a few seconds looking at her body is what he'd wanted to transmit to him (or her). He'd never touched her, not out of any moral conviction other than his old mania for order, not mixing business with pleasure. Before, he dreamed of everything he'd do to her when the shoot was over... Now he's convinced he'll never go to bed with her.

Something makes her untouchable. It's not her body or what the eye detects in its search for pleasure, but rather something photographs reveal. Maybe the mark of that unknown man (unknown to Bruno, anyway) no one can measure up to. What did he do to her, for God's sake, what did he do? He doesn't dare ask.

Could she explain it in words? Perhaps, but what good would it do? Something weighs her down, the great sorcerer senses it, the ghost of something indelible, something she's lived through, something that drags her toward dangerous, unnavigable depths and banishes the happy frivolity of his art.

He gives up, exhausted. With as much courtesy as he can muster, he tells her they've finished for the day. He tells her nobody sends anyone packing in the rain, she can stay till it lets up, if she likes. She gets up without a word and walks to the corner farthest from the light where she'd left her clothes very neatly folded on the back of a chair. She doesn't seem upset. Of course not. Why would she be? All the anxiety falls on Bruno's shoulders, he has to deal with it. The shoot's over for today. And tomorrow? What'll he do tomorrow? He hasn't the slightest idea. What's he going to do with you, E? How will he pose you? He's down in the dumps, the enthusiasm he felt at first is gone.

He calls to her and a voice answers him from the corner with the chair and the shadow: "Yes, what is it?"

"E, you realize it isn't going well, don't you?"

"Yes, I realize that. I guess you'll have to find another girl."

"No, E, I don't want another model."

"So, now what? What do you want me to do? You say don't smile, so I don't. I really don't. But you're not satisfied. What do you want from me? You don't let up. You say I keep on smiling. I'm driving you crazy and all that. The problem is you don't like my face..."

He interrupts her, "That's not it exactly..."

She interrupts him, "Well, something like that. I didn't know my face was that important in this kind of photograph."

"I didn't either. To be honest nothing like this has happened before. But tell me, have you done this before?"

She emerges from the shadows, dressed, with a lit cigarette. Thunder drowns out her "Yes, once. But that was different, very different. *He* liked my face, he liked everything I did." E's eyes shine with a radiance almost as ambiguous as her damned smile.

"Do you still have those pictures? I'd like to take a look at them. If you don't mind."

"I don't mind. I only have one left. The others got lost or were confiscated when everything blew up in our faces. But you're in luck, at least in that way: I always carry it around with me."

She digs around in her leather bag while Bruno asks himself if

122

he is the "he", the unique lover, and he asks her what blew up, in whose face.

"Everything! Everything! People don't understand, you know? There was a trial," she shrugs her shoulders the way the great sorcerer's seen her do so many times over the last few days.

"People said horrible things. Afterwards I lost track," her sigh is full of a very old hatred. "I never heard another word."

She holds out a black and white photo, the size of a postcard, with very ragged edges and curled up corners.

"First time I've shown it to anyone."

Bruno carries it over to the lamp and what he sees catches him off guard. There before his eyes (accustomed, as you might imagine, to all kinds of tricks and lunacy) the light makes the inexorable image of E leap off the page: she's stark naked, stretched out, in a full frontal pose, arms behind her head and one knee flexed so you can see the mole on her thigh and more. Charming, smiling, a little queen, already sure of her power ... seven or eight years old.

Translated by Pamela Carmell

WOMEN OF THE FEDERATION
Francisco García González

She's stretched out on her back on the bed and I know she's having a lousy day. She has the complexion of a fresh apple. Sometimes I keep this to myself and other times I get a kick out of telling her so, depending on how things are going. Pretty corny. I'm always thinking it, but I only say it out loud once in a while. I look at the magazine that hides her face. I run my eyes over the sweet fingers of her sweet hands and the sweet freckles where her shoulders begin and the sweet breasts drifting toward her armpits. I look at the magazine and I wonder what she can be reading since she only knows about five words of English. "Goodbye." "Boy." "Girl." Maybe "Nike" if not "night," because women are so smart — about brand names. I'm sure she's gazing at the barefoot models or reading the names of the face creams and vitamins for the skin, or just casting her eyes over the pictures of overflowing platters of luscious-looking food. She loves lotions and constantly frets about the sun because her complexion is so fair. She's an active member of the Federation of Cuban Women, a food service worker, wears a uniform and black stockings, and, contrary to what you might think or she might hope, she is always ravenously hungry. I love her complexion and her appetite, her sweaty sheathed legs. I call her my yummy Pudge, my scrumptious pink Piggy, and watch how her nostrils dilate. Because Pudge or my little Piggy are invocations, triggers that unleash whirlwinds of desire. Followed by stiffening nipples, pupils rolled back, uncontrollable gasping until the spasm of release, feet kicking the air beneath or on top of me. I give her a whistle, ask how she's doing just to say something. I see her legs poking out from under the sheet and her underpants bulging around the double sanitary pads, so I know it's the third day, when her flow always seems even heavier than last month's. She doesn't answer. I go into the bathroom. Poor baby; I know she's having a bad day. I open the window. The book of word games is on the toilet tank. She's good at word puzzles. She left the last Find The Word page half done. Topic: soccer. Words to spot: goal, contract, penalty, score, winger, corner, line... I reach into the hamper and touch her soiled clothes. I pull out her work stockings and some white panties, yellowed by pee stains. I suck in my breath until my lungs are filled. Man, this is my girl's smell. I look around for the toothpaste and my toothbrush among the empty face cream jars and shampoo bottles, then I go back to smelling those yellow pee stains on her panties and I think how intimate and tender my girl's world is. Sometimes I'm part of her world, but other times I feel like an intruder. I give my dick a shake and the last drops spill onto the floor and onto the edges of the toilet. Pudge threatens that someday she'll stick a hose onto me every time I take a leak. Men's pee stinks worse than women's, she claims, and she says I manage to drip all over the place so it reeks like a bus station latrine. That's what she says and I get a kick out of thinking how wise women are and how they can do everything better. I finish brushing my teeth and count the napkins in the open packet: Pudge should have enough for this month. She's still got one more unopened packet. So she'll get by until next time. It doesn't help to tell her to think positively. She's cheerful, even joyful and optimistic, until two days before the cataclysm strikes. And then, all of a sudden, she wakes up one day and her breath smells different and she's got that look on her face that neither one of us likes. And sure enough, the next day the bleeding starts. Spotting at first and then a heavy flow, with clots in it. I've seen them on the tiles in the shower and in the toilet bowl when the water's off. The image of a clot on a tile floor is the very embodiment of abandonment and desolation. But a clot floating in water is something else, it remains diaphanous and intact even while those little protuberances like the pseudopodia of a handsome amoeba are swaying around. With time it begins to dissolve and tints the water until it becomes an intense purple as the clot disappears. It's beautiful. She finds it disgusting. I like it, but I don't tell her so, any more than I tell her I smell her panties, pee stained and unwashed. I leave the towel on the rod and count the napkins in the packet again, and the used ones in the waste basket. The total, figuring in the two she has on, confirms my guess: she'll have enough for this month. So that's good. I stand on the scale. From the bathroom I can see the magazine and her fingers. She's lying on her back on the bed and I know she's having a lousy day. I give her a whistle, but she doesn't answer. She goes on gazing at the barefoot models and the delicious platters of food, even though I can't imagine that she's feeling very hungry right now. On days like this I exempt her from everything. Pudge, I'll make my own breakfast, and I'll leave a nice lunch all ready for you,

125

and you can just stay there in bed until I get back, my lady love, my madonna, my nymph, and that way you can listen to the soap operas and watch the noon preview programs and finish your word game and listen to all the tapes you want. Anything, Pudge, just don't look out the window to see if the smokestack off in the distance is belching smoke up into the sky or if it remains silent and lifeless, shut down yet again. Because, Pudge, today is a gray day which is doubly bad for you, so tell the world to go to hell and just stay here resting until your *papi* comes back. I never knew what that distant chimney was until she moved in with me. It was during our first menstrual period together. On the third day I found her on her knees, gazing out the window. She gestured for me to come over and asked me if I knew what that chimney was, the one we could see in the distance between the gray stone buildings. And here I'd been thinking that she was engrossed in the trees in the park, or was watching the kids running around benches in the little plaza. "That's the smokestack of the sanitary pad factory." I looked and saw how lifeless it was, without a single plume of smoke against the sky. She didn't have to explain anything to me. I rinse out the glass and go back into the bathroom. A new pad count, more drops on the floor and on the edge of the toilet bowl, again the fragrance of Pudge's pee. She gives me a hug and says not to be late, I tell her I'll call her at noon. I feel her fetid, familiar breath on me and I think if a guy can feel desire for someone who smells this bad, he should be called a hero. I avoid the second kiss with a loving bite on her right ear and I tell her that I can't wait to get past the next few days so I can nibble on her little ear again and see her panting with her eyes rolled up. She believes me and hugs me and I believe me too and I hug her back and I don't avoid the third kiss because I am a hero and tomorrow or this afternoon I'll desire Pudge even though she doesn't like it this way in the midst of so much blood. And in the midst of the kiss and hug it occurs to me that if, as we've been taught, heroism is based on the amount of blood spilled for a worthwhile cause, among other things, then women are the true heroines. The fact that they menstruate just because they are what they are, well, we men should not only tip our hats, but take them off altogether. They are the true heroines, women are, and I shouldn't say I'm a hero just for breathing in her infernal stinking breath. What does it matter that women, at least some women, turn on the tears easily. At first, every time we'd find ourselves at the climactic moment of the primordial act, Pudge would burst into tears. Her sobs drained my enthusiasm and I lost my momentum. I never figured out whether she meant it or not. If it was a farce, I was sorry I was taking it seriously, and if it wasn't, it was just too pathetic. The only interesting part was the taste of her tears: salty sweetness of a landlocked sea. But all that spilled blood, and having to put up with it! Pudge, I forgive you the ocean and for drowning me in your eyes. The topic gets me hot again, and Pudge complains that I could break her thorax. I blow her a kiss from the doorway and she tells me to watch out for cars. I blow her another kiss. She's the one having a lousy day, not her bicyclist.

Pudge isn't pudgy at all, and she has apple skin and she's a heroine because of all that spilled blood.

But the street is something else, man. Another part of the same thing. The air is just right today because the cold wind has blown away the last of the fog. This is something only a cyclist would notice. He's on a bike. She's on a bike. They're on bikes. So are we, so are you. The asshole pal I inherited the bike from when he decided to leave is still up there in the States, far away, and since he's a sentimental guy he writes to me once in a while. In his last letter, he told me about how he'd had a dream where I was riding my, *his*, bike thinking about fucking every woman who crossed my path. Just then, like those things that happen in dreams, the person who crossed my path was the Pope, who was here on a visit. A truck goes by almost sideswiping my bike and leaves me wrapped in a dense cloud of black fumes. The guys riding in the back yell at me – either they want to encourage me or else they're just making sure I notice that they're moving a lot faster than the guy they're leaving in the dust. It's a show of strength. "*Tarrú*," I manage to make out, "Asshole!" In the dream of the pal who left me the bike, nothing else happened. I think about what it would be like to meet the Pope somewhere along this highway. His Holiness the Pontiff comes along in his special popemobile, going the opposite direction, and something — he never told me what — makes him notice me. His motorcade comes to a halt. The sun gleams on the keys of Saint Peter's emblem on his limousine. His aides lead me over to the Vicar and I try to act as natural as possible. He still hasn't opened his mouth and I ask him how's he doing and what's he doing on this highway. He tells me he's going to the hospital, because today is the day of his encounter with the world of pain. Then he asks about my bicycle and I tell him that it was left to me by an asshole pal who feels bad every time he remembers that he had no choice but to go off and leave me this pile of shit, this junk heap. Junkip? His Holiness asks what "junkip" means. I explain to him and his mouth twitches in what looks like a laugh. Then he asks where the owner of the "junkip" (like that, all one word) is and says something about the grievous separation of the family. He too had had to pedal hard in Krakow. I laugh thinking about the Pope having to ride a bicycle back then, and in Krakow because it's the only city in Poland, besides Warsaw, that I've heard people talking about. If the Pope and I met, there'd be lots of photos. Before he went on, he asked me first if I've been baptized by the Holy Mother Church and I tell him yes, I was, and he says that will do. And then, if I fear God. Yes, sir, sometimes I'm scared of God. That, too, is sufficient. Since the motorcade is going in the opposite direction, to its encounter with the world of pain, no one offers to give me a tow. The Pontiff makes one more joke about my "junkip" (like that, all one word). I should skip over the fact that one of the aides gave me a T-shirt with Saint Peter's keys on it, and a cloth patch with the image of Mary on it. Once again, the same fumes on the road and the same or other shirtless black guys are yelling at me. This time I do understand. There, from the truck, proletarian-truck, the black guys yell that I'm an asshole and that I should get out of the way and they're also going in the opposite direction from the Pontiff. Although they (the black guys) and I are going along another road (which is the same one, not the only one) toward the world of pain. And what if I'd told the Pontiff that my girl's home in bed and if I'd told him about the sanitary pads and about the worst days when my heroine just stays in bed? For sure he'd scratch one ear and would recommend me to his pupil, Mother Teresa, who might well be here and not so far away, unreachable Mother of Calcutta. Today the north wind has blown off the fog and the wind shoves me along, and I catch up with other cyclists. An old man. Another old man. A guy with a bored expression, even though the north wind pushes him same as yesterday and tomorrow. By now Pudge has probably tired of her magazine and gone back to the Find A Word game. Penalty. Contract. Run. Goal. Pudge is really good at finding the words. The cyclists are left behind and the bright, soft sun, cooled by the north wind, gleams not on the emblem of Saint Peter's keys, but on the roadside stand where they sell cane juice, *guarapo,* to people coming and going along the highway. I might invite the Pontiff to have a *guarapo* with me. I'll bet no Pope has ever had a *guarapo.* The Pontiff's in luck: they have ice. I order two *guarapos.* The kiosk owners refuse to charge the visitor. His Holiness admires the machinery that crushes the cane and spits the stalks out in bits. The owners recommend we add lemon. We do so. Tasty. Delicious. The aides try the drink, too. The owners tell the Pontiff that they work in a cooperative named "Cuba-Laos Friendship." Cuba-Laos Friendship? Wow, he says to me, that must be very important. It is. I ask the owners if they know where Laos is, and they answer that they do not, that when they got there, that was the name of the place. I understand, says the Pontiff. This machine is a "junkip" (like that, all one word). We all laugh. I almost laugh and I finish drinking the *guarapo.* No ice today, the guy in the cap tells a taxi driver. Did any Pope ever really drink *guarapo?* What will the friend who left me the bike think if I tell him how I've improved upon his dream? The taxi driver doesn't much like warm *guarapo,* either, so he orders just one. While he drinks, he notices that the business belongs to the "Cuba-Laos Friendship" cooperative. He asks about it. No clue, pal, when we got here the place was already named that. The taxi driver and I pay. Tomorrow there will be ice, then we'll each have two and eventually someone will tell the owners where Laos is. Tomorrow or never.

The other item in my friend's dream isn't quite true. While I pedal along, I'm not thinking that I want to go to bed with every woman who comes into view. I'd have gone to bed with Pudge if today were a good day for her. And there are no women hitchhiking, standing in the shade of the trees along the side of the road. No. It's Lisanka I'm thinking of. I should admit it, the dream is partly about her. I've given Lisanka the best thrusts of all in my mind and on this bicycle. Once I told her about it and she told me I had a sick mind and that's what she liked about me. Lisanka is different from Pudge. At least that gives our relationship some meaning. Otherwise, why bother? I met Lisanka not long ago on a bus. I met Pudge at some friends' house. When I saw Lisanka hanging onto the bar trying to read a book, I stood right behind her, leaving just enough space so it could be accidental or on purpose on my part. It was a book of poetry. "If everyone riding a bus read a book, we'd be closer to the sun." She laughed. You couldn't begin on a higher note. The day I met Pudge, I had to use the bathroom. That underwear couldn't belong to anyone else. The olfactory memory, the girl they had introduced me to had to be menstruating. That may not have been her day, and that's why she hardly paid any attention to me, there are meetings and then there are meetings. Lisanka tells me not to exaggerate, the fact is we were pretty close to the sun in that bus, otherwise why would we have been sweating so much. And since sometimes I manage some mental agility, I scolded her and said she shouldn't confuse hell with the sun. In hell, it could be cold, too. Cold and hot. I asked her to read me a poem. Just then we were pressed tight against each other. Lisanka closed the book. *If some day the waters/ drown my memory/ from the first scolding/ to the final holocaust...* the poem was hers. Lisanka belonged to the "Rabindranath Tagore" literary workshop. Lisanka was a writer. Pudge was studying gastronomic science when we met. The day after we met, she had a practical exam and had to present a main dish. She was complaining that she wanted to make stuffed peppers and she couldn't find the two peppers anywhere. Everyone in the room was complaining. Pudge never suspected that her smell and her skin interested me. I offered to look for the peppers. They tried gently to dissuade me: it was a pretty risky business. Pudge was having a really bad day. Lisanka said that Rabindranath Tagore was a Turkish poet with a very long beard. I could get into that. *Like the pocked sea/ the waves boiled/ in such gray display/ close by other rocks.* You just can't let a poet with such an elevated idea of Turkish poets get away. I pressed her on the nationality of the poet. Right. Turkey, over there by India. If I hadn't seen her eyes I'd have thought Lisanka might be leading me on. But Lisanka is incapable of lying, I picked up on that right away. Rabindranath Tagore was Turkish, from over there by India. Women do things that just kill you. I didn't wait for my bus stop. Want to go sit in the park? Lisanka's skin was white with delicate black fuzz on it. It was a risky enterprise, something that added to her attractions. I spent the afternoon walking the city, and Pudge ended up with not two but five handsome peppers. Under the trees, Lisanka read the poem again... *And perhaps you will arrive invading/ before and after, you/ alone at the helm, your back to time.* Things wouldn't — a question of chance — have progressed past the enchantment of listening to each other, if Lisanka hadn't revealed the mystery of her name. Lisanka was the name of the mare that belonged to a character in a Soviet novel, a book we'd all read in the crowded military barracks in the 60s. *Whipping his gallop/ quick to retreat/ like the pocked sea.* A shame not to be the Ivan or Boris who could go for a gallop on this Lisanka. The woman laughed and I thought how long her face was, and what big, strong teeth she had, and what a black and gleaming mane. And the image of desire was a woman-mare who wrote poems and trotted in the solitude of my bicycle journeys. But I knew that no matter how much the poet aroused me with her neighing, it was my displaced apple I really wanted to bed, although sometimes with desire stimulated elsewhere. A week after the exam, Pudge came to my house and repeated every detail of the exam in my kitchen, barefoot and aproned. Pudge laughed her way around the house, inspecting and tidying up. I followed her around because I was so taken with her legs and her barefootedness, until she stopped in front of the window and pointed at the dreary smokeless chimney. She didn't explain then what it was about. I'd rather gallop and savor an apple, says a banal — that is, astute — pop tune.

I swerve around an ambulance and turn my attention back to my pal's dream. I had never thought so much about a Pontiff before. We ordered two *guarapo*s and stood back from the counter. Behind the *guarapo* stand, the slaughterhouse butchers of the "Cuba-Laos Friendship" cooperative have done their usual stuff. Right by our feet runs a stream of water red with the blood of just-butchered hogs. I'm afraid my guest will ruin his white cassock on his day to visit the world of pain. We stand there looking at the blood, and I'm sure his thoughts flow toward the earth where the blood will turn to dust tomorrow or the next day. And maybe because I see him so deep in thought, I ask him if by any chance he remembers a Soviet novel where a character had a mare named Lisanka. He sighs, stands there gazing at his glass, and then confesses that he has never been able to get through a Soviet novel. I trade confessions with him: I haven't either. What do you think we've missed, Your Holiness? What do you think we've been spared, son? Eating apples? A good gallop?

The street is one thing and work is quite another, man. I don't know who the hell this "man" is. It's not Pope John Paul or my bicycle buddy. The secretary has left me a note. She's had to go to the hospital with an asthma attack and won't be back until afternoon. Clients won't come either, which makes me pretty happy. You can expect all the extremes of behavior, good and bad, from these guys, never the normal thing. I shuffle through my papers and a picture of my pal with the bicycle falls out onto the floor. He rode that bike to work for two years. He had a job in a cemetery. When he walked into his office to deal with death, he'd say hello to the woman in charge of death certificates. At noon, she'd come in and they'd screw on his desk. She complained about this a little. Afterward, they'd pee in a potted plant. The plant seemed to thrive on this. It's complicated, but we've kept in touch. He's never met Pudge. I'd like to tell him about Lisanka and her poems, about how, contrary to all expectation, we've never gone beyond some affectionate making out, even though my ideal desire fantasy is the woman-mare strumming a harp and neighing in my ears. Ah, Lisanka's mouth. On the back of the picture, my pal wrote that someday we'll have to compare notes. He's put on so much weight that he looks like a different person. He and Pudge could cook up some good dishes in the kitchen. What would it be like to have a three-way conversation between him, the Pope, and the heir of the bicycle? We'd talk and we'd drink *guarapo*, watching the blood — the hogs' blood — run along the side of the road until it soaked into the earth and the dust. For sure we'd tell two or three good jokes that we'd have to explain to the priest. I put the picture and the papers away. I take a look at the newspaper. Italian Robbers Drugged Their Victims. Police detained four Albanians who had been breaking into victims' houses, and knocking them out with drugs so they could get away with all kinds of bad stuff. Rape, robbery. New members appointed to the Socialist International. Alleged fraud in Special Oympics disputed in Mexico City. "Troyano" disguised as Y2K error. Called FIX2001, the virus infiltrates computers, disguised as innocent electronic message. Before I folded the paper back up, a letter to the editor caught my attention. A lady's companion has gone from one province to another on account of a death in her family. The wake has made her realize that coffin manufacturing is a disaster in her town, while at the same time she praises the good taste and efficiency of the operations of the funeral home that tended to her relative. The list of manufacturers' shortcomings in her native Guantánamo fall like hammer blows on stone. Green wood. Skimping on nails. Poor quality lining cloth. Delays in delivery to the family. A shoddy product. Her complaint is going to the sanitary authorities of her town. She ends by congratulating her colleagues in Bijarú. Bijarú: now there's a place where they know how to treat you right on your final journey. Bitter words from a *compañera* now sitting in her armchair, sipping coffee after coffee. The moment comes for us all, and one coffin is not the same as any other. We want to do it right when we die. A letter like this merits serious action. This heroine, apart from the blood she has spilled during her life, is the defender of a cause that is surely transcendent. I cut the letter out carefully. I'll send it to my bicycle buddy, so he can see. Better to send him the entire paper. I put water on to boil. Just as I put the kettle on, the electricity goes off. I look over the clients' requests one more time. It would be better if they didn't come, at least not today. At first sight, the operation doesn't seem complicated. I go through the document and by the end I can hardly believe how tortuous and eccentric a procedure it is. New winds of consumer awareness are blowing. Someday everyone everywhere will have coffins like the ones in Bijarú. At noon I call my heroine. Nothing new, the word search for soccer terms is giving her a headache. I cheer her up by suggesting that she look for a topic she likes better. Before hanging up she reminds me to bring her the magazine with the article about Lady Di's death, she wants to read it again and loan it to some friends. The day they issued Cuban stamps with Diana on them, Pudge wanted me to get her some. Neither one of us has ever collected a stamp. The Diana stamps are under the glass top of the dresser with some postcards of the movie *Titanic*. I promise her I won't be late and I'll bring her the magazine. A little while later the phone rings. Neighing on the other end, that seductive voice reels me in. Lisanka is alone and wants me to have lunch with her. I feel like I'm throwing myself off the top of a roller coaster. I feel bad about Pudge, but the poet mare is the vivid, single image of desire right this instant. Despite her pleas, I detect a sad tone in her voice. I'm a pushover. There's a silence after we hang up. Behind the indecipherable noise I know there lurk surprise and the mystery of poems I'll never understand. I feel bad again. Without victims or perpetrators, how could heroines exist?

The street is one thing, and work something else, and this chasing after another woman, can't even talk about that one, man. I hadn't seen or talked to Lisanka for three days. Down the roller coaster I slide, and my hard-on is the bicycle's horse. Nothing matters, not her sad tone of voice, not the war in my diaphragm, not Pudge or the Pope or the dust soaking up the blood spilled by the slaughterhouse butchers and by my heroines. This chasing after another woman, man. This hiding my desperation when I get to her door. The exquisite detail of Lisanka's white fingers on the brass doorknob. "Hi there." The silky mane brushes against my cheeks and the scent, that distinctive scent of this Lisanka, who stands there with her hand on the knob, tells me her body fluids are awash in an elemental mix of woman and beast. Down the roller coaster, man. Excuses, but there's no action brewing here, nothing to excuse. And before Lisanka even says a word, I know, feel sure of it, that today's not her day. Lunch was just a pretext, even though the french fries, canned meat, rice and beans, and the two beers are right there. I dish some up for her and help myself. Great potatoes and meat, and Lisanka watches me chew as though seeing me eat were a banquet for her. Today is not her day. Yeah, I know, I tell her. She smells different. The Soviet hero's mare runs her fingertip through the sweat on the glass. The mare isn't hungry. Her parents get home tomorrow. She asks me if I think she's fat and if I want her lunch, she doesn't feel well. It's all a terribly domestic, and even heroic, scene. I feel the tension in my diaphragm subsiding. Will Lisanka's clots, on the bathroom tiles, be the very image of desolation or will they waft like beautiful amoebas in the water in the toilet bowl? I tell her it's fine with me and I'm glad she felt she could call me when she feels this way. I get her to stand up and I pull her onto my lap. Lisanka relaxes against my body, I stroke her mane and she lifts my hand to her lips. She kisses my fingers. She bites them with her square, equine teeth. If she has called me today, it's because she takes me seriously, she assures me and that, for now, seems okay to me. She has several things to tell me. Things she can't tell anyone else. On days like this, she thinks nothing she does matters. The last poem she read at the "Rabindranath Tagore" workshop, named for the Turkish poet, was a great success. But she doesn't believe it. *This December day, / the forest is so heavy / it hides mockingly / amidst sips of solitude.* How can she have any doubt about such moving images. The weight of a forest hiding mockingly. Lisanka shouldn't even question the beauty of something like that, I assure her, hugging her. And it's not that I'm being an asshole, leading her on, but right this moment, a heavy forest hiding mockingly amidst sips of solitudes are words that embody a beauty that is total, possible... *often piling up*

debris / beside old ants / hanging from my eyes. I think Lisanka
has talent, and I hug her close again with my arms that have been
the victims of simultaneous natural cycles. Lisanka's weight on
my knees begins to bother me. *Sustained by the gaze / of sterile
rains.* We kiss, a key move, man, when you're trying to keep
from inhaling bad breath. *Perhaps wisely / I could bear no more.*
Man, I like this poem, what does it matter whether R. T. is
Turkish or Malay or Australian. I move out from under Lisanka's
weight. In vain, I look in the bathroom for trophy by-products, the
package with whatever napkins are left, clots, old pee-stained
underpants. Then we sit on the bed. Will the day ever come when
we won't doubt what we do? Doubt has no sex (SHE) (THEY),
Lisanka. I've written a story, too. A story, Lisanka? It's called
"Blame the river." Hardly letting me ask about it, the mare
cleared the next hurdle without a hitch. Marisol meets Miguel at a
meeting, Marisol goes to live at the guy's house. One day,
without any explanation, Miguel commits suicide. Marisol, who
is pregnant, is rejected by Miguel's parents. She goes to see the
dead man's aunt and uncle. Miguel was HIV positive. Shock.
Then I...? Positive. Marisol-Ophelia-Alfonsina Storni (the river
connection), instead of heading home to her parents, leaps into the
river believing that she sees Miguel's face in a small, luminous
window in the middle of the rapids. Miguel is calling her: "Come
on, darling, come on." Marisol-Alfonsina-Ophelia doesn't know
how to swim. The end. She hasn't read the story yet in the R. T.
Workshop. I scratch my head. Lisanka is waiting for my reaction.
I don't know, right on the spot. I'd have to reread it. You should
let me have it, and tomorrow I'll tell you. Lisanka moves her ears
and her mane. From this angle she looks more attractive. We fall
into each other's arms again. I liked your story, but I don't know.
The heroine opens her legs and makes space for me down there.
We can't do this, I don't feel well. You don't have to tell me,
Lisanka, today's a bad day for everyone. About that guy with
AIDS, that's strong stuff, man. Strong stuff. The heroine pushes
me away slowly: now my weight bothers her. I go back to
variations on my buddy's dream. The Pontiff swirls his *guarapo*
around. The hogs' blood runs right by our feet. All rivers flow
into the sea. Even the one Marisol leapt into, without first
checking with the Center for Hygiene and Epidemiology just in
case. I tell the priest I'd like to confide in him. I'm attracted to
two women, sir. My guest finished his drink and shrugged his

shoulders. There's sin along all of life's roads, son. He tells me this, he, a priest, a man, an old man. Then he says goodbye to me through the window of the popemobile. At my side, my pal drinks his *guarapo*. It's been years since I've had such good *guarapo*. We both gaze at the mix of blood and water running into the ditch. Cuba and Laos can do a lot together. No one laughs. I tell my pal I'd like to confide in him. I'm attracted to two women, bro. My pal finishes his drink and shrugs his shoulders. Don't leave the main road for a detour, my friend. He's saying this as a man who's monogamous and who's seen the sun set over the mouth of the Hudson River. I get off Lisanka. We'll have our trot another day. That's strong stuff about AIDS, man. Nothing more demoralizing, man, than AIDS and pornography. The one castrates you, and the other is too perfect, and excludes you. Now Lisanka can breathe better and asks me what kind of music I'd like. The mare walks past me and her strong odor hits me in the stomach. Anyone who is capable of desiring someone who stinks like this is either a hero or out of his mind. This is the second time I've thought this. And while Lisanka fusses over the music, I inflate a condom and paint little eyes on it, and a smile, and an "I Love Lisanka" and below that, the head of a mare with very long eyelashes. When Lisanka comes back, I toss the zeppelin into the air. The poet neighs with pleasure and I'm glad she's pleased. We play a little volleyball. A condom, man. A condom for Lisanka. I hear the sound of Silvio Rodrígues on the record player. I tell Lisanka I didn't think anyone paid attention to Silvio Rodrígues any longer. I think he's great. I bet you do - I can't stand him, I think he's really trite. How could I have guessed that such a casual remark would upset her so. I got tangled in a stupid explanation and I finally said she was right. Silvio Rodrígues is a great guy. If my friend the midget heard you, he'd throw a brick at your head. The midget, Lisanka? But no one else counts here but us, and certainly not a midget, right, my mare? *How could it be/ how could it be/a steed without a rider ...* A great guy, Lisanka, just like that midget who heaves bricks. Anything you want. Silvio Rodrígues is the best Turkish crooner I know, no matter what the midget says. Anything you want, go on and bleed today, and tomorrow then, we'll get on with it with spurs and riding boots and the bridle that's...

The breeze wafts the condom from one side of the room to the other. Lisanka goes back to bed, her ovaries are still aching. She's glad I'm keeping her company. With her legs half open and lying on her back, obviously every month she wishes the earth would swallow her up. Again she apologizes for taking advantage of my patience and my time. I tell her that if it were up to me, I'd spend all afternoon with her, but I'd better get back to work. Just a minute, and the mare heaves up on her haunches and goes over to the cupboard. Help me, would you, before you go. Lisanka spreads a sheet on the bed. If she cuts it into strips, she'll have enough for the rest of this period and next month, too. Okay. We set to work. If the Pontiff and the pal with the bicycle saw us, they'd for sure insist on the road of life, sin and the detour. Two heroines are too much. So far Pudge-Apple hasn't had to resort to this extreme. We finally count up sixty strips. At this rate, I'll sleep on the bare mattress, she tells me, and it sounds frivolous and absurd to me. As absurd as asking the Pope in the middle of the highway how things are going. Once again in each other's arms. Pats on the haunch. The heroine will end up with no sheets. If I offered her Pudge's contacts for buying contraband napkins or cotton, it would be a double betrayal. One is enough. And before I leave, I go over to the window and I ask her if she sees that tall tower there in the distance. Well, that's a sanitary products factory, they make napkins. *White on the outside close up / not from far away...*

I leave and Lisanka remains standing in the window. I look from the street and to my surprise the smokestack begins to emit swirls of smoke. Then on my bicycle without a Pontiff and without a pal, without *guarapo* or seeing the blood run along the earth, I think about what I'm like, an it seems to me that I, too, am the very image of abandonment. A clot on the tiles, an inflated condom, pulled here, pushed there, pushed and pulled. It's all one thing, man, and this is something else.

November, 1999

Translated by Mary G. Berg

ROOMS
María Elena Llana

What a shame, Olga said as she ran her sad eyes over the Christmas tree's beautiful landscape—now out of date. The Three Kings had left their gifts at its pleasantly snow-covered cotton base twenty-four hours ago. Marina, who was in a benevolently indifferent stage at the time, shrugged and told Olga that if it was so heart-breaking she should not take it down.

"Should I leave it up a few more days?"

"No."

"So... what then?"

"I just said not to take it down."

Baffled, Olga looked at Marina and understood the silent message delivered by her authoritative greenish eyes. It clearly said «Leave it up forever». Olga nodded, perplexed. She then covered her mouth to stifle a laugh, "A permanent Christmas tree!"

And she didn't touch it. The kids were happy to find it there when they came home from school, but a week later the tree started to get on everyone's nerves a bit because every single visitor asked what was keeping them from finally taking it down.

It was then that they decided to move the tree to the back room, where from that moment on it would always be Christmas. They'd be spared the wait for December's decreed blessed joy. It would be enough to enter the room and, it goes without saying, dine on suckling pig and radishes the twenty-fourth, carve the turkey the twenty-fifth, devour twelve grapes the thirty-first, and let the carols flow, all without seasonal limitations. And of course, on the morning of the sixth, gifts at the foot of the tree.

Rene said they were getting nuttier every day. Esteban didn't even push aside the armchair, where he had his cup of coffee every day after lunch, in order to make the move a little easier. So, Olga and the kids proceeded through the hallway with great difficulty while Marina, in the back, said: "Careful, slowly, a little more to the right, the star's falling down, okay — now you've got it, go ahead!"

This initiative was the first of a series of other schemes. If there were more rooms in the house, why not have them all celebrate a seasonal occasion? The Circus, the kids demanded. Carnival, suggested Martica, who was just coming of age and liked a good party. If that were the case, added Marina in the neo-devout nature she acquired after turning fifty, then we shouldn't forget Holy Week.

Collective enthusiasm moved the project forward splendidly. By March, in addition to the Christmas tree room, we had one with streamers, balloons, masks, and a good supply of harlequins, skaters, and gypsies. And another had religious images and deep-purple drapery, with Handel, and whatever other *requiem* we came across through friends, in the background.

There was no longer any peace and quiet. Busybodies were always dropping in and fake visitors came over with no other purpose than to snoop around — but every institution has its pitfalls. The men declared themselves in favor of a plan for an eternal summer which resulted in digging an in-ground pool in the basement and attaching a bar where there always seemed to be a crowd of visitors hanging around. And if that wasn't enough, Rene Jr. insisted on putting a call girl up in the empty room on the roof — the only space left. There was some rationale for this. If everyone else got to enjoy themselves at home, why did he have to exercise his adolescent passions elsewhere, when it was so simple to screw in a red light bulb and bring in a bleached-blond? Fortunately, she turned out to be very easy-going and got used to eating at the patio table with the circus troupe who had installed themselves in the garden around the old lion's cage (the lion-tamer doubled as the acrobat who exchanged incomprehensible lampooneries with the clown). The group also included an equestrian who neither had nor requested a horse. They'd all arrived having undergone some failed venture along life's paths, following the bright star of gossip that had shone from our project.

When someone realized we didn't have a Hurricane room things got ugly. All of the other rooms were in use. In the end we deactivated a huge bathroom in the back that at the time was only used by an old ghost in his morning coat. We installed a strong fan, a brightly-lit lantern, and a small stove to make the hot chocolate associated with the storm. It turned out to be surprisingly rewarding—some friends amused themselves by sending us victim-relief donations.

How long could we keep time at bay, isolated as we were from the world in our own house? I don't know... I guess the enthusiasm lasted as long as it could. But the kids grew up and, in this era of rock-and-roll, no longer had any interest in our fantasy-land project. René Jr., who graduated with a degree in Fjordic Engineering, left for Holland after he married a tourist from there who was headed for Aruba but ended up on the wrong island. Olga, creaky with age, hums her carols no matter what corner of the house she's in and can therefore do without the rooms. Marina, ever more devout, prefers the parish congregational life. Their respective husbands, retired, spend most of their time in parks, where they get together with their contemporaries and usually talk about the rooms as just another of the bygone things from the good old days. Martica obeyed the Biblical mandate to obey one's husband, a Barabbas who steers clear of reproduction by blaming her for I don't know what chromosomal deficiencies that make everything her fault.

In short, I am the only one who still walks through these rooms filled with our happy memories and decorations that crumble just by looking at them... I get together regularly with the troupe who, after the lion died, had no place to go — except for the equestrian who found a job with a foreign balloon-inflating company.

We eat together at the kitchen table and once in a while we put together a Christmas, a Carnival, a Hurricane or a Holy Week. On these occasions, the big-lipped clown is kind enough to put a red ball on his nose, and the girl from upstairs one of her see-through dressing gowns. Generally, we look at each other with affection, fearful of doing or saying anything out of place, because, well, for some years now we haven't been quite sure which room we are in.

Translated by Barbara Riess

A FIVE-HUNDRED YEAR OLD RUM
María Elena Llana

*It was useless to make demands of
someone who was already dreaming
of what lay behind the horizon.*
  - Alejo Carpentier, "Like the Night"

for Marlene Vázquez

"Shit, Lazarito, you can't do this to me."

"Get off me, dammit, they'll leave without me!"

"But, Lazarito, I want to go with you!"

"You can't! You won't fucking fit! The raft is chock-full—
I'm lucky they gave me a break!"

She watches him walk off, towards Prado Blvd., knapsack
slung on his shoulder. She doubles over, clenching her fists,
beating her thighs and head. Then, she runs over to the corner,
takes out a bottle and holds it up to the light. She takes a swig and
starts to sob. Don't leave, Lazarito, don't leave me. I don't want
another man, dammit. She takes another long drink. The rotgut
rum traces a shiny gleam across her lips. She licks them
anxiously. The only thing left for her to do is to scour her stash
for enough for a fifth, a ten-peso half bottle; but there is nothing
— *nada*. Unable to stand her room, now her tomb, Izzy goes out
to the street. She sets off through the archways along Prado Blvd.,
anguished and lost in herself, as if she had buried all of her
strong-minded *mulata* spirit.

"Shit, Lazarito, you can't do this to me!" She yells down
Consulate Street, yet his name has already faded into nothing
more than a shadow, a shadow in the shadows that make their
way toward the *malecón.** Where would they leave from, for
God's sake? Please, *virgencita*, let him get to Miami, don't let
them catch him! Son-of-a-bitch, why didn't you take me with
you? Just then she remembers that last minute gesture, when
Lazarito stuck his hand down her shirt and she, experienced,
dodged what she thought was a feel. She digs around and finds a

---

* The word malecón refers to a cement sea wall found in many Latin American cities.
Here, it refers to the area that lines the Bay of Havana, a popular meeting place and
site of the 1994 maleconazo protests and departure point for rafters during the
migration that followed.

five-dollar bill. Her jaw drops; she's touched: ¡*cinco fulas*!

"Ay, Lazarito, you left me all that you had. But it is you I want, you, dammit, you!" she cries, leaning on a pillar, doubling over again in pain. Without thinking twice she looks for an open kiosk, the ones with the colorful umbrellas, the only flowers open this time of night, and soon she grabs hold of a bottle of the real stuff, the one with the *Giraldilla*, the weathervane cut-out figure of a woman appearing to challenge the wind. She knocks back her first drink — to Lazarito, the one who's leaving, who won't listen to her, who makes fun of her by saying that she won't fit on the raft (as if one more doesn't always fit on the raft). She downs another, long and gurgling, to stop the wound from burning like it's burning, to help her sleep until tomorrow. Tomorrow Lazarito will be far away; he won't be that shadow that runs down Prado Blvd. — that same Prado that turns suddenly dark and bare, no trees, just bushes on both sides, no lion statues no sidewalks— Obatalá,[*] I'm going crazy—Where am I? What bottle did this forsaken place come out of? And that feeling that I'm seeing it for the first time, but not now, before, a long time ago? She runs, tripping through muddy tracks she can barely see, sobbing, until she bumps into someone, another shadow in the shadows, and a pair of hands hold her up.

"I pray thee, what seems to be the problem?"

Just what she needed, a Spanish tourist! "The problem? None!" she responds aggressively, but the stranger is moved by her whimpering.

"Come, now, it cannot be that bad..."

"That bad? That he's gone North? It can't be that bad?"

"The North amazes them! Tomorrow at first light, my husband departs."

"It's not the same, damn it! You guys can come and go as you please, and by air, but — "

She takes another long swig that washes away any apprehensions and she hears herself telling this woman she knows nothing about what's tearing her apart inside: how he jumped on the shitty raft that the sharks and the waves will do away with in a second unless some larger boat rescues them, but not even then... and how, of course, if they get there, they're saved, they'll take

---

[*] Obatalá, in santería or Regla de Ocha, is the deity attributed with sculpting humans. She is associated with purity and presides over thoughts and dreams.

care of themselves, but they have to get there, just set foot on land, and it's almost impossible!

"...Just set foot on land," the Spanish lady says to herself, "What a strange expedition!"

But Izzy is unstoppable, telling her that Lazarito didn't really have too many problems living here. That he'd managed to find a bit of cash and didn't need to rush into this venture. That what happens is that his friends get him all excited telling him all those tall tales of fame and fortune.

"Always, it has been that way. Those tales of wonders! Neither Ponce's bad fortune nor Narváez's sufferings are enough to get Hernando to reconsider. It must be Sir Alvar Núñez who has driven him mad — the mysteries that surround what Cabeza de Vaca had seen in Florida have decided his fate."[*]

Izzy stops mid swig and sways a bit. "Alvar Cow's Head!" She lets out a laugh and is about to comment on the swell partners they've picked — that guy must be in all of the police's computers for meat trafficking — but the Spaniard keeps on:

"It is in pursuit of his stories that Hernando leaves for Florida. His presence in Cuba is but a pretext for this great venture. He departs — " she goes on, her voice breaking, "and I remain in a most terrifying solitude."

It's Izzy's turn to feel sorry for her. And, with the rum making her all warm and feeling like she can't keep her dollar-bought bottle to herself, she holds it out to the tourist, who drinks hesitantly. The bottle goes back and forth and they both end up seated on the muddy ground, leaning on an unfamiliar wall barely lit by a far-off flame that lets them make out diffuse stains of men and barrels, without the *mulata* having the least idea what street they're on. Yet, the breeze on her face swaying her blouse feels to her like... She shakes off her stupor:

"Hey, sister! What happened to the Morro's light? Don't tell me they've shut it off too!"[+]

"I know not of what thou speakest"

---

[*] Juan Ponce de León (1460-1521); Pánfilo de Narváez (1478-1528) Spanish explorers who met their deaths on their expeditions to Florida.

[+] Álvaro Núñez Cabeza de Vaca (1490-156?) Spanish explorer who survived for eight years among the natives of what is now the Southern United States and Mexico and returned with tales of the Seven Golden Citites of Cíbola that probably inspired Hernando de Soto's voyage.

"Hey, you still haven't seen the Morro? You've just gotten here, huh?"

"One year ago."

The *mulata* scratches her head. Something's not right about this chick who, while telling her story about her husband leaving, is also drinking up her Havana Club. She's about to set things straight but, because the tourist seems captivated by the picture on the label in spite of the darkness, she surprises herself by coming out with the tour-guide speech: "That's the *Giraldilla*, a tiny statue from way back that's on one of the old castle-towers, but we can't see it because of the damn blackout."

"A small weathervane, in the shape of a woman," the Spanish woman murmurs, "Does it have some special meaning?" To which the woman she asks shrugs, "It's like the symbol of Havana, or something, but don't pay me no mind."

The Spaniard nods and adds discreetly, "Could it be that thy husband took some of that liquor in his provisions?"

"Do they have rum with them? You bet sister!"

"Rum... rum..." the other repeats as if she had just learned the word.

Izzy can't take it, and goes from benevolent to challenging: "Listen, girl, no one dupes me. That man of yours has got to be up to something. In Cuba, we're the only bastards that can't go nowhere. No Spaniard has to come here to get all jazzed about going to Miami. What mess is your old man involved in, anyway?"

"I understand thee not, but if of my husband thou speakest, I can tell thee that Sir Hernando, a gentleman of fine Extremaduran line, has been granted his title of Captain in Peru, valiantly, justly and with honour."

Izzy yells out a laugh and slaps her thigh; "I shoulda' known! Peru, Colombia — same thing! Must be a big deal going down, but ya' know they can really bust you for that, not just that Cow Face guy, but your man — and you, too, sister," she says, taking a big swill.

The other woman smiles. "Thou sayest things to which I know not how to respond. I only find it clear that we both suffer from the same cause."

Salt in the wound. The word "suffer" touches Izzy, who loses the attitude and tries to think: "But — well, 'splain yourself a bit, lady. You both came to Cuba, now your hubby's leavin' you and takin' off for Miami."

"He leaves for Florida..."

"Ay, *chica*, same thing!"

Her new friend, fond of the bottle, takes another sip. Izzy tells herself not to get upset; after all, her guest barely wets her lips. Lost in thought, she smiles as if she's happy to finally tell someone her story:

"I knew I would not go with him since we met due to his conquistador fame — "

"You like being conquered, eh sassy?" interrupts Izzy with a conspiratorial slap on the knee. But her friend continues, unfazed:

"Before Cuba he made Castille's gold—Nicaragua, Peru. He returned to Spain with his coffer full, but I was captivated by his demeanour, dost thou know of what I speak? When a man has challenged the perils of unknown worlds he returns home with such a manner as if all of his muscles were relaxed beneath his silk doublet like a tiger or a cat moving in rhythm, harmoniously, free of the cuirass and the arquebus — and grander for them. Hernando's azure eyes seemed to look upon me from all distances; his smile revealed his alliance with God, for he did return victoriously from places seeded with soldiers like himself, many of them mutilated savagely, always failed in their unfulfilled dreams, worse in their fortunes. And full-knowing that neither reasoning nor begging would deter Sir Hernando from his goal, I did not object—for I want not the silence of a man who had renounced dreaming of his own world. Cortés and Pizarro were only able to posses what they had dreamt of before.[*] Because they followed their dreams, they thus made them real. Hernando was in search of what Ponce de León left waiting for him and I was pleased to be wed to he whom His Majesty, King Charles, would first name to come to Cuba. He was finally ridding himself of those quarrelsome and gregarious Columbuses who strove to rule everything from Hispaniola.[+] Imagine, governing the world from a small island!"

"No, no, no way sista'," Izzy's now slurring her words, "No way! I ain' cooked 'nuff yet to talk politics, you hear me! You the one with the passport, not me."

---

[*] Francisco Pizarro (1475?-1541), Hernán Cortés (1485-1547), explorers attributed with the conquest of Peru and Mexico, respectively.
[+] Name given to the island currently made up by the Dominican Republic and Haiti.

Absorbed in her own thoughts, the tourist reaches for the bottle, and her story takes an almost private turn, "Besides riches, he might also find the fountain Ponce so looked for," her voice becomes dream-like. "Will he be younger upon his return?"

"Sure will! Juz like Alfonzo the Noze! When he leff', he was skin 'n bones and pale as death, but after three years of good eatin', his skin stretched out 'n he came back all plump and rosy like a baby!"

"Could it be that they have already discovered it? Sir Alfonso, from which family is he? Under which Captain does he serve?" she asks, almost intrigued, yet instantly returns to her naturally distracted self. Meanwhile Izzy wets her whistle and thinks, going back through the story — well at least the Spanish lady's looking on the bright side. Who says the guy won't be back soon? Maybe he's just gone to have a look. "Hey, when d'ya say your husband left?

"Tomorrow he departs and I remain in his place, as Governess of the island."

"You don't say," Izzy purrs a philosophic laugh: men are the worst—they do, they undo, but always sweetening the pot—this one's given her a title, mine gave me five bucks and thanks to him, we're sitting here through this hard time together. Then she turns magnanimously to her new friend.

"Listen, sister, to each his own, right? Govern all you want, and one of these days, he'll appear, and you'll give him a fresh start, right? Me too. I'm going to keep going, and who knows, in a couple of years Lazarito'll come for me and I'll go back with him."

"What sayest thou?"

The *mulata*, fighting to get the last fumes out of the bottle, gives up. "That this baby's dead, dead! We've gotta get another, sister. Your hotel bar'll have one, even if it's dark. Right? It's your turn to pay, right? Yes, yours. Thouz!"

"I must return to Sir Hernando," Isabel replies, standing up. "Go with God," she turns and says cordially before setting off, and leaves so definitively that the other, despite the buzz, can't believe it.

"Hey, wait... your turn to buy, isn't it?" But Isabel is seen no more, lost in the darkness of the only night ever that Izzy hasn't seen the Morro's light shine. "Where am I?" she asks, trying to get up without letting go of the bottle while telling herself that her new friend sure did have a lot of nerve. After managing to steady herself, Izzy in all her anger and impotence, yells defiantly into the shadows, "Who do you think you are?!"

The faraway response comes to her in circles, in a swirling whisper of dry leaves, "Madam Isabel de Bobadilla." Instead of telling her to go to hell, Izzy raises the bottle up to her lips — a useless attempt that leaves her cursing anyway. Lázaro dropped her like a hot potato and now this smart-assed tourist, not a hair of Madam or dumb-dilla[*] in her, leaves her there on the ground like a used rag. With the cocktail the rum and fury are churning inside her, Izzy hurls the bottle onto the ground. On impact, it seems that all the glass in Havana shatters. Startled, Izzy looks back and forth: the Morro's searchlight has thrown its beam, the streetlights light up, and she sees that the muddy road and brush are transformed into the stone walls of the Castillo de la Fuerza. She crosses the wide sidewalk and starts running toward the *malecón*, her head pounding with the sound of the breaking bottle, a sound unthinkably amplified, reverberating loudly enough to hear five centuries back in time.

"What was that?!" Hernando de Soto springs up with a feline quickness and tries to look through the barred window onto the street. He then moves to the door in his wood-and-tiled Governor's mansion. "Servants!"

Isabel, her cheeks burning, quickly slips her head back onto the leather headboard. She congratulates herself on her secret escape to those muddy paths they call streets. It has so calmed her troubled mind on this spring night of 1539, the eve before the expedition was to set sail for Terra Firma to the north.

"'Tis nothing, Hernando, worry not," Isabel says to detain him, with a serenity that seems to ridicule his fear.

"I see thou art very calm, my wife."

"After acceptance of your departure, a small noise from oft the ruddy street outside our treacherous palace does little to scare me."

"I pray thee, forget not that this is a world not yet born," he admonishes.

"If in Florida thou findest more than this, a world already born shall we say, perhaps in a year or two's time thou willst come for me," and she adds, both hoping and challenging, "I, too, could invigorate my fervour with the waters of the fountain of youth."

[*] Boba, the first part of Isabel's last name, means stupid or dumb.

De Soto looks at her in reproach. "Some short time ago you were lamenting my departure; now, thou dost not hide that it is Cuba that has defrauded thee."

"Cuba is a fraud, Hernando. Without gold and without hope. Between those that leave for Mexico or other parts of Terra Firma, and the privateers that continuously pillage her, she is but a rung in the sea. Even for thyself — has Cuba been any more than a departure point in the middle of this New World?"

His wife had never spoken in such a way to him, but on this evening Hernando de Soto must not have realized it.

A servant enters with a piece of glass in his hand. Isabel smiles. The governor concentrates on its inscription, some sort of cathedral picture, the likes of which he had only seen in stained-glass windows. He examines one side and then the other. The lady goes to his aid by putting the *Giraldilla* in the vertical position: "Observe it thus."

"Dost thou know what this is about?"

"It is a weathervane in the shape of a woman, see? This staff, the Cross from the Order of Calatrava as its crown must hold the banderole that blow in the wind."

Sir Hernando nods. His wife has always been quite logical. For this reason he's made her Governor in his absence (although he has also appointed a military lieutenant to assist her). He disregards her guessing-game and returns to his own deliberations. His nine ships have been provisioned, the horses sum two hundred thirty seven; the men, six-hundred. By sunset everything was ready — except for loading the water-barrels. The night had swallowed up the port's hustle and bustle that would be revived by the first light of day. De Soto is lost in the fantasies that have beset him since childhood, intensified through his own experiences: not only would he accumulate more treasure than Sir Francisco or Sir Hernán, but he would finally debunk Alvaro Núñez's pretension of being the only one to have survived Florida. Florida will flourish for him, captain Hernando de Soto, to whom fortune and glory are no strangers!

"It were a fine weathervane for the Fortress."

Hernando does not answer. Isabel's eyes draw back to his profile, to the line of his forehead crowned with reddish hair that gets lighter with the sun; to the eyelids that can barely contain the spark in his eyes that turn blue when near the sea and darken with adversity, now burn with desire. She speaks again, raising her voice left husky from the sore throat that befell her on the crossing from Hispaniola to Santiago:

"Dost thou agree?"

He turns his head, startled out of his remoteness, "Thou sayest?

"I say, that when finished the Fortress, thou couldst commission a weathervane such as this one, cast in bronze, to orient the ships."

De Soto nods. Another honor conferred upon him by his majesty: to erect the first military bastion in these Indies, may God preserve them. He responds kindly, to the gracious lady to whom he was wed in his father's, the Count of Gomera's[*] palace, the lady who undoubtedly married him — not only in admiration of his chivalrous and Christian letters but of his share in Atahualpa's[+] treasure — with great satisfaction.

"Thou shalt order it, my lady," he says gently and returns to his fantasies on the eve of his grand voyage — before the words Alabama or Mississippi mean anything to him. Knowing she is no longer in his thoughts, Isabel rubs her finger on the moist edge of the piece of glass and raises it to her lips, reviving a sort of fire that this liquor seems to produce in her very blood and turn her quite strangely desirous.

Feeling the quiet burning in her gaze, Hernando de Soto gets up and comes towards her. Although the last eleven months as supreme authority on the isle had been one giant party after another for him and the noblemen of the expedition — more than ever seen before in these lands — and despite having had some very secret escapades with many of the most willing natives and even ladies from his own entourage, this night he was to fulfill his duties with his wife Isabel. Tonight he would leave his print on the pillow he is sure no other will warm. Besides, his wife is particularly beautiful this evening with that glow on her cheeks and a sort of drunken smile on her lips. He goes to kiss her mouth and she offers him her breasts that swell when brushed by his beard and are crowned with ruby-hard buttons. For an instant his dreams of sails and rigging are sunk into these ductile fruits that mold so well to the pressure of his hands. They go into the

---

[*] One of the Canary Islands.

[+] Atahualpa, the last Incan emperor. Hernando de Soto was the first European to make contact with the emperor, who was later assassinated (by order of Francisco Pizarro) despite the enormous treasure his subjects raised for his release.

bedroom. For the first time in their two years of marriage, Isabel looks at her husband's body in all of its splendor. She clings to it, runs her lips across the rough waves of his chest, licking the marks left by his zeal for Terra Firma, bites his hips, slides down to his groin in search of the mainmast, stiff as never before, to assuage her palate. Wildly, he who before sought pleasure now finding himself so pleasing, he returns each stroke with the same, he rubs, caresses, squeezes, sucks, tastes, massages, gasps and exhales yesses. He snorts, exhaling as he wets his face in the fountain suddenly gushing from his wife's unfamiliar fortress, his battering ram heading towards the soft tunnel tarred with burning almond juices and finally reaching the deep bastion. It is handed over without surrender, flags waving, engaged in a combat that captures his spear in the gears that turn to the rhythm of each charge and retreat, in increasing urgency, until they both are mutually conquered, possessing one another in unison, in such a way that had never happened before — to him for his speedy exploits, nor to her for the shame that, until now, had restrained her pleasure. Both the conquered and conquerors, they watch the dawn entwined. In their peaceful bliss neither he feels the euphoria of his departure, nor she its anguish. As they get ready to untie their bodies, Isabel voices an unusual appeal:

"Hernando, if, on thy way to Florida, thou findest a small boat, deny it not aide."

"Such would carry only fugitives," he answered, still relaxed.

"Hear, my husband, my last request: Hoist the unfortunate onto thy ship and whence ye just set foot on land, they will care for themselves. Be certain thou willst see them not again. And, take care to scorn not," the lady says with a mysterious and knowing smile, "the liquor they offer thee."

To evade deciphering the words that for him are telling of the upheaval caused by his departure, Hernando caresses his wife's cheek. "I can deny thee not, Isabel. I am bounded to thee for always. Pray for me and await my return."

"I will wait for thee while still in this life. And, in death, thou willst find my spirit in the weathervane that looks to the sea."

"Defying the wind, as does this city."

"And fulfilling her fated duty to worry for those who leave it."

The captain deserts his bed.

Izzy puts on the coffee.

Translated by Barbara Riess

MIRAGES OF DAILY LIFE
Alexis García Somodevilla

The Buildings

The trucks pulled up by a vacant lot that was yellowed and covered with caked sludge. Just looking at it gave you a backache. When he looked more closely at the nearby houses, Daniel remembered that a long time ago, in that same place, he'd worked on building some houses. But he could be wrong about that, since he hadn't been a bricklayer for long then, and when he thought about it all these places looked pretty much alike anyway.

Just to make sure, he asked one of the guys right after they got out of the truck:

"Hey, weren't we here before?"

The guy nodded as he looked around the lot indifferently.

"And the houses we built – where'd they go?"

"They've disappeared." the guy said.

"What do you mean disappeared? Who can steal a building?"

"No one has to steal them. They just disappear." the guy said, sounding almost amused.

"So we're just working for the hell of it?"

"Of course not. We get paid. Don't you get paid every two weeks?

"Yes, but that…"

"So what if the buildings disappear? Even if we don't come back to this site, we'll keep putting them up in different places. Unless you get a different job."

"Is there any job where things don't just disappear?"

Suddenly Daniel's fellow worker turned very serious.

"Look, kid," he said to him, "don't complicate my life. Think whatever you want to think. Either way, I'm going on vacation tomorrow."

The Punching Bag

The police car screeched to a stop and backed up. When the car was right across from Daniel, the cops got out.

Daniel stood up, worried. It's true that at that hour of night you weren't supposed to be stretched out on a bench.

"What are you smoking?" asked one cop, grabbing at a twig sticking out of Daniel's mouth.

"Smoking? I'm not smoking anything."

"What have you got in here?" asked the cop as he pulled open the backpack.

"It's sawdust for a punching bag."

The cop dumped all the sawdust out of the pack.

"What're you practicing for?"

"Nothing. I do it to unwind. I hit it with whatever comes to hand. A stick, a rock, a pole, anything."

"To unwind from what?" asked the cop.

Daniel made a vague gesture with his hands. They were staring hard at him.

"To unwind from whatever. You know how it is. Tension, too much work, all that... you know."

The cops turned their backs on him and got back into the car.

Daniel watched with relief as they sped off.

The Chimney Sweep

Any chimney sweep's destiny is the destiny of all chimney sweeps. No one can change that. To change it would be to steal the secret of such a noble job, to snatch the broom and the ladder from the chimney sweep and throw him into the water. And what good is a chimney sweep in the water? Usually they drown. The truth is, they don't know how to swim.

Because of this, when as small children they go up to the rooftop and start talking about chimneys, the best thing their parents can do is encourage their inclination and send them to a chimney sweeping school. They will ask to go. They will keep asking until you send them.

The chimney sweep in our story was like the others, but a bit more talented at climbing trees especially fruit trees. He finished the chimney sweep schools for beginners and continued in the advanced schools, which dealt with huge chimneys. He was very diligent. He practiced every day, and even a cat would have a hard time beating his agility on a rooftop. Finally he completed his studies. He finished them while he was still young and returned home triumphantly, with all sorts of awards and a diploma bordered in gold.

The welcome he received was extraordinary. The boy came home a man, a man with useful skills. His diploma said "Chimney Sweep, Specialist in Heights" and they hung it on the wall. He hardly got a chance to sleep because so many people came around wanting to see it. They'd come bursting in the door rudely and stand staring at the certificate. Everyone in the family knew that there weren't many expert chimney sweeps and even though he had not yet started his work, he promised to be one of the very good ones.

But disappointment wasn't long in coming.

The first day the chimney sweep went out to work, he couldn't find a single chimney anywhere. Not one. He confirmed this by standing on the roof of the tallest building in the city and looking in all directions. Furious, he went back home and he asked his parents what it meant. They told him it couldn't be, that if there were schools for chimney sweeps, it was because there were chimneys to clean and if he couldn't see them it must be due to poor vision. They recommended that he go see an eye doctor. But since the chimney sweep knew his eyesight was fine, he didn't waste his time – he went out to the street and asked all the people who walked by. The results were similar. They pointed out invisible chimneys.

His inquiries continued until the inevitable happened: he was taken to a psychiatrist and sent to live in an asylum.

When he got over the shock, he found himself surrounded by truly insane people, dreadful cries and strange conversations. Every morning they forced him to walk around a muddy lawn with some empty benches in the center. It was the usual punishment for annoying the guards.

But our friend soon discovered that he wasn't alone. Several men from his class and others who had graduated earlier were there. He learned that many chimney sweeps lived in the asylum and that more continued to arrive from all over. His case was not unique. The others had all suffered from the same symptoms before they were brought in. They had all manifested the same symptoms before being sent there.

You probably think that life in the asylum was terribly boring for the chimney sweeps, but nothing could be farther from the truth. I mean that there they were actually able to do something. In the kitchen there was a red brick chimney, not too tall, that had been constructed by the first chimney sweeps who'd been sent there. It was behind a wooden shack, and it gave off the whitest, cleanest smoke imaginable.

A great crowd of chimney sweeps were lined up outside the shack, waiting for their turn to clean the chimney.

Translated by Mary G. Berg

THE GREEN VIOLINIST, AFTER CHAGALL
Anna Lidia Vega Serova

Now that I've found you,
Known you, lived you,
Why are you leaving,
Love?

Mornings, she could be seen out on her balcony with her birds and her plants. She wore thick Coke bottle glasses and a stupid hairdo. Every day she'd greet us with the same smile that seemed somehow snooty, as she went by with her violin in its case on her way to her job as a receptionist at the cultural center.

We're pretty sure she doesn't play the violin. At least, no one's ever heard her. "What a dried-up old maid," we'd say to each other.

When she moved into the building, people began to check her out, but nothing, we didn't find out a thing. No one ever took a step through her door.

That's why the whole neighborhood was in an uproar when we saw her with that Chilean or Argentinean (we couldn't figure out which). They went in and closed the door. Then we got into the building just across the street, someone brought some binoculars, and we saw them sitting across from each other talking. He was talking; she was looking at him through those Coke bottle lenses, mechanically smoothing her unsmoothable hair. After about two hours we got really excited: she brought a bottle and two glasses out of the kitchen and began to talk. They changed places; now they were sitting next to each other. We almost got into a fight over the binoculars. The most daring of us were betting that he'd be on top of her in a half hour. The skeptics were a minority. The binoculars went from hand to hand. We were disappointed: when they stood up and we assumed they were about to get to it, but what they did was head for the front door.

We went on talking, trying to figure it out, and when we saw the two of them come out, we decided to send a group to follow them. We were annoyed that they were moving so slowly, but nobody wanted to miss the show.

They say they went to the beach. He was carrying his wine in his hand, and she had her useless violin. Some say that they heard

154

them saying really stupid things about human nature and that stuff, but I think that's a lie: no one can overhear what's said two hundred meters away on a noisy evening. They sat on the seawall, and he put his arm around her shoulders. When it got dark, she took out her violin, but he was the one who played it. They say it was one of those Mozart things you hear on Radio Encyclopedia. Then they went back. Most of us went home at this point, but a few of us stayed to see what would happen. They talked. All they did was talk. Around five, we went off to sleep, but by eight some of us showed up to cover them again. What we saw startled us and amazed us. She was on the balcony without her glasses, with her hair loose and a pink bathrobe that revealed her you know whats. She was smiling. She leaned over and greeted us, asking:

"Is there going to be okra in the market?" Lord knows what okra has to do with all this! He was helping her with the birds and the plants.

A little later she went off with her shopping bags in the direction of the market, smiling and humming to herself. She walked by us and took our breath away. What a woman! There was no way to prove it, but we decided that they must have done it. A woman doesn't change completely overnight just by talking. A moment later a guy came along. We didn't like the look of him. He asked where she lived and we had to tell him. We found out what he does: he's a musician. He plays in a group that practices at a cultural center and he's traveled a lot. The foreigner opened the door to him when he knocked and they started hugging each other like old friends. Pretty soon the foreigner grabbed his backpack, left a paper on the night table and went off with the musician. Some say it was his photo he left, others say it was dollars or maybe his card. What we know for sure is that they walked right past us saying things like "remember so-and-so?" and "how's old Joe doing?"

She came back from the market smiling and humming with two shopping bags packed full. We tried to help her but she said "they're not heavy," and it was as though she didn't really think they were weighing her down. She was floating.

She knocked on the door, waited a moment, and still smiling, opened it with her key. She lugged the bags in, looking in all the corners. When she saw the paper, tomatoes, oranges and everything else went spilling all over the floor.

We felt really bad about this and we wanted to help her, but she wouldn't open the door. Some of us peeked in to see what was going on. There she was, sitting on the floor with the fruit all around her. They said she wasn't crying.

That afternoon the woman in the other stairwell got into a big fight with her mother-in-law and we gave up on the old maid, who is still living there now with her birds, her plants, her Coke bottle glasses and that stupid hairdo that keeps people at least ten feet away from her all around.

She carries the violin upstairs and down again, but we know perfectly well that she doesn't play the violin.

Translated by Mary G. Berg

PAPER LOVE
Anna Lidia Vega Serova

For María Gala, my inspiration

The smell of dampness, of rancidness, of cold sweat, of ancient corruption. The mother puts her little girl to sleep in the room's only bed, the same bed where she'll receive whichever lover comes tonight. She turns out the light, she gropes her way in the dark, she undresses, opens the door a crack. Everything is odors, whispering voices, the muffled creaking of the mattress, rocking and throbbing.

The child falls asleep right away. Her mother won't allow her to wake up, but still, she does: every night she wakes up for an instant when the bed suddenly stops rocking, always abruptly. She hears the heavy breathing beside her, she listens to her heartbeats growing louder and expanding through her body, and the bitter stench and the panic. But she doesn't move; she hardly breathes; she doesn't dare confront her mother's anger.

During the day she looks around for traces to prove it wasn't all a dream, that it's not just a nightmare that recurs night after night. But there's no evidence or she doesn't know where to find it and she goes on that way, full of doubt, always suspecting, in a state of permanent fearfulness.

The house, the smell of the closed-up space, the heavy odor you can smell even from outside, gets in your clothing and your hair: a chronic inescapable foulness. "You stink," her grandmother would say when her father took her to visit once in a while on a Sunday, only very occasionally. Her large black grandmother would heat water and scrub her body with a bundle of herbs until her skin burned. She'd rub her with talcum and cologne, trim her finger and toenails, dress her in her cousin's bathrobes, and sit her on the doorstep for the rest of the afternoon. The cousins beside her played with dolls in elegant outfits or with miniature kitchen sets or with coloring books and magic markers and they'd ignore her. She ignored them, too, not out of indifference or pride, but out of fear.

Only as she returned to her street was the little girl aware of the stench of her home; she'd recognize it from out in the hallway before she opened the door, a bitter wave of smell, then she'd get used to it again.

The mother sleeps late and the child gets up cautiously and slips over into the corner where she has her kingdom: bits of paper, some pencil stubs, empty matchboxes she makes into furniture for her paper dolls. She has a large paper family, ever growing and more united: they marry, have children and grandchildren, and they're very happy. They're a little like her own family, like her mother, who is the Mom, and her father, who is Dad, and a Grandma and Cousins, who are all charming and affectionate. She spends a lot of time with her paper family; she gets to know them better and better and care more about them. They keep seeming more real to her, as if they were replacing the everyday world, taking on an existence of their own, forming a solid family circle, in a secure and loving space.

When her mother wakes up, she gives her milk and bread, and goes off. Her fear looms larger: it's in the humid pattern of the fogged walls and in the shrieks of the crazy man on the floor below and in the spider webs hanging from the ceiling. The child and all her paper relatives hide from fear in the bathroom, that has the only window that opens out onto the street; there's a little light there, a breath of air, and the noises of the outside world can be heard there - sounds that don't frighten.

Sometimes her mother stays. She makes her move around from one place to another. She always seems to be right behind the child as if on purpose, while she tries to put their home in order. She scrubs and shakes the rugs, swirling the dust and stirring up the cockroaches. The little girl watches her, seeing her tired sweaty face and her mouth twisted into an exasperated expression. Then she sees her give up, sees her abandon the whole huge, useless, sporadic effort.

Her mother weeps, lying in the bed, covering her face with both her hands. Her mother cries and swears through her fingers, her shoulders shaking. Her voice is high pitched and grating. The child watches her from her corner, her eyes huge and unblinking, without tears. She never cries, not even when she sees her mother weeping and she's afraid she's going to die, that she's already died, that nothing more can happen after that. But it goes on, it's prolonged for an eternity, for longer than an eternity. The child drifts off and at some point she falls asleep. When her mother, tired of weeping, lifts her head and sees the little girl sleeping, she shakes her and wakes her up. She tells her she's hard hearted, that

158

she doesn't love her mother, that she should hug and kiss her. Then the child realizes that it wasn't death that was happening. With passive resignation she puts her arms around her mother's neck and waits for everything to finally be over in order to finally, finally die.

Her paper Mom only cries from happiness. The child cries from happiness, too, sometimes, when she hugs her paper Mom. They hug each other and say loving things to each other. Then the paper Dad comes and takes them to Grandma's house. Paper Grandma has fixed lunch for them, all the child's favorite foods. The paper cousins play with the little girl on the doorstep. The little girl has lots of dolls and she loans them to her cousins. She loans them her bathrobes, too; she has lots of bathrobes, one in every color, and the cousins tell her she's the best cousin in the world, that they love her a lot, really a lot, and they hope she comes back soon. Grandma kisses her on both cheeks and tells her she is her favorite granddaughter, and gives her a bag of caramels for the trip home. The child returns home with her paper parents. She takes a bath, puts on violet perfume, and climbs into a bed that is her very own bed, all her own. Paper Mom pulls up the covers and tells her a story about princesses, and paper Dad plays the guitar and sings her a song. Mom and Dad kiss each other, smiling, then they lean down and kiss the little girl. They wait until she falls asleep, then they tiptoe over to their big bed.

Sometimes the paper family gets worn out with so much hugging. Sometimes they get tears in their necks, the weakest part of them, and the little girl has to make new ones. She draws great big eyes on them and smiling mouths. Every time someone gets torn, she makes a new one, but she never throws the old ones away. She puts them away in the shoebox where she keeps her treasures. She has lots and lots of old paper family members in there. The one she has most of is Mom, because she has hugged her so much. There's nothing better than hugging paper Mom while they say loving things to each other.

One day, in one of her spasmodic housekeeping attacks, her mother grabbed the shoebox that held the child's treasures and emptied it into the trash bag where she was stuffing the garbage and litter that had accumulated in the corners. In a single instant the child saw everything disappear: her drawings, her matchbox furniture, the two-color pencil her father had given her, and her entire paper family. She didn't react, or make any sound at all, not a single complaint or lament; she just mentally relived over and over again her mother's gesture as she tossed her treasures into the bag. Her mother kept on moving randomly around the room, picking things up, straightening things, but the child no longer sees her mother, she only sees the odious person who has deprived her of her world. She feels more horror than she ever has before, a painful horror that impedes her breathing, clouds her vision, makes her arms and legs tremble. She keeps watch on the odious person, studies each one of her movements, waits quietly until she comes close and leans over to pick something up off the floor; her neck is close, her exposed, fragile neck, and in a single animal leap the child fastens her teeth onto that neck, bites down hard, blindly resisting the jerking and tugging, the contortions, the blows of the person who is trying to pull her off, but is unable to. The child pours all of her energy into that bite, all the stored up energy of her resentment and her deprivation, her fears and her love.

They fall together, for the first time really together, child and mother, for the first time in their lives the two of them united in a true embrace and that gushing of blood and that unending stench.

Translated by Mary G. Berg

DREAMING OF SHIPWRECK
Anna Lidia Vega Serova

My steps slow down and my heart pounds faster as I walk up Prado Avenue. The lions look at me indifferently, men call out appreciative comments, the sun burns me and something within me begins to tremble and melt away. The stretch to the Hotel Inglaterra seems interminable. I can see Paul in the café; he waves to me and smiles. I try to greet him with the same enthusiasm, but it's such an effort that he notices and asks what's going on. Now's the moment. I should close my eyes, say it once and for all, and be done with the anxiety that's stifling me. I close my eyes and smile. "Nothing," I answer.

Yesterday everything was different. It's as if there were an impenetrable wall between Yesterday and Today. An abyss. Yesterday was bright and vibrant, as if it would go on forever. The chance meeting that wasn't chance at all but destiny, a Miracle. Because it couldn't be just by chance that Paul happened to be renting the car at that very time and that he didn't have a route planned out, that he should just happen to drive along the Malecón right as I'd finished my shift at the Almejeira Hospital and was standing at the intersection thumbing a ride as the light turned red. It couldn't be coincidence that of all the girls who hope for luck at that corner it would happen to be me who got a ride, that he'd be French, that he'd be listening to Enya, that his work was also related to medicine, that he was a redhead, and that his voice, and his eyes, and the way he looked at me…

I avoid his insistent eyes while I trace circles on the table with the bottom of my glass. I have to say it, otherwise I'm lost. I rehearsed my words a thousand times at home and all along the way here. I have to say it. I drink, but I don't manage to gulp down the huge lump of sorrow in my throat, a barrier that only trite words can get through. I say things about the situation in Cuba, about how hard it is to survive, about the scarcities, the gap between salaries and prices. Paul listens to me with a polite smile even though I can read disappointment in his eyes. He must be wondering how it can be possible that I'm the same woman with whom, only yesterday, he felt such a sublime connection, such intimacy, such a communion of souls.

Yesterday. He said he picked me up because of my nurse's uniform; he told me how he was in Cuba to install medical equipment, that he's headed in two days for Brazil and then on to Peru to do the same thing, that it's the first time he's been here and that he rented the car in order to see a little more of Havana. Eagerly, I told him about how I'd spent a week in Paris, on a sightseeing trip organized by the Youth Corps; that's my most marvelous memory. I talked to him about the City of Light, all its streets, churches and museums and the nice people I met over there. We'd gone through the Bay tunnel when he asked me timidly if I'd be his guide in the city. I answered before I thought twice about it: "turn to the right here," and then I thought about how Mom would be worried, waiting for me with a hot supper and bath. But we were already climbing up to the Morro Fort, where there was a good view of all Havana, a sensual panorama of my city.

"It's gorgeous," you said with a sigh and I sighed with the same emotion and then I pointed out the dome of the Capitol and the Girardilla tower and the spire of the Bacardi building. Later we got into the car again to have a close up look and were astonished again by its beauty. We drove around until we were dizzy. We stopped at the Floridita bar and you said you wanted to check out whether Hemingway had been right when he said they make the best daiquiri in Cuba, and we went from bar to bar ordering the same drink in each. In the Cathedral square we embraced, just as a trio in the Patio restaurant began to sing "Bésame mucho," and we danced gazing at each other, and our hands danced, and our lips drew closer and closer and we kissed for the first time.

I watch Paul eat. I watch his mouth move, his hands holding his knife and fork, his eyes, his red hair, just like the prince of my childhood dreams. I am unable to enjoy the flavor of the rice and beans, and the seasoned yucca; my insides are knotted in sadness and there's no room for food. I'll tell him after we have coffee, I decide with the courage of the condemned.

All women have their Cinderella hour, and my time was almost up. I was uneasy about Mom at home alone worrying about how late I was; I should have gone home hours ago. It was painful, as if suddenly this man I barely knew had become the closest and dearest man in the world. "Will we see each other tomorrow?" he asked in a pleading tone, and in his eyes I saw that for him, too, this separation was agonizing. I kissed him again as an answer. Of course I wanted to see him again, endlessly, infinitely.

We said good-bye in the car, and I went off feeling happy. I ran up the stairs like an adolescent. I opened the door and collided with Mom's anger. Instantly, I knew that it had all ended, that there is a fatal equilibrium between joy and despair that had just been shattered. And while she hurled sentences of pain and anger at me, I gazed at the second hand that pointed to past midnight, that hour when all enchantments come to an end.

The refrigerator motor had burned out. The mechanic had said it would cost fifty dollars to fix it. Where could we find so much money, how will we live without it, what little food we have will spoil and I hadn't come home and she was going out of her mind, on the verge of calling the police, I'm a good for nothing, I come home drunk at midnight like a tramp. Mom cut off the barrage and wept. I hugged her and calmed her down. "Don't worry, I'll figure out something tomorrow. Go to bed now." I cried silently all night long.

Paul puts his cup down and I explain my problem in a stifled voice, repressing shame and pain. When I finally have the nerve to lift my eyes, he is counting out money. He puts it on the table in front of me. I realize he didn't believe a single word I'd said. "They'd told me all Cuban women were whores." His voice is like a whip lashing me. He pays the bill and leaves without saying good-bye. I stare for a long time at the bills on the tablecloth like the remains of a shipwreck victim. I pick them up one by one but I can't keep from sinking deeper and deeper into that bottomless void.

Translated by Mary G. Berg

WAITING
Ronaldo Menéndez Plasencia

"You're the Chief, eh? No offense, but around these parts, Chiefs have faces showing the years they've been on the job. I hope you don't take this the wrong way, but I wasn't expecting a kid fresh out of the Academy, like you guys say. I met one a long while back, which was the only time I set foot out of Los Hoyos and that was because no Chief ever made it here. That one had a thin mustache, like you, but he didn't have your build and he had lots of years etched on his face. He also had an unexceptional scar halfway down his cheek. Sorry if I'm beating around the bush, but I don't like getting down to brass tacks right off because that confuses people and keeps them from seeing eye to eye. Understanding between two individuals starts to spark halfway through a good bottle of rum, so tell those two men at the entrance, which isn't really an entrance because nobody but me will be coming through it, to go fetch us some more rum since this is going to stretch out for most of the night. To be honest, I'm nothing but an informer and so as not to have that make me feel bad, I'd like you to treat me like a guest and not like one of your workers, if you get my drift. Like a guest who's about to tell you quite a story, which is the excuse for not wasting this bottle of rum.

You came to Los Hoyos to investigate a death under your charge. But you do know you're not on your turf. How else can I put it? You really don't know the people here or the lay of the land. And the land doesn't matter, because I, who's never really traveled, picture the planet as just miles and miles of grass and hills, with the sun and moon shining above it all. I know some travelers, and they tell me that people are people everywhere. Sure, names change, but people are people and names are names and the difference between *man* and *pan* is one measly letter. Your father was a Chief, from the old school, and though you're fresh out of the Academy, you know I'm right. You say that years ago, your father was investigating another murder under his charge that dead-ended here in Los Hoyos. Whatever comes from there to here seems to disappear. Your father never solved the case so now I've got to hand it over to you even though you're fresh out of the Academy and your father didn't have the nerve to go into Los Hoyos. Who knows, maybe it was fate for you to

164

become Chief, from the old school, and for me to turn informer.

So I'll tell you about your father's dead man, who was never really dead and what happened to your dead man, who really is dead; you saw for yourself when they dug him up with a hole through the forehead.

Years ago, *El Negro,* your dad's dead man — a pussycat who thought he was a tiger because he could shoot straight — came into these parts. He had two friends from around here that were good and dead, even back then. That's lesson #1. Let me explain. The three of them got together and went into the gorges. No matter how loud you scream there, no one'll hear you not because of the distance, but because the land dips and forms walls. That's how it started... Put down your glass now; this booze's having such a good time it doesn't give a shit about us. Well, our little pussycats went way down in the gorges and as luck would have it, they found a boy all by himself. God knows what that kid was doing there; maybe he didn't mind being in the gorges alone. These three decided to grab him up — maybe because youngsters around here think they're all so smart. I won't bore you with details anyone can imagine, but not one person saw how it all started. Hold on, I'll explain. They fucking tortured him, did whatever pigs do to make themselves feel superior. But they went way too far. Someone who shouldn't have seen the rape saw it — another of those odd twists of fate. After all, this is a story of coincidences. Like you and me sitting here with a bottle of rum between us, you solving a crime and me snitching. Understand? I believe there's a reason for everything. Hmmm. Do you know *El Viejo*? He owns the ranch where they found your dead person. Do you know why they call him *El Viejo*? Back then he wasn't old, he had a regular name with a Mr. in front and a whole life ahead of him. He was a widower whose wife had died giving birth to their only child, the boy the three troublemakers ended up sodomizing. And it wasn't a coincidence that there was a witness. Without getting off his horse, this sharpshooter dropped to the ground someone who a second earlier had been jumping around and laughing. With a mocking laugh turned frozen, he sent him to his death. The second shot made the horse jump a foot or maybe sheer rage clouded *El Viejo's* eyesight. But he missed the assailants and killed his own son. A hole right through the neck. *El Negro* hightailed it out of there and hid in the brush. The other assailant stood over the stiffening body, not knowing what had happened, till he was pulled up by the hair and stretched out flat. *El Viejo* didn't kill him right off, which would've been better. Instead, he pulled out a shearing knife, the kind that glints from side to side. The man who lost his son went crazy. Believe me when I say he used him as bait to get *El Negro* to fight. But *El Negro* wouldn't show his face. Since *El Viejo* lacked imagination, his torture consisted of slicing the skin along the fingers, all the way down to the wrists, and then shooting off the hands. Everyone says this was the only time a scream escaped the gorges. *El Negro* was reputed to be a good shot, but panic must have overtaken him in the brush because he missed. *El Negro* actually aimed for *El Viejo*'s chest but hit him in the shoulder instead. And then he scampered off. The wounded father finished off the others, calmly got back on his horse, which surely gave him an advantage, and chased after him. But *El Negro* had the devil running wild inside and when he finally made it back home, without getting hurt, just past the barbed wire, he came face-to-face with that Domingo Suárez, who twenty years ago was waiting with his saddled horse alongside. Not asking but not really stealing, *El Negro* just mounted the horse and disappeared. *El Viejo* never caught up to him. That's it, Chief, the story of your father's dead man; now you know he never died but disappeared terrified.

There's just a drop of rum left so I better cut this short. Everyone in Los Hoyos knows and remembers this tragedy. We buried his son and burned the others so your father, the Chief, wouldn't find any clues. Oddly, *El Viejo*'s hair turned gray over night. Sure as you're looking at his white hair that's exactly what he looked like after burying his son. That's why they call him *El Viejo* and everyone is scared shitless of him. He spent a month looking high and low for *El Negro*. He didn't find him and he went nuts: he couldn't believe that *El Negro* had escaped. *El Viejo* suspected that he had never left Los Hoyos and that one of us was hiding him. That's why he's sniffed around here these past twenty years waiting for him to reappear...One last drink, Chief, 'cause here comes the hole-in-the-head dead guy you dug up this afternoon, the one named Domingo Suárez. I'm sure you can finish the story. I'm told that Academy-types are pretty good at constructing stories. For some reason, Domingo Suárez decided to come back to Los Hoyos yesterday morning. Do you know what he did? Out of pity or fate or because he couldn't resist the urge of telling what he thought the other person wanted, he went straight to *El Viejo* and told him how the story ended, how a frightened *El Negro* lost himself in the brush. Imagine, *El Viejo* took out his gun and put a hole in Suárez's head — a beauty mark—right above his eyes.

We're out of rum, Chief. There's Domingo Suárez's body; he thought that *El Viejo* needed a tiny bit of truth. And Chief, do you know why I'm here snitching? *El Viejo* asked me to, saying there's no point waiting any longer. So put a rush on it, Chief, shoot him first thing in the morning. It'll give him some pleasure.

Translated by David Unger

SHE
Marilyn Bobes

All my sweetness held fast in your hands.
Now I'm a flask empty of perfume.
- Alfonsina Storni, "Dulce tortura"[*]

She had barely opened her eyes when the stiffness and pain in her arms returned. She tried to lift her head and felt dizzy from pulled muscles in the back of her neck. God only knows what vertebrae had been injured by the strain of lifting those inquisitorial iron weights. Gaston had assured her that exercise would firm up her breasts and restore elasticity to tissues that had gone limp. For forty-five years she had managed to get away with just sporadic gym visits and no real fitness program.

Now things were changing. Simple aerobics or swimming three times a week wasn't enough. She was lifting weights and relying on the draconian approach of an experienced physioculturist who was famous among actresses and models. Clients swore by him. Gaston's techniques made liposuction and reconstructive surgery unnecessary. Just a few months of his systematic exercises plus a diet of fruits and vegetables and the body would regain its natural qualities, they assured.

The past eight years with infrequent workouts and only occasional swimming had taken their toll on abdominal muscles now invaded by fat and on muscles gone slack from lack of exercise. Mario himself, who was usually reluctant to make unpleasant observations about her body, had pointed out that her waistline was expanding. His comment, said almost in jest, wouldn't have worried her if it hadn't come at the very time that he seemed to be losing interest in her physically. Now the phone rang barely once a month to announce her lover's rushed visit— one in which he blamed his exhaustion and lack of libido on an excess of work and mental fatigue. The purported change in work pace didn't really make sense, however, since Mario had always been very busy. He was director of one of the country's major publishing houses. Thanks to his work he brought her publications that were helping build her modest library.

[*] Alfonsina Storni (1892-1938), Argentine poet whose poetry lamented sexual injustice and raised women's consciousness. Her verses are filled with despondency and dismay and became increasingly angry. In October of 1938 she walked into the sea. The poem "I'm going to sleep" (1938) is considered her suicide note, and has been put to music under the title "Alfonsina and the Sea."

It was also true that Mario's gifts of late had been limited to a mediocre anthology of contemporary short stories and a Japanese novel called the *Palace of the Sleeping Beauties*. The Japanese work had proved both morbid and fascinating. The plot revolved around a group of old men who paid to spend the night with attractive young women but were forbidden to possess them. The old geezers had to content themselves with simply being onlookers as the sleeping beauties lay drugged, on their sides. The novel had left her with a vague feeling of fear, disgust and depression — such a different set of sensations from the spontaneity she felt in reading Alfonsina Storni's poety. Storni's book of poems had been a Valentine's Day gift from Mario. She could still remember the first lines of the poem "Lyrical Letter to the Other Woman:" *I do not know your name and have never seen your face.*

When she first read those lines she hadn't seen the face of the other woman. Now she knew the face belonged to Beatriz, because they'd had a chance meeting the previous afternoon at the gym. Beatriz had uncombed hair that was pulled back in something resembling a bun; she wore no makeup and her face had a tired, pitiful look. They stared at each other for a moment as if they might exchange greetings. Then the other woman immediately averted her eyes, holding in check a friendly impulse and pressing against her chest a copy of Virgil's *The Aeneid*, a book that was one of Mario's favorites.

Mario had been reviewing an edition of the Roman masterpiece during the month of July and that was the last time she'd seen him. He hadn't even bothered to tell her that he would be going to the beach house in August. She had to wait get the news from Rosita, his secretary. In better times, Rosita had treated her like a girlfriend and played the part of a faithful accomplice, but now the secretary seemed evasive.

Yesterday afternoon, feeling bored while she waited for her lover to show up, she had called his office and was surprised to find that her name meant nothing to the new girl. The distant impersonal voice on the phone gave no acknowledgement of her standing: "The director is not in. Would you like to leave a message? Unprepared for the formality of the reply in Mario's office, she went blank and said nothing.

She clung to the idea that maybe the director hadn't returned from the beach, although deep down she realized that such a notion was impossible. It was now mid-September, and if he were still at the beach she wouldn't have run into Beatriz, Mario's wife

— the woman who shared her name. Now looking back on that day at the gym she thought she detected in her rival's countenance an expression of regret far more profound than simple unhappiness.

She had never blamed herself for any lack of happiness that Beatriz might feel. After all, Mario had taken other lovers before her and surely his wife knew he wasn't monogamous. What's more, she harbored the idea that her namesake wasn't the type to worry about a husband's infidelity. Most likely Beatirz was content to claim the respect she was accorded in her role as legitimate wife. Besides, Beatriz led a life full of things to keep her busy. She traveled extensively. She was always flying off somewhere, although she never looked happy. Unlike most who travel, she came back from trips abroad wearing the same cheap, tacky clothes and sporting the same tired, dull hairdo. If was as if she wished to disguise her enormous imperfections with a studied lack of interest in physical appearance. Being unconcerned with her looks gave Mario's wife the ideal excuse; she could seem careless rather than unattractive. But decidedly, Beatriz was more than careless. She was ugly. With her too-wide face and oversized head on a small body, she resembled a bigheaded puppet. The short neck and robust but disproportionate body overshadowed alluring hazel eyes and luminous white skin, which constituted her only charms.

Beatriz, the other Beatriz, had observed Mario's wife closely the day they arrived at the gym at exactly the same time. The married Beatriz took little interest in the other woman. She looked away quickly perhaps to dispel a lack of confidence or perhaps to ignore any contrast with her physical appearance. It was probably for the best. Her relationship with Mario didn't seem to be grounded on physical attraction.

Clearly Mario maintained an ambiguous attitude toward his wife. He was somewhat ashamed of her, but compensated for it by ascribing exceptional qualities to her that only he could see. His comfort level with Beatriz, his wife, obliged him to love her, in part because a woman like her, with low self-esteem, would put up with his peccadilloes. On the other hand, he was sure that she, his other Beatriz, would never lack lovers. Even so, his jealous eye had become less obvious. And, as Mario's jealousy faded she started to worry that his trusting attitude coincided with her lack of suitors. It made her recall a saying of her mother's: *I realized I'd gotten old when men stopped whistling at me.*

There staring her in the face was the truth: almost

imperceptibly, men had stopped whistling at her. Once she noticed the change she caught herself searching desperately for reaffirmation from the lips of any man on the street and made a conscious effort to elicit the kind of flattering comments that once sprung spontaneously from street corners when she passed by. Surely Beatriz, the other Beatriz, had never faced that problem. Since she'd never been a woman whose looks stopped traffic, there would be nothing for her to miss. To have lost beauty would always be more terrible than to have never had it. The other Beatriz could be content just being Beatriz. But she needed more and she needed it above all because of Mario.

It was naive to believe that he would always love them both with the same intensity—although in different ways—as he claimed. Perhaps he had never loved his wife the way he loved her. But now that she was forty-five, things that had once been in her favor turned cruelly against her. Mario seemed uninterested in what she was thinking; his comments all had to do with her feminine qualities. He had never shared experiences with her that weren't sexual and even discussions about literature had become a kind of necessary foreplay. Things that don't grow old — conversations, business concerns, illnesses and habits — belonged entirely to Beatriz. The wife was irreplaceable, and she, the other Beatriz, interchangeable.

Then last night all these realizations reached a crescendo. Just after seven o'clock Rosita's voice on the phone—it was unmistakably Rosita, though she didn't identify herself — asked for a *Doctora Fernández*. That's when she felt for the first time the tightening in her chest and the certainty that something had changed. She knew that Mario had been suffering digestive problems and had recently consulted a doctor who was the daughter of one of his subordinates. Ever since then Mario's visits had grown fewer. A renewed interest in how his shirts looked, about his weight, and about his performance as a lover seemed directed not to her but to a third person who was just beginning to take shape in Beatriz's imagination. The other Beatriz, Mario's wife, had long ago gotten used to avoiding such anguish—the kind of complications that get you nowhere.

She spent the night awake, trying to endow the phantom doctor with some precise traits. Mario had assured her, affecting nonchalance, that the doctor was a very intelligent woman, a recent graduate. *So that's how you are? Tell me if your mouth has the humming of honeycomb. / If your ears are like rose petals, softly curved.* Oh Alfonsina Storni, we're back where we started: *I do not know your name and have never seen your face.* What did Beatriz's name and her sad, round peasant face matter now?

Now this bitter fatigue stirs within / this silence of the soul where I take refuge. [*]

Eight years down the drain. Lost, as her mother used to say. Eight years—the prime of her life, maturity, and her waning youth squandered at the side of a man who offered her only books and who, to top it off, had for some time been aloof, indifferent, and distant. Of course he was growing older too, but in her eyes the signs of his dwindling vitality were her fault. She didn't reproach him for his lack of libido. Instead she blamed herself for supposedly lacking the charms to keep the flame of Mario's desire alive. She observed with alarm his sudden interest in pills and illnesses.

Panicked, she recalled a story she'd tried to forget: about her friend Adelaida's affair with a married engineer. Finally after a year or two of vacillation the engineer decided to get a divorce. Then a few days before the wedding, Adelaida had a woman visitor. The groom's ex-wife hadn't even bothered to learn her name but the woman on her doorstep had been the engineer's lover for fifteen years and was showing up to claim her rights as spouse — as if there were a pecking order. Adelaida had been upset by the pathetic fifty-year old woman's complaints that she'd dedicated the best years of her life catering to the whims of an ungrateful man who was now abandoning her for a third woman.

Many times at night she'd recalled the story. Which was sadder, the role of an abandoned woman played by the engineer's lover or the role of a seductress? Her other friend, Isabela, was a living example of the seductress, always on the prowl for the occasional young boy or a chauffeur who would enjoy her car for a few weeks and then go about his merry way.

Poor Beatriz. She was in pain, hungry, and smeared with creams. She rose at dawn to sweat blood at Gaston's place trying to get back what, deep down, she knew was gone forever. And now the thought that Mario was probaby at his beach house with the doctor.

She leapt from bed and looked in the mirror to confirm that despite six months of effort her abdomen was still big. She'd given up on having children thinking that when the time came her figure would be better for it. It had all been pointless: her struggles with the cello, three years of studying architecture, her

[*] From "Lyrical Letter to the Other Woman" by Alfonsina Storni.

fling with a judge in 1969 when she had been chosen for her beauty as queen of Carnival.

She grabbed the phone off the hook and dialed Mario's office.

She'd never known his home number. It was one of her lover's unalterable secrets. Before making a decision, she would have liked to talk to Beatriz, her namesake Beatriz, to compare stories, to analyze Mario the way you do an insect, maybe even plan his murder. But she had no way to get in touch with Beatriz. Tomorrow the other Beatriz would find out when the scandal broke. Rosita asked her to wait a moment. After a five minute pause Rosita informed her that the director wasn't in. She didn't have the slightest idea when he'd return, and didn't even know if he was back in town. "Tell him I have his appointment book," she lied, convinced that nothing was more important to him than that.

She took out the book of poems by Alfonsina Storni that he had given her on February fourteen years ago and opened it to the page she'd re-read so many times:

Teeth of flowers, hair a web of dew / hands of grass, you gentle nursemaid / give me smooth earthen sheets / and a quilt of pure moss. She wrote in the margin of the poem: "It's all Mario's fault," and the date.

She didn't think twice. She got out the bottle of alcohol and poured it over her head until she was soaked all the way to her feet. She made a special point of covering her bulky abdomen with the ethereal, flammable liquid. She reached for the box of matches and let the match head flare.

The last thing she heard before her body started to burn was the ring, the insistent ringing of the telephone. Storni's suicide poem floated into her thoughts. *Oh, please give him a message / if he calls again / tell him to quit trying. / tell him that I've gone.* [*]

Translated by Pamela Carmell and Anne Fountain

---

[*] From "I'm going to sleep" by Alfonsina Storni

WHEN LIFE GIVES YOU LEMONS
Mirta Yañez

My blood still boils when I think about it. Seems like it was only yesterday. There's no word for what this girl had to go through back then. You couldn't make me return to that life, even if you held a gun to my head. And don't give me that crap that I'm brainwashing you. That's not it at all. You see, I've learned a thing or two in my time. So now you're going to hear everything, from A to Z. Those stories are stuck in a corner of my brain and no matter how much I try to forget them, they come out for a little stroll once in a while. When I'm done talking, you'll be so worked up we'll have to swab your forehead with alcohol to cool you off. But that's how it is. When certain things happen in a woman's life, she decides it's better to keep it under wraps than to spread the details all over town, spoiling everybody's day. Who hasn't been through something that weighs you down over the years. You'd rather walk in front of a train than talk about it. So why do you want to drag this nonsense out of me now? Sure, you've just told me how you're leaving the country and how you plan to whore yourself to survive up there. And with a tongue looser than shit, you've reminded me that until just the other day (as they say) I was a whore, though now I'm trying to pass myself off as a decent woman. So I'm going to tell you even if I have to haul you to the emergency room afterwards. At first, I wasn't one of those girls who had nothing better to do than hang out with low-lifes. I was the cream of the crop, all things considered. My old man, may he rest in peace, well, sure, he was knotted up inside by what he had to give up and the anger he must have felt for so long, but he taught me to read and to write with neat Palmer-method penmanship. Before misfortune came around our house with my old man's illness and my brother Quique's death up north, I considered myself a well-brought up young lady, and I even spoke a bit of broken English with some Swahili thrown in for good measure. So, when I first started living that wicked life, I was a stuck up, classy girl. Not for the average Joe. And boy did a girl have to get thick-skinned about the things she had to do! I even felt superior to those other girls who had to walk the streets, when I was set up in a place all neat and clean, where they treated me like a queen.

And when a *mister* came calling, I never doubted he'd ask for me. I'd even come home with some new English word I'd picked up and repeat it not knowing what it meant. My old man sitting there in his arm chair would blow a gasket and turn blue in the face because he'd been a waiter in Texas and he knew a thing or two. Even though I was the one who brought home the bacon, many times I had to stroke the old man's ego and butter up Mama so she wouldn't start to cry. I'd say that better times were coming. Better times. What a crock! To this day when I remember what happened, I don't know whether to cry or what. They say misfortunes file in like ants. First it was my brother Quique: out of the blue, a letter arrived telling Mama "Damn it, I'm dying," and then came a postcard from I don't know who, telling us he was dead and buried in a town whose name I can't remember. Then Papa gets sick and loses his job; Mama with her bad heart and me having to start a new line of work. At least we had enough to get by, pay the rent for our tenement room, and buy food every day. Then one fine day everything really fell apart. Every blessed thing. The police came and had a row with Señora Obdulia, the storefront madam. Murderers: strolling in their fine linen suits on Sundays, their wives on their arms. Then when they patrolled the neighborhood, they'd steal our money in broad daylight. And if Mrs. Obdulia didn't pay right on time, they'd cut our kite strings. Don't get me started on that! On the very same day, I found myself out of a steady job and lost my old man. Back home in our lousy tenement room with the bad news, I couldn't get the words out because I ran smack into Mama hugging Papa who'd just keeled over, deader than a doornail, coffee cup still in his hand. And he hadn't spilled a drop, ladies and gentlemen. Our last dime flew out of our hands for the wake and to dress the old guy in decent clothes. By the day of the funeral, he was so stiff, it was a royal pain to get a guayabera shirt on him and we never did get it on right. But finally it was over and Mama was satisfied. I said to myself: what now, dear Mother Mary. I had no choice but to pound the pavement and see what it was like to wait in the cold and rain, hoping to reel in some customer, ready to latch on to anyone who came along. I'd strut my stuff, but no one came. I'd go back to our miserable room empty-handed and Mama would look at me like a lamb with its head cut off because she hadn't had a hot meal in a week. We considered those burgers they sold on the corner a real feast. As for me, it'd been three days since I'd eaten anything at all. I'd buy Mama a burger and hand her the line that I'd eaten mine on the way home. The half a block I had to walk from the burger stand to the tenement was torture. I'd look at the burger in my hand and tell myself she wouldn't notice a little bite and if she did, I'd say they sold it to me that way. I'd pinch crumbs off the edge of the bread and put them in my mouth. That only made it worse. By the time I got home I could've eaten a whole cow if they'd put one in front of me. I gave Mama that measly burger and washed my hands in the wash basin in the hall because just a whiff of that greasy little thing made my stomach turn somersaults. I felt like I was going to faint right then and there. So that's how I headed off to work all those nights during hurricane season. I had so few customers, there was no end in sight to that hunger. On the eighth night this dolled-up old broad parked her long-finned Caddie at the corner where I was showing off my wares, stuck her head out the window and looked me up and down. "I sure don't need this aggravation," I said to myself, and turned my back and pretended to be looking at the mannequins in a store window on Virtudes Street, keeping an eye on that old bag to see if she'd left. But after a while, something told me to look over my shoulder and there's that woman, who'd seen better days, she must have been at least eighty years old, covered in gaudy jewelry, her head cocked, looking at me like I was some monkey in the zoo. "It's my son!" she blurted out, as if she wanted to close the deal fast. I kept my mouth shut; to tell the truth I didn't know what to say. Next thing I knew, she was pulling me very slowly toward her Caddie. I got in without a second thought, already plotting what I'd do with the money. Sure, it was a strange situation: a hi-toned lady out at eleven o'clock at night looking for a girl like me for her son, but, at the crossroads of life, your thoughts take off like a rocket and I couldn't quit thinking about the feast we'd have the next day. So I said, "OK," and went with the old girl. At first she didn't even look at me, but after a bit she took out a large bill and looked me straight in the eye. Sizing me up. There was something fishy about the way she said "twenty now and twenty *later,*" just like in the American movies when the gangster gets sent on a difficult job. Maybe it was the way she said *later* or maybe it was how much she offered me. You felt like a millionaire with that kind of money in those days. The thing is, I got a knot in my throat, but I told myself don't be a shithead, take advantage of your good luck, a chance like this only comes along once in a lifetime. My head

was in that tug of war as the Caddie slipped through an iron gate
covered with huge, blood-red hibiscus and I thought I must be
uptown, in Miramar. I've tried to find the place again so many
times with no luck. Sometimes, in the Cerro neighborhood I'd tell
myself, "This is it. But no. I walk around the Vedado district.
with all its mansions, and the thought "Here it is," pops into my
head. But I'm wrong again. There's no other gate like that one,
with the bedraggled hibiscus hanging from its iron fangs. It's as if
the earth had swallowed it up. When the old lady parked the car
and told me not to make any noise so I wouldn't wake the
servants, I was completely freaked out. If I'd pinched myself hard
to see if this was a nightmare, I'd have left a huge, bloody black
mark. We crossed a kitchen five times bigger than our room in the
tenement. On the table they'd left a covered glass bowl filled with
chicken and rice, and my eyes went straight to it. The old lady
noticed and repeated, *"Later."* When I heard her say that again, I
looked down and saw a crisp twenty peso bill in my hand, a sight
I hadn't seen for a long time. It smelled wonderful. I tucked it
safely away and told myself, come what may, that bill's already
in the bank. Just in case. It felt like a thorn sticking in me. As we
were climbing the stairs, the old woman seemed to want to tell me
something. I was so cocky that I said, "So what's the deal?" She
looked at me and didn't say a word. I felt like a rag only good for
mopping the floor. That's when I started to look around for an
escape route in case the deal went bad. Right then, we stopped in
front of a door propped half open, and the old woman spoke to
me. Her words are stuck in my brain. I'll take them with me to the
grave. As if I were a stray dog, she said to me, "Behave yourself,
my son is very special." *Very special.* That phrase sill haunts me
and makes my blood boil and I feel like I'm about to explode. I
went into the bedroom and know what I saw? On the bed was a
kind of pasty-white creature, with a sheet pulled up to its chest.
Unshaven. At first glance I didn't catch on, but then I saw the
guy's big hands flapping around, slobber running down his chin
and heard grunts coming from his throat. I shouted, "But señora,
he's a freak!" She looked at me with eyes hard as dog's teeth, and
answered, "I'll pay." And I remembered the new bill, and the
other twenty she owed me, and Mama back in our room with her
bad heart, and the three months' rent we owed. Even the chicken
and rice popped into my head, because now I was thinking rapid
fire, like a machine gun. I saw that bowl growing, blowing up like

a balloon there in the kitchen. rice spilling out from under the lid; the voice of the radio announcer back in our room in the tenements, our room overflowing with chicken and rice and that damned *jingle for Jon Chi* Rice: *big plump kernels. Jon Chi Rice, bursting with flavor. Jon Chi Rice, You're gonna love it.* And I looked down at that fat slob and felt that knot again. This time it sunk to my stomach, then rose to my throat. Despite all that, I told the old bag I was OK. When life gives you lemons... Just as the lady was to leave the room, that knot slid down my chest and I think it nicked my heart. I crumpled to the floor. That must've caused an uproar in the house, because the old lady thought I'd died. And I think I did die a little. When I came to in the Caddie, the man driving said he was the chauffeur and that all the racket had wakened everyone in the mansion, that the lady ordered me to forget the whole thing, and that the twenty pesos were mine if I kept my lips zipped. She told him to take me to the hospital. And I said to him, "Over my dead body. Do me a favor, pal, let me off at the next bus stop." I got out of that Caddie as fast as the devil carries off a soul.

But why are you looking at me like that? Don't make that face. You look like you're about to croak. You don't think your mother's telling you lies, do you?

Translated by Pamela Carmell

FIGURES
Raúl Aguiar

How long would you have to wait, you were wondering, until Lezama Lima and Chinolope showed up.

In a way, you got your answer. You were sitting on the bench in the Plaza de Armas, facing the park and the Céspedes statue, your back to the Palace of the Captains-General, watching sparrows peck at crumbs tossed by charitable diners in cafes so venerable they deserved coats of arms and liveried retainers at their gates. You were happy, if I may say so, because landing on this island was like falling into a hole, an island-tunnel where you could be just another face, a bit out of the ordinary but not strange, a place where you could walk the streets with fine friends like Retamar or Lisandro or Lezama himself, that intimidating *slow volcano of words.* You could sit down to rest in a park without having to sign autographs or hide behind sunglasses — just be there, maybe respond to someone asking you the time, or answer a friendly greeting as if you were one more piece of flotsam in the stream. You could feel at home here, on a January day like Parisian summer, far to the southwast of any publisher, journalist, or dyed in the wool fan — and you would be, besides, in a fulcrum of new futures and fates. In Cuba, that is.

All that, yes, sir, but unaware that you, girl, were headed right this way, down Obispo, letting the beat of the old city wash over you, trying to hide how many tears you'd shed, how sad you were, how sorely you needed a little magic, a few words to comfort you. An old man stubbornly tried to sell some tourists a coin with Che's head on it, but they just laughed, shook their heads, and turned their eyes to you, looking you up and down, with desire perhaps, not knowing that today all you had to offer was emptiness and silence, that you couldn't turn the clock back because time was so sneaky and irreversible, so you were thinking the best thing would be rebirth in the style of the phoenix, becoming an echo, a resonance, much better than this tearful remembering of what had happened just a few hours ago: after taking the drug you couldn't feel anything at all, so they used you like some throwaway, not even paying you when they were done.

So here you come, girl, along the side of the Palace and then crossing the street into the Plaza, with your head down, without noticing you, sir, sitting there on the marble bench, just as unaware of her. You sit down next to him, while you stop your reading to observe out of the corner of your eye, to see her eyes with the make-up all smudged. She seems so lonely she reminds you of some small abandoned animal, and you'd like to ask her but you know you're not a very amusing conversationalist, so you go back to reading, yet the silence is too heavy, so you tell yourself there's really no reason to go through life on tiptoes, hiding or withdrawn — nor to be so Argentine, baring claws and casting aspersions, because in the end those poses are no good, and what's the point of that kind of vanity on a planet where everybody shares the same heartbeat, the same mistake, and in the end we all have to eat from the same plate — but not yet, never quite yet. That girl seems to be barely breathing through the scar left by some awful defeat. She has the look of somebody unsure how to go on living at all. But you don't want to be impolite, so you decide to make like a tree for a while more, tough and indifferent, while you, girl, are just looking for that encouraging word which might anchor you again to terra firma after that night in the grasp of the beast.

You pull out a cigarette and then root around in your backpack for the lighter, but it's gone, lost forever in that damned room. So you check out your benchmate, surprised by his height. The tallest man you can imagine, with a boyish face and eyes set so far apart. "Got a light?" you ask him, and that, well, sir, it cheers you up. Suddenly the Plaza is bathed in the seven colors of the spectrum, and you pull out your lighter, from which you, girl, light your cigarette, and you take two drags and try to smile. "What country are you from?" you ask, addressing him as *tú* without any to-do, while this quality, the way these Cubans never think twice about *tú*-ing everybody, is something that fascinates you — that is, *usted*. It's like stripping naked all of a sudden, like one might do at the edge of the sea. Maybe that's the explanation, you think — the sea always there, never more than a few meters away. But you picture her lifeless among the weeds and know you can't go on washing your hands of her. "From Argentina," you answer, and suddenly you miss Aurora and a good bottle of wine. There's no wine in Cuba — well, there's that bubbly orange one, but this is no country for wines, because rum drove them into full retreat.

"Are you a singer?" you ask him. "Or an actor? I know I've

seen your face somewhere."

You look her in the eyes and shake your head firmly. "A writer," you say.

"Oh. What's your name?"

"Julio."

"I'm Karla."

"Pleased to meet you, Karla."

"You're a writer, from Argentina, and named Julio. I suppose Cortázar would be your last name?"

"You've heard of me?"

"Are you kidding?"

"About what?"

"You really are named Julio Cortázar too?"

"What do you mean, *too*? Is there another one?"

Suddenly she seems annoyed. "Of course not. That would be too much of a coincidence. Anyway how could you not have heard of him? Everybody knows Julio Cortázar, they even teach him in school. I think he died about fifteen or twenty years ago."

You think about the rhythms, about how people insist on this term "coincidence" for events that follow laws not yet understood, though they may be just as causal (or inevitable) as the marvelous fact of waking up every day.

"Are you sure that was his name? And that he was Argentine? You couldn't be confused?"

It looks, you think, like this guy is going to keep playing games with you. Well, at least it will help you forget the mess — and the blows — that changed your life forever a few hours ago. You're just like your mother's sister, had to go through the same damn thing: fall in love with a fool, with the worst of imbeciles, and then come home crying like a good girl on the rebound, begging forgiveness — if you don't decide to throw yourself in the ocean, to swim until you wear out and then let the waves lap away your life one swallow at a time.

"Of course not. Everybody knows Julio Cortázar wrote *Rayuela*. I haven't read him very much, but...."

"Wait. Did you say *Rayuela? Hopscotch?*"

"Uh-huh. And a lot of stories about cronopios. And 'The Pursuer' too."

Suddenly you think she must be pulling your leg. These Cubans, always such jokers. But the girl sounds too serious, as if she really believes what she says. Of course, she could be crazy, or this could all be a dream, though it doesn't feel that way.

"The other day my father was reading one called something like *Modelo para armar.*"

"*62: Modelo para armar A Model Kit.*"

"That's it."

Now you've found the false note, the Telltale, something that refuses to fit within the structure of Reality at all. She can't know that book, because it hasn't been published yet. You haven't even finished writing it. Could you have mentioned it in some interview? You don't remember doing so. It's disturbing. You're always dazzled when something like this occurs.

"I'm that Julio Cortázar. But as you can see, I'm not dead."

"Cut it out. I don't like people playing with me. Believe me, right now, that's the last thing I need."

You try to get up, girl, but you, sir, you grab her by the arm. Your heart is hammering, beating like a drum. "Wait. There's something here that doesn't make sense." You fumble in your jacket pocket, then hold out your passport flipped open to the photo page.

You read what it says and look at him in fear. "I don't understand." You open your backpack, reach inside, and hand him your own ID — and now your eyes are fixed on her date of birth. Everything points to this being a dream, which allows you to decide to go ahead.

"Really, I'm as confused as you. You tell me that other Julio has died already. What year? When?"

"I don't know for sure. In the eighties, more or less."

"The eighties? What year is it now?"

You shake your head, incredulous. "2003."

Silence. You decide this is all an after-effect of the drugs. Hallucination. But you sir, believe in oneiric possibilities. A confluence of time streams? Or did you really die, and who you are now is just a ghost? No, you prefer the first explanation, although it seems so science fiction-like. But Cuba has always felt a bit surrealistic, neither fully real or fully fantastical, somewhere in between — an island full of people on the border of those two worlds. "Wait," you say, slipping out of *tú,* detaining her now with an Argentine *vos.* " You think I'm a dream. I think the same. Sooner or later, we'll wake up. So why don't we accept that, and talk a while? I'm really here in the Plaza de Armas, waiting for Lezama Lima and Chinolope, the photographer. It's January

1967. I'm in Cuba as a judge of the Casa prize. You've heard of Lezama, no?"

"Of course. And I too am in Havana, in the Plaza de Armas, but the year is 2003."

You feign an aplomb which you're far from possessing. "And you don't notice anything strange? Can you tell me what you see?"

You look around, and for a few seconds you get carried away by the hubbub of the city, the clowns on stilts, the flocks of tourists besieged by newspaper vendors and *jineteras* selling themselves. "Why?" you ask him. "This is all nuts. You're a hallucination of mine."

"I don't think so. Remember, you lit your cigarette with my lighter. You can touch me. I'm quite solid. Solid matter, I mean."

"That's true."

"And if this is only a dream, or a strange voyage in time, put yourself in my place. It's still a marvel. Suddenly I can talk with somebody who knows the future."

"I don't think that will do you much good. As far as your life, I mean. Or as far as literature. I know you published a ton of books, and you're very famous, but that's all."

"It doesn't matter. There are other things you could tell me about."

"Such as?"

"I've got a thousand questions. Was there another world war, or not? Apparently not, or we wouldn't be here. Have men landed on Mars? And the Vietnam War? Have any other peoples in Latin America freed themselves? What's happened in Cuba in all this time? Is Fidel still alive? And Che? Has socialism triumphed after all? And Argentina — do you know anything about that?"

"Che. . ."

You're about to tell him, and then pity takes over. A suffocating sadness. Through your dark glasses you see the other reality, and your eyes start to burn. You know that these days of pale imitations and how-much-does-it-cost have changed everything, that almost nobody understands about dreaming, that it's all about the iron chains of selfishness in a world that cranks out wolves and smart bombs, robots born of the fire of words, this damned new millennium, and what is the statue of Céspedes saying to the alcoholic beggars, to the booksellers pitching their used tomes, to the vendors of sex, like yourself, girl, who have forsaken truth for clothes, food, or flight? Adjusting forever to things as they are, life in suspended animation. You, at least, feel like you're free of hopes and expectations, except there was that blinding moment transformed into a wrenching memory. Yes, but how to tell him, it's no simple trick of the lips, nor is it like deciding to believe in horoscopes, just look at him there. So you're thinking, girl, but you, sir, you're waiting — your frank eyes, your old fashioned suit and all the brash innocence of a writer of the '60s fascinated by the Cuban Revolution, by Che's guerrilla, by so many things. . .

It would be too bad, you think, to wake up now and find yourself back in the hotel room, staring it its four walls. Suddenly you wish you'd been born in his day, without all the accumulated garbage of these forty years, and you wish you didn't know. You wish you didn't know, because of course you could break it to him gently, you could speak of far-off wars, story-book adventures, or you could just tell him the good things, you could talk in parables, in riddles, you could even lie, invent an alternate reality about the collapse of the capitalist bloc or something like that, because after all you're just a character in a dream. But no. You can't do it, because he deserves better than that. So you make a decision, take a deep breath, and as you're about to tell him, what do you do, sir? You get up, say, "Excuse me a moment," and go to greet a fat man who has just walked into the park. You speak to him excitedly, leading him toward the bench, saying "Let me introduce you. This is Lezama." Only it's too late for you, girl, because you see how the edges of things are growing fuzzy, and Havana disappears into weird geometric figures. "Who were you talking to, Julio?" your friend asks, and you can only make a shrug of resignation, gesturing toward the now-deserted bench. While you, trying to hold onto your last glimpse of his oblique eyes, suddenly want to laugh or cry. Now, you think, you're really going to have to start reading, whether you like it or not.

Translated by Dick Cluster

UNDER THE WEEPING WILLOW
Senel Paz

I wake up in the morning, and I feel good. I hear the cows mooing in the corral and the voices of my grandfather and my uncles yelling at them. None of the cows is as disobedient as Caramelo, a rust-colored cow who knows she's the prettiest in the herd. At sundown, I climb on the fence to look at them and Caramelo comes slowly down the hill, the one with all the flowering pine nuts on top, so that I can admire her. And I look at her and I see how the first evening star is framed by the sloping arches of her horns, and she and I talk. Grandfather gets up at three in the morning when everyone's alarm goes off. He calls my uncles who are getting back late from visiting their girlfriends, and the three of them go out looking for cows. This time, I don't hear the alarm clock, nor do I hear it the second time at four thirty. Then it's Grandmother who gets up, makes coffee, sits down to wait for Grandfather to come back with the first bucket of milk, boils it, and sends breakfast to the corral. What wakes me up are her bustling about in the kitchen, the crackle of firewood in the stove, the sound of a dish hitting something, and the two of them whispering. Or perhaps it's the light from the lantern and the stove that reaches the dining room from the kitchen, turns toward the room where I sleep and comes in through the half-opened door. At this hour, I am alone in the room, and I like seeing that sliver of reddish light and listening to all the sounds: the cows, the voices, the mice, an occasional horse, and then feeling the shiver of cold from being alone, with my mother far, far away from this house. That's when I'd like to talk to the plants or the animals. I let myself get carried away by my thoughts, and I'm riding horseback as well as Uncle Armando, I'm Isabel's boyfriend, Uncle Alberto's girlfriend or I've just arrived from the Canary Islands, and meet Grandmother after selling a tobacco farm, and I'm wearing a new guayabera made of fine linen, and we get married. That image fades, and I imagine I've found a lot of money and given it to Mother, and I get a house for her and we all live together. Because there are four of us: my other grandmother, Mama, my sister Gloria and me. That grandmother works in Gavilanes harvesting coffee. I like the fact that she works there because she always brings cheese and guava sweets, and all her stories are new, although she says that Gavilanes has outcroppings and hills where if someone falls he's gone forever. And I always want her to show up not only for the paper-wrapped candies, cakes, and dark-sugar cubes, but also because when she visits me she sits in the dining room facing the other grandmother and they talk about people they know. I look at them, trying to decide which of the two is prettier or which one I love more. If there are a lot of pieces of sugar candy and cakes then the grandmother who brought me the treats wins, but if the other one just recently took me to look for hens' nests or to the rose apple pond and I got to swim, then she's the winner. Mama comes to see me less than Grandmother; she works in the town and is the one who buys clothes and shoes, and my sister is in her godmother's house. Sometimes I am the one who stays at the godmother's house and my sister stays here, or both of us are at the house of one of my Mother's cousins, Clotilde, or at the house of don Gervasio, who is related to us in some way I don't quite understand. Sometimes they leave me at Mundito Gutiérrez's place — he's the compadre of my grandmother — but they don't leave my sister there because she's big now and so is Mundito's grandson, who may have turned out fresh like his father — may he rest in peace. Grandfather says that Gloria and I can't be here at the same time, though this is where we most like to be, because for starters we raise a ruckus around Grandmother and we get sick at the drop of a hat, and there are two mouths to feed. But first one and then the other, well that's fine. Another thing he says is that Mother can come and go in this house any time she wants, day or night, and that when's she here she should be looked after and given the best there is because Mother is not to blame; Father is the one to blame, and my sister and I are not responsible. My three maiden aunts are the ones who don't want Mother coming to the house and who put brooms with salt behind the door and hide in their rooms with their thick lips puckered and pouty until she's gone. And what they like least about us is that we shamelessly pee in bed even though they tell us not to. The only place we can pee without getting people riled up is at cousin Clotilde's house because there we sleep with all the other cousins in one bed, and in the morning you can't tell whose bladder was to blame. But as it turns out, at cousin Clotilde's house, neither my sister or I, buggers that our little wee-weers are, ever peed in bed. I'm not sure if Grandmother likes for Mother to come because she receives her in the living room and offers her coffee and tells her stories about how obedient and well-behaved we are, almost as if there weren't kids in the house and that if it weren't for the question of food we could both stay. Even so, all it takes for us to stay is for Grandfather to say that we can stay and for him to say that mother can visit for her to visit us because nobody dares to contradict Grandfather. Not even Caramelo.

But that's not what I was going to talk about nor why I am under this weeping willow tree since dawn, in my dress pants and a shirt, all combed and not taking my eyes off the road for a minute. Early this morning I was talking with Grandmother in the kitchen hoping that the mist would lift so I could go to the corral and see the last cows being milked, and Grandfather came in and abruptly turned to me and said: "Do you know what day it is?" I didn't know and I looked to Grandmother for help. "Today is Christmas Eve and we're going to roast a pig," he said. "But the important thing is that today your father is coming to meet you. Make sure he's combed and dressed early on and doesn't get dirty so he'll look good for his father." Then he just looked at me, and I looked at him and looked at Grandmother. "Let's go sleep a little while longer," she said when Grandfather left and she picked me up and carried me to bed. But I didn't sleep. The first thing I decided was I wouldn't eat any tangerines or guava so that I would be really hungry and eat a lot in front of my father when they served the meal. And when my aunts found out that today my father was coming, they really perked up and said they were going to dust and mop the house and clean the furniture, and they combed my hair and dressed me. I went to the courtyard of the house, wearing my hat, to choose the place where I would wait for my father. "Hey! Who's that guy all decked out? Who does he think he is, Mundito Gutiérrez?" said the hens when they saw me come out. But I paid them no attention and told the ten o'clock carnations to open today at nine and the night jasmine to disperse its perfume in the daytime, and the butterflies to be ready to flutter the moment Papa appeared, and the cats that they should each hunt a mouse and have it ready in their mouths to welcome Papa by showing him what good hunters they are. I planted myself in the middle of the roses with the idea of staying put and not letting on when I saw my father arrive, so he could ask "And that man over here taking care of the shrubs, who's he?" "Him? He's your son," responds Grandmother; but then it got really sunny and I went to the shade of the large *Guásima* tree in the courtyard and picked up a hatchet to chop firewood so that Father could say, "And that man over there who's working so hard, who's he?" "Ah!" Grandmother says, "that's your son." But I think maybe not because the trunk of the *Guásima* tree has a very ugly termite nest near the top, and so I came to this weeping willow, and here I am waiting, standing spread-legged like a cowboy. "Who is that serious, respectable-looking man standing over there?" Papa will ask. "That's your son!" Grandmother replies. "You don't say! He's so big and so good looking! Come over here, Son, I want to say hello to you and give you presents. How are your sister and your mother? Tell them I said hello." And when I get close he'll say, "Why, he's just like me. Now I'm going to look after him; I'm going to take him to Camagüey and put him in school." Papa will appear on the road riding a white horse, his saddlebags full of gifts. As he crosses the stream, he will stand in the stirrups and shout "Let my son come greet me!" and I'll run as fast as I can with my hat in my hand, and he'll lift me up into the saddle and the white horse will snort and his body will quiver the beautiful way horses do, shaking his mane and tail, eyes open wide with excitement. My father is my father, and I want to meet him. That's why I'm staying under this weeping willow without changing my cowboy stance. There's a photograph in the living room of my father on horseback when he was a young man. He's had more girlfriends than Uncles Armando and Alberto together says Grandmother, and not because he's her son, she says, but there was no one around as handsome nor one who could invent a better country ballad. My sister saw him once and told me that he's taller than Grandfather, heavier, but he has the same voice, Uncle Armando's laugh, Uncle Alberto's eyes, and only his nose is like Grandmother. Uncle Albert is the one he resembles most; the way he walks, his eyebrows, and the way he talks, seeming to push the words through just one side of his mouth. Both of them like checkered shirts, black hats and standing like the cowboys they are. I resemble him, too. Everyone says so; they recognize me by his traits, and the fact is, I think of the same things; I have the same birthmark, the same way of walking, and sleeping, all this without ever having seen him, except in the picture in the living room, because the blood runs true.

Grandmother says that when he was a little boy, he was small and thin, too, and people took pity on him, but he hardly got sick and he worked harder than I do. At home, I can't mention him. When my mother's relatives say he is shameless and that my mother is very good, and that when I grow up, I have to look after my mother, and if he needs me, I should say no and remind him that he didn't look after me when he should have, I just say yes, that's what I'll do. But it makes me sad that my father is such a scoundrel that everyone says bad things about him. It's probably a potion some woman gave him. At times, I imagine I'm my father and my picture's in the living room on that same horse, and then I go to town and I bring Grandmother the things she likes so that she can put them in the old cupboard. First thing I do is get married to Mother again. Other times, I think my father's the one I'm sleeping with and not Uncle Armando and that he's the one covering me so the mosquitoes won't bite and it is even better when he, not Uncle Armando, takes me for rides on the old mare, we talk, and he asks about my sister, and I invite him to visit us.

But he hasn't come, and I had to eat a tangerine, and I ate another without realizing it and then a guava without thinking. I missed seeing the pig speared, didn't see how the tip went in nor what a slaughtered pig looks like inside. My aunts just finished straightening up the house, and the last one is in the bathroom. Grandmother told me that yes my father is coming, that he'll be here any minute, and I went as far as my friends the palm trees and told them that he's on his way, and so now they are just waiting for him to appear so that they can greet him. My aunts cut fresh flowers for all the vases and Grandmother laid her white embroidered apron on the kitchen stool so she could put it on as soon as he got near. Every few minutes, she looks out to the road or asks me if I see him. "He'll get here around noon," she said. But twelve o'clock came and went, and I had to tell the ten o'clock carnations not to close up at one and ask the night jasmine to keep on spreading its perfume. It's just as well that the birds are having a party in the *Guásima* tree. And here I am, melting because the weeping willow really doesn't block out the sun much. If my shirt gets dirty, I don't have another. For sure, Mother will ask me: "What did your father say? Did he think you were big, strong, and handsome? Did he ask about us, about your sister? Did he give you money?" Me, I just want him to get here.

"Here comes Joaquín!" I suddenly hear my aunt Rose call from a corner of the porch, and she drops the broom and runs inside smoothing her dress.

"Here comes Joaquín!" repeat my other aunts and Grandmother from the kitchen, and my uncles rush off, leaving behind the pig they are cooking under the star apple tree. Only Grandfather stays put, straightening his hat and belt. The cats look for mice. Caramelo comes toward the fence, the roof of the house glistens, the butterflies flutter about, the birds sing in the bushes, and all the hens come to the front of the house, as if it were feeding time.

Joaquín is my father, and I finally see him on his white horse, appearing and then disappearing between the palms, but there on the road. He will get to the gate, and he will take the narrow path. We don't have to rush out to meet him yet, not until he crosses the stream, and his horse begins to climb the ridge and comes slowly under the generous shade of the *Bienvestidos*. Then I'll see his face. Grandmother has left the kitchen wearing her white, embroidered apron, wiping the soot and grease from her hands. Then come my aunts, all smiles, with flowers in their hair, and then my uncles. I just stay where I am under the weeping willow, with one foot on a stone and a hand on my belt, as if I were Uncle Alberto carrying on a conversation, and now everybody comes through the garden. The ten o'clock carnations, the night jasmine and the roses all release their fragrance. Now my father is crossing the palm grove; he's almost as tall as they are and the palms have run up to the edge of the path and are applauding him. The foot-long *biajaca* fish in the stream jump for joy. The white horse is enormous, and you can see Papa is smiling and my chest swells with so much pride that I burst a button. Grandmother can't resist the temptation and runs. She reaches Papa in the middle of the pasture. I hear her laughter, and he stretches out his arms and lifts her on the horse. Grandmother laughs and kisses him, and he takes off his hat. I should go cut firewood under the *Guásima* tree but now there's no time. My aunts are waiting at the door to the old sugar mill, and my father's dog has reached the courtyard. Papa lifts Grandmother to the ground, jumps down from his horse and hugs and kisses his first sister, then the second one before the first one lets go, and the third one before the first and the second and Grandmother let go, and then it's my uncles' turn. From where I am, I can hear the backslapping as everyone hugs and laughs. I wonder if father likes grapefruit juice like I do. Now the second button on my shirt pops off, and all the birds in the bushes begin chirping because they want to see my father and his horse, who is following the welcoming party, very proud of being so white and so handsome. Now they arrive. At last I see my father, who hasn't seen me. I get a good look at him. From now on I'll always remember him that way, smiling, with his teeth so white, looking like he'd just bathed; I standing under the weeping willow and he against the sun. How big he is! I'm sorry that I can't say to him: "Good tidings, father. How are you? And your wife?" And can't answer now if he asks me about my sister and my family because... how tall he is, what a grand mustache he has, what a nice laugh, and how deliciously the others laugh, and I feel ashamed because I'm not laughing, and they're coming this way. He's going to pass right by without seeing me. I better change position without seeming any less of a cowboy than he is. Now I know: I'll cough, I'll say something. "Aunt Rosa, you, haven't seen my jump rope have you? Grandmother looks at me. It must be she who looked at me. She's the one with so many embroidered flowers on her white apron. Now I'm sure. I love her more than my other grandmother. In all the family uproar, she makes a path between me and Papa with her arm and pointing to me she says "Look Joaquín, this is your son." Now why is it I don't have my lucky snail shell in my hand? I'm about to run right to him, but his look stops me, and I wait for the words he will say: "He's bug-eyed like his mother's family," he says, and closes the family circle, and they head for the house where Grandfather greets him with open arms. "I was beginning to think you weren't coming," he says to him. They stand there hugging. I'll bet they'll go to see the roasting pig.

Me? I think I'm just going to go eat a tangerine and keep on looking for hens' nests.

Translated by Anne Fountain

BLACK AND WHITE
Aida Bahr

Rebecca's daughter

I don't know whether to think you're a saint or a fool, Luisa, although maybe they're the same thing. Did Rebecca's phone call really upset you so much that you had to go hide? The living room smells like death. How long is it since anybody's been here? Even the mailman knows to come to the back door. You've created a boundary, an invisible line that says that the house starts at the dining room. It's probably so you can imagine Rebecca still here and Leon still alive. And if you keep the lights turned off, it must be because darkness allows you to imagine furniture and curtains that haven't been here for years. And it's all a shame, Luisa, because now this house belongs to *you*. Rebecca's not here to tell you what to do. She's lost her rights — if she ever had any — when she left. And it's pathetic to hear you cry talking to her on the phone. Don't give me that "she was crying too" bit since we both know what her tears are worth. Remember how weepy she got when they came to inventory her things before she left and they seized the wedding photo? "Oh, no, not that," she said with rivers gushing from her eyes. So they gave it back to her but she didn't take it after all because without the elegant frame it wasn't the same. If it wasn't going to take center stage on a coffee table where everyone could admire the pearls, fancy beadwork, and intricate lace of her wedding dress, it didn't have the same appeal. You're the only one who believes she got choked up just talking to you. She didn't call to find out about you, Luisa; she still wants to order you around. For her, you've never been more than a servant.

Luisa

That's not true. Rebecca and I are more like sisters than cousins. She and I are the only descendents of the Ricardo family because Mama and Aunt Amalia, even though they got married young, didn't have us until they were in their forties — Mama because she always lost the baby in the third or fourth month and Auntie Amalia because she never got pregnant. At age forty Aunt Amalia had Rebecca and the next year I was born, as if Mama had been waiting for a signal. Rebecca and I were always together.

They even dressed us alike, except that on Rebecca the clothes looked beautiful while on me they seemed to be hanging from a hook. I turned out like Papa: tall, thin, and gangly. I don't think Mama ever forgave me. Sometimes she looked at me as if my very existence was punishment for some unknown sin. We never really got along. Mama tried her best to mold me and she used to say: "Even though you're younger than Rebecca, you don't always have to do things her way. Sometimes you should be in charge. Tell her you want to play with dolls instead of playing doctor." I tried that, but it always turned out that when Rebecca wanted to play with dolls, or felt like playing nurses, she made it so interesting that I agreed with her. That's just the way it was. At some point Mama got tired of trying to change me. Perhaps it was after father died and we were in mourning, I for a year and she in perpetuity. Neither her body nor her soul ever really gave up mourning. It even offended her that I got to the point of being able to laugh again. That was the worst period of my life because I discovered I could never fill the emptiness that my father's death had left. Rebecca was my salvation. Every time she went out she came by for me and begged so much that mother ended up letting me go with her. Thanks to Rebecca, I went to parties, saw friends, and took walks. If it had been up to mother, I would never have seen a single movie. And was it Rebecca's fault that she was pretty and cheerful while I was unattractive and withdrawn? Anyway, I never felt ill will or jealousy because people preferred her. On the contrary, I had fun because of her romances and many times I helped her arrange to be alone with a boy. Nothing serious happened until Leon appeared, and then it was clear that he was something different. He was twelve years older than Rebecca and was a respected physician. Even before the engagement she paid him special attention, and wouldn't dance with anybody else. I was the beneficiary of her exclusive focus because when boys asked her to dance and she said no, they turned to me. But none of them interested me, and after Leon asked for Rebecca's hand, no one dared to approach us. I didn't really miss the male companionship. Leon was so kind that he never made me feel like a chaperone, or someone extra. It was marvelous. Something in his way of looking at you made you feel protected, safe from everything. He treated us like little girls and brought presents for both of us. He was crazy about Rebecca: when she spoke he smiled, and you could tell that he was not just listening but also looking, drinking her in with his eyes. With me, it was what I said that mattered. Leon and I always found it easy to talk to each other. One afternoon we were discussing a biography of Marie Antoinette by Stefan Zweig, a book Leon had given us and that I, as usual, had read and then summarized for Rebecca. The conversation was about more than an aristocrat facing the guillotine. It was about whether the punishment was fair or not. Rebecca saw Marie Antoinette as a young girl who had done nothing more than amuse herself and said it wasn't reasonable to expect more of someone who became a queen at age sixteen. I argued that Marie Antoinette was a grown woman at the time of the French Revolution and that by then she should have gained some degree of maturity. Zweig (for his part) seemed to me to be enamored of the idea of a beautiful queen meeting a tragic end. To all of this, Leon smiled. He praised my intelligence and said I had common sense, which was rare: "We'll have to take care of you, you're the sort of woman who's becoming extinct." Rebecca thought he was making fun of me and scolded him, but I took it all seriously. Their courtship period was a beautiful, harmonious interlude, but it didn't last long. The wedding was a big deal, first the ceremony in the church and then the festivities. Mama didn't want to go but Aunt Amalia interceded for me and we went for about an hour, enough time to see them cut the cake, sip the cider and kiss. On the way back I cried, but mother didn't even pay attention. At the time, she was already sick but didn't know how serious it was. In any event it didn't matter to her. During Rebecca's honeymoon — days when I never left the house — I realized that mother was going to die. One night while we were eating I asked her if I shouldn't study typing. "Don't be ridiculous," she said, "you have your pension and the house." Mother faded little by little without complaining. The last thing she said was, "I'm coming to join you, Antonio." Not a word for me. I, who cry about everything, was dry-eyed, and empty. It hardly seemed that mother had died but rather that she'd left me alone on purpose. At the funeral itself, Aunt Amalia asked me to come live with her. I said no, and it took Leon's help to convince her to let me go home by myself after the burial. I went to sleep and slept like a rock until the next morning. In the morning Aunt Amalia came back to try to convince me, and I told her I would think about it, and when she left I said to myself: I've got things to do, and I set to cleaning. I washed doors and windows, swept the roof, and scrubbed the floors. People came to give me their condolences and they couldn't even step inside the door because of all the water from my scrubbing. Rebecca came in the afternoon and found me scouring the cement steps that led to the patio. She completely forgot to mention mother. She sat in the kitchen, and I offered to fix her coffee, but she wouldn't let me. "You're coming with us," she said. And it was just like when we played as children: I knew that she was right.

You were born with a silver spoon in your mouth, as might be expected of Rebecca's daughter. Pretty as a picture. Your grandmother Amalia used to say: she'll be a fashion model. Rebecca dressed you up in such frilly and beautiful outfits that you looked like a princess, and even people who didn't know you felt like they had to pay compliments. One time they gave you three polished, jet-black *azabache* pendants out of fear of the evil eye. And in one of the carnivals they dressed you up as a harem girl and painted your face. They had you ride right on the hood of the car. You surely remember that because it was the happiest moment of your childhood. Three years old. And there you were: a precious little doll seated on top of the hood throwing streamers and kisses.

Rebecca's daughter

The earliest thing I remember are the bars of my cradle. I played that I was a lion in a cage. I crawled and roared. I also remember that the only one who listened to my stories was Leon. He listened attentively and discussed them with me seriously. Rebecca insisted that if I kept it up I'd end up telling lies. I'll never understand her. The day that I ran away from home, the only thing she did was to laugh at the sight of me with high heels, jewelry, and makeup. They found me three blocks away from home, and I hadn't yet started school so I must have been less than five years old. I suppose that in those days I was happy, but I can't remember that happiness, just a few good moments that fell my way like the aces from a deck of cards. One of my best memories is of an afternoon on the patio when I was alone, seated on the ground with a plate heaped with caramels. Other good memories are when uncle Pedro taught me to play cards in the middle of hurricane Flora; well, I know it wasn't exactly a hurricane because he never left the farm, but still it was raining really hard that afternoon. He also taught me to ride horseback and drink sugar cane juice. The farm was a paradise, but we didn't get to go very often... Rebecca always complained about how far it was, how bad the road was, about the mud and the insects—about everything. When she wasn't around Leon, she was disparaging of uncle Pedro, who was such a macho guy that he and Leon hardly seemed like brothers. But guess who always came to our rescue. The trips to the farm are among my happiest memories. Another time was when Grandma Amalia and Grandpa Enrique went north, their kisses wet with tears as they said goodbye. Of the trip to Havana, the one where they said they took me to the city's Coney Island Amusement Park, I don't remember anything. Oh, and of course there was the beach. Rebecca would lie in the sun wearing her Hawaiian pareu while Leon taught me how to swim. One day we couldn't go in because the sea was so rough and the waves so furious that they could drag down a grown man. While we were sitting on the beach an old man with white hair walked by all bent over and alone. He was all by himself. He didn't dare go in the water but he got close enough to bend over and splash a little water on himself when the waves came in. But then he got knocked down by a big wave and the poor old man had to retreat. I felt sad seeing him so unhappy and defenseless. It made me angry that he wanted to bathe in the ocean and the sea wouldn't allow it, just like if someone came to knock on your door to ask you for something and you threw the person out. Alms. Oh yes, the question of charity. That's something for which I'll never forgive Rebecca. I used to save coins to give them to the old people who sat in the doors of the church. I'd go to nine o'clock mass so I could sleep in the morning. After I had my first communion, they let me go to seven o'clock mass and I didn't see any more beggars. But, before, when I used to go with Rebecca, I did see them. There were three old men. I would go up to them and give them my coins, two or three to each one, and they would smile and say thank you and God bless you. Rebecca never gave them anything. I went up to them all by myself, a good little girl giving alms. One morning there was a younger woman there and when she saw the three coins she threw them on the ground. I was shocked because she said "shit," just like that, "shit," and then Rebecca came and rescued me while the woman said, "Money, what I need is money — not these shitty coins." The old men had never protested. Rebecca said they must be millionaires with all the alms they got at every mass. And I was giving them coins. I'll never be able to forgive or forget that incident. I was just a little girl and I didn't understand, and Rebecca in her own way helped me to understand.

If you don't want this letter from Rebecca to end up in the bathroom wastebasket, don't leave it out where it can be seen. After all, you're the one who wants to know how she's doing. And you needn't make an effort to tell us that she still hasn't found work and that she's living with Bonnie and not Carmela. Everything that the letter says we already know; there's never any mystery with Rebecca. It's was obvious that she wasn't going to stay with Carmela after Pedro kicked her out. Carmela is cheap and Rebecca likes luxury. Didn't you say that Bonnie has money? Leon's inconsolable widow won't be looking for work. She's not like you, Luisa, almost going crazy and asking God to help you get ahead. Now, there's nothing left for you to sell. Well, yes, there're the hidden jewels, Rebecca's famous emeralds that matched her eyes. You looked almost comical when you said you'd rather work like a slave than sell them. But you'll have to do something. Yesterday you cried after refusing the chickens that Manuel brought and nobody knew if you cried because there wasn't any meat in the house or because you couldn't believe that Manuel wanted you to pay. And what did you expect, that he's going to just give them to you because Pedro was always kind to him? In any event, Manuel was working for a salary, and if he was Pedro's friend, something no one can prove, you're really nothing more than the cousin of the wife of the brother of his friend. That's a pretty distant relationship, don't you think? And the fact that Pedro's niece is in the middle of it all hardly matters either. You should be thankful that he is bringing you things, because many people would have to go to him to buy them. You also have to remember that if he keeps coming in vain, he's going to stop coming. But don't worry; you have rice and beans and there's meat once a week. Isn't that right? So be happy.

Luisa

Ever since '59 everything's been falling apart back there. Well, maybe since '60, because in '59 there was all the rejoicing over the triumph of the revolution. Leon laughed because he said that all of a sudden we discovered that everything was linked to the date July 26, and how could you explain that Batista had lasted so long.[*] From '59 I just remember one bad thing; that's when Bonnie, Rebecca's best friend, went North.. While Bonnie was here, Carmela was nothing more than an acquaintance. Bonnie was nice and spoke a kind of comical Spanish. She used to say: I am (*soy*) really confused, I am (*estoy*) clumsy in Spanish, getting our two ways of expressing "to be" completely mixed up. She could never understand the difference between "ser" and "estar." Her family had extensive holdings, and they left sometime between May and June of 1959, while we were still in the period of euphoria. Later everyone said that they had had foresight. First because of the hassles about ownership and then because of military conscription. Rebecca's friends kept leaving until only Carmela Aguirre was left. Aunt Amalia and Uncle Enrique left shortly after the money was changed. They had theirs all hidden away in the house and they were ruined. They tried to convince Leon to go, too, but he had lived in New York before he got married and had no desire to return. He did, however, give them a blank check so that they could use money he had left in a bank there. That money ended up being a big help because six months after they got there Uncle Enrique suffered a heart attack and couldn't work anymore. Even now they're still living on welfare, which is why Rebecca couldn't stay with them. Another person who suffered a lot was Pedro. The second agrarian reform law took away almost all of his farm — the best land according to him — and he became bitter and left. When he came to say goodbye and bent down to kiss me, I realized that his hair had turned white. That's how we ended up being alone. Pedro prospered in the U. S. and offered to help us come whenever we wanted. From the very first, Rebecca wanted to go. Every time a letter from Pedro arrived she argued with Leon about it. In May of '67 she insisted for the last time. I can remember it vividly: Leon seated in the rocking chair and she on the footstool to the side, leaning on his knees and begging. His response had always been that he wasn't missing out on anything. This time he said: "Here I have a name and I'm respected." "You can make a name for yourself there as well," she said. But looking at her with sadness he replied: "Not now," and she understood and ran to the

[*] July 26th - After the 1959 revolution, much was made of the date July 26 to commemorate the July 26, 1953 attack by Fidel Castro and his followers on the Moncada Barracks in Santiago. A Cuban song includes the refrain: "For us, it's always the 26th."

bedroom with tears in her eyes. They didn't speak of it again, not even when Carmela herself planned to leave. I'm not sure why it took so long for Rebecca to realize about Leon's state of heath; perhaps she wanted to hide from reality — stick her head in the ground — like an ostrich. I understood from the very beginning. When Leon had to work at night I was the one who stayed up to heat his meal and talk to him. One day the hospital called to say he was doing an emergency operation and would get home late. When he arrived it was after midnight and he was not in his own car. They brought him home. When I went out into the hallway, it scared me half to death to see him; he had to lean against the wall to be able to walk and seemed a shadow of himself. I helped him sit down. What's the matter? What happened? I asked. No answer. I asked him if I should bring him some food and he nodded no with his head and just stayed seated, leaning back, with his eyes closed. He was breathing so weakly that I could hardly hear him. I'll call Rebecca, I said, but he took my hand in his. What is it, Leon? What happened? He spoke with long pauses, as if he didn't have sufficient breath for a whole sentence. "There was an accident. In the middle of the operation the man's heart stopped. I couldn't pull him out of it. I couldn't." I tried to console Leon: I'm sure you did everything you could. He closed his eyes again and said simply: "The patient died and I'm alive." And it was then that I realized that Leon had suffered a heart attack at the very time he was fighting to save another man's life. He hadn't been able to go on. No doubt they tended to Leon more than the other man, so he felt guilty for having stolen another man's chance to live. The remorse of that incident devastated him as much as his own illness. He was never the same after that. When he tried to tell a joke, he ended up wanting to bite his tongue with regret for having spoken. It was then that the really bad years began. 1968 was the worst. We lost Leon, which meant losing everything; it was the greatest sorrow of my life. When Papa died I was just a little girl; then when Mama died the sensation was very different. When Leon died my world came apart, and I couldn't even cry because someone had to look after the house and Rebecca had to be sedated three times during the wake and couldn't make it to the burial. The next few days we were like ghosts in the house. Carmela came every day. I left her alone with Rebecca so I could take care of the household chores and could cry alone in the kitchen. If I had money for all the tears

I spilled in that kitchen, I'd never be hungry. One month after Leon died, we went to take flowers to the cemetery. There at Leon's tomb Rebecca told me that she was going to seek permission to leave. I looked at her without knowing what to say and she explained: Mother will take care of the legal matters and Pedro will give us the money. You're coming with us aren't you? No, I said. The people I love are buried here and I'm staying here with them.

You must remember about all of that. It wasn't when you were really young. I'm sure you remember because it was the time you began to change. You went from being a sweet, outgoing, talkative little girl to becoming a silent and withdrawn human being. Everyday you hid a bit more of yourself. Rebecca always tried to get you to go out with her, and you always said no until at last she gave up and began to go out by herself. The more you refused to talk, the more she herself talked. Couldn't you see that she was about to go crazy? The culmination came when it was time for Carmela to leave. I know it must have been hard for you: the day you turned twelve you didn't even smile when Rebecca woke you up with a kiss and congratulations. This year the nightmare will end, she said, and she was right, except that your nightmare and hers were different. Once the unpleasantness of the pre-departure inventory was over, Rebecca seemed to be humming with happiness. You, on the other hand, seemed to be dying inside. The night you and Rebecca were headed for Varadero you had us worried. You'd never before thrown a plate of food on the floor. Then in the station you sat on the floor and acted deaf when they called, and had to be put on the train. Your eyes had a vacant look as if you weren't going toward Matanzas and from there to Varadero, but rather toward hell. What happened next only you know.

Rebecca's daughter

Torches and smoke. That's my memory of the station. A very long black train seen as if I were looking at it from outside my body: I saw myself seated at the edge of the platform with my legs dangling. There was a drunk lying on a bench like a bundle of rags. I even thought that I was dead and that my body had been thrown out, but I don't remember much more. Just scenes and sensations. The bathroom of the train wet with puddles and full of paper. The metal door felt cold. I remember how that cold penetrated. The trip made me seasick. The trees ran backwards, and all of a sudden a station would appear: they were always the same: the same fence, the same building, the same benches. The train blew its whistle and lurched forward, and the trees began to run backwards again. I'm not sure how long it took or what Rebecca did. When we got to Matanzas a man in the station was selling Caracas cakes or some kind of bread like that. I asked Rebecca to buy me some but she put me in a rented van where we were all on top of each other on top of the luggage. The man with Caracas bread remained behind; people were buying, breaking off pieces, and eating. Rebecca tried to give me some of the meat pie she had brought, but I wasn't hungry. In Varadero we stayed in the house of a woman who rented out space to people who were leaving; it was the same place where Carmela had stayed. The woman already knew about Rebecca, greeted her as if they were old friends and even fixed her coffee. They sat in the kitchen and talked for a long time. The woman told Rebecca that they would make her give up her wedding ring because it was gold and suggested that she swallow it. Just pretend it's a pill she said. The house had a wood swing on the porch, and I spent some time there. I suppose that at some point, I bathed, we ate, and that they gave us a room to sleep in, but I don't know, I just can't remember. I was on the swing when Rebecca called me to get dressed. I wanted to stay dressed in pants but she made me put on a gingham dress. I closed the suitcase and heard the car honk outside. Hurry up she said. As I left the room I saw her on the sidewalk with the man who was going to take us to the airport, a fat man with a double chin that almost reached his chest. He looked at Rebecca as if he were going to eat her up. They were standing next to each other and their thighs were touching. I didn't think about anything; I didn't know what I was going to do. Instead of walking to the sidewalk I went to the patio. Something snapped inside my head; I saw the zinc fence and jumped over it. Behind the fence was underbrush. I began to run, but at first not very fast. Then I heard shouts and realized that I was escaping or rather that I could escape. I ran like crazy through the countryside falling down and getting up and running again and when I had to stop I lay down between some rocks and a thorny *marabusal* bush with my throat dry, scared to death like in hide and seek where you know they are looking for you and that if they find you, you lose. Nightfall came and I stayed put, paralyzed, not daring to move. Suddenly I heard noises and a flashlight beam was on me. Someone pulled me up by the arms. I saw some very blue eyes, thought it was an American, and began to shout that I didn't want to go, that I wanted to stay in Cuba. Then I saw a dark haired man and realized that they were both dressed in olive green. I tried to walk but I couldn't; the one with the blue eyes carried me to a jeep and they took me to a guard post. I heard them talking on the phone and they mentioned Rebecca. I shouted again and grabbed the arm of the official: Don't let her take me, please, don't let her take me. She can't take you because she's already gone, he said. I looked at him stupefied and began to laugh and cry at the same time. They brought me a glass of milk and then I fell asleep and didn't even dream.

Seeing you place flowers on the tomb, dressed in mourning, anyone would think that you were the widow. Leon was a lucky fool. Instead of choosing you he married Rebecca and got you both. An ideal combination: a beautiful lover to show off and a perfect housewife. How could you stand it? Your mother was right to be irritated with you. You could have married, had children, your own house, your own life, but instead you preferred to be a shadow of Rebecca. If you'd wanted to, who knows. After all Leon was closer to you than to her. The way in which he talked to you, looked at you, smiled at you. If you'd wanted to…

Luisa

I've been happy. Very happy. Perhaps I've had more than my share of happiness. Life is never black and white, or rather it *is* but the two colors are mixed: nothing is entirely black or entirely white. All those dances, those strolls in the park, so many lovely memories that can't be separated from Rebecca; thanks to her I enjoyed them. Should I have gotten married? I had some suitors before mother died, but not a single one stirred my interest. If I had stayed in my house perhaps others would have shown interest, and probably not because of me, but because of the advantages of my being a single girl with a house. When I lived with Leon and Rebecca I met many men, friends of Leon, and occasionally one would pay me a compliment or drop a hint. But I never encouraged any of them; I didn't need to. I've lived the life I chose and the bad things that have happened were not anybody's fault in particular. The break-up of the family, Leon's heart attack: Rebecca suffered more from them than I did. She always needed things that weren't of interest to me and she kept losing them one by one. For example, she loved candy and Leon would get it for her two boxes at a time; even more when she was pregnant. She always insisted that I eat one as soon as she opened the box because her craving was so strong that she could eat the whole box in minutes and would then feel sorry that there wasn't one left for me. In some ways her weaknesses were not her fault. She was always spoiled, pampered, and treated like a doll, but she was also sweet, cheerful and good-natured. She simply wasn't prepared to face life on her own. She'd always had someone to do things for her: first Aunt Amalia and Uncle Enrique, then Leon, and at the end just me. If she is living with Bonnie now it's not just for economic reasons. Every time we talk on the phone she ends by telling me: I really miss you. She feels my absence much more than I feel hers. It's always been that way. It was always up to her to give and to me to receive.

You were very sentimental as a little girl; you had a special capacity to enjoy love. You don't remember it, but one time you saw Leon and Rebecca kissing on the lips and you ran out to tell everybody you saw: my mother and father are going to get married. It was the same with the gift of *La Edad de Oro.** Do you remember that you decided that you would begin to read it on the very day of your birthday and that you've kept it on the night stand unopened until this very day? Leon was sorry because he understood that you would have wanted such a special gift to arrive—not on just any day—but on some important date. At the same time he was proud that you would organize things that way; he said that it was good that you were capable of wishful thinking. Now, on the other hand you've become hard and practical. You're obsessed with all of Rebecca's supposed failings. And now you don't even call her Mama.

Rebecca's daughter

Carmela's house was just like her. From the outside it seemed like a lovely big house. but once you went through the door you found sagging furniture, cobwebs on the lamps, pictures and

---

* *La Edad de Oro (The Golden Age)* - famous book of children's literature written by the Cuban national hero, José Martí. It contains stories and poetry and is important for its moral lessons as well as being a source of information and entertainment.

door-molding and rooms that were empty because she had sold off everything. The first room was full of cardboard boxes, piles of cardboard boxes, who knows for what, and two more rooms that were empty, and then her room which led to the hallway of the patio and the bathroom. Her room did have the bedroom furniture intact. In the patio, grass was growing between the cracks in the cement. The garden wall and the wall of the bathroom were covered with mold and bracken. Apart from the living room, that room and the kitchen, there was no place to sit down. They sent me to the patio and I sat down on the floor of the hallway. I don't know what they were thinking when they told me to amuse myself back there. How did they imagine that an eleven-year-old would amuse herself? While Leon was living we never went to that house. He probably didn't allow Rebecca to go. After he died we would go two or three times a week, with me always as a cover. The unhappy widow paying social calls with her daughter. Rebecca never went to the cemetery because it depressed her. She said that Leon wasn't really in the tomb but in her heart. How ridiculous! Leon in Rebecca's heart in Carmela's house while the two of them whispered and laughed and made me leave if I tried to come in. They talked on the telephone very softly. Until that afternoon when Rebecca said she had a terrible headache and Carmela said she should lie down a while and then insisted that I go with her to the park. Like I was some five-year old or an imbecile. They would have given me candy if they'd had some. When we got to the park, Carmela sat down on a bench and said: Run around over there. As incredible as it seems, I sat down and asked God to send a downpour — a great, huge deluge that would soak her completely and it wouldn't matter that I got wet as well. I asked it with all of my heart, but God must be deaf. People walked through the park and went in and out of stores. Why couldn't I become one of those people who were walking all around me? A little girl fell down, scraped her knee, and cried. The mother came running to pick her up, carefully cleaned the knee, blew on the wound to dry it and then carried the little girl away. Was it that afternoon? Was I perhaps the one who fell? The park smelled wet but it never rained. The sun was an orange you could look up at. The air around me was suffocating and I couldn't take it any longer. Why didn't I run home without saying anything to Carmela? She would have looked for me for a while and then would have gone to tell Rebecca: "She got lost in the park." She might not even have been alarmed. I was so well brought up, so obedient: "Let's go look for mother, let's go, let's go." And she: "let's wait a while, would you like to look at the stores?" "I want to go, I want to look for my mother!" I can still remember the warm flush on her face. "Trouble-making, ill-bred little girl." A snake hissing the words. I didn't grab her by the hair and drag her through the park. I didn't rip her dress and leave her naked in front of everyone. And I was capable of walking along with her to the house, crossing the living room and the dining room to the patio, the hall to the room, the room empty, the bed empty, the bedspread and pillows on the bench in front of the dressing table and Rebecca's belt, watch and necklace on the dressing table itself, and Rebecca coming out of the bathroom combing her hair. What happened? Rebecca finishes combing her hair, applies makeup, and then puts on her watch, belt and necklace. And the whole time Carmela is opening and shutting her mouth, talking, getting worked up, becoming hoarse, and her sounds are swallowed up by the bed, empty, white, and sunken in the middle. Carmela's bed.

Luisa

Rebecca should not have done that to you. She was a widow and free and she didn't need anyone to serve as a cover. I don't know why she was so worried about what people would say when she had already decided to leave the country. Of course the criticism would have been harsh. The husband barely two months dead and she's already out seeking consolation. People judge just by appearances, even you. I don't know if I should tell you this or if I will help destroy the only thing you love and respect, but I feel dirty hearing you talk that way. I hope you can understand. When Leon died, it had been over a year since he and Rebecca had sexual relations; they slept in the bed like brother and sister. She was young and full of desire. She never complained and I'm sure that if he had been living she would never have gone near another man. I could tell you that the cause of all of it was that he had had a heart attack and in one sense that would be true, although not entirely true. You said that Rebecca had been the lover and I the wife. Ever since I came to this house I began to take charge of things and little by little Leon got accustomed to discussing all the daily details with me. Rebecca didn't want to be bothered with that sort of thing. One night, one of the many nights when Leon got home late and found me awake he stroked my hair and told me: "It took me a long time to learn how to see you, Luisa, and now I can't offer you anything. I'm sorry." I answered him: I have everything I want. And that was true. I loved him from the very beginning, from those first days in which he took an interest in Rebecca and I was happy with his affection and kindnesses without hoping for more. I suffered the day of the wedding, for the first time seeing them kiss, realizing that he would not be mine, and that I could not touch and embrace him like she could. When they were on their honeymoon I suffered more. I understood that my life would be worth nothing without seeing him, speaking with him, or touching his hand or arm just casually. Rebecca made that and much more possible. I shared everything with him except his bed. After that late night conversation, he allowed himself to caress me sometimes, always careful to not go too far. Then came the first heart attack which affected him some, but not totally. Rebecca cried with me in the kitchen all morning. "He just can't any longer" she told me, "he's not well." "Give him time," I advised. She looked at me. "You understand him," she said; "help him." I felt confused and embarrassed. "Ever since I came I've done nothing except try to help both of you." She shook her head. "I know, but he needs you more now." I didn't know how to take her words. I turned them around and around in my head and the night we stayed together very late watching a movie, when he began to caress my hair and kiss me on the neck I decided that Rebecca had wanted to give me a great deal of leeway. I never dared to let her see; neither did he. We kept up appearances because we felt that it would be a big problem if she had to face it, but I've always believed she knew. That day in the cemetery when I told her that I preferred to stay in Cuba where my loved ones were buried, her response was: "they're more yours than mine." And when she called from Varadero, gone crazy, crying, and talking incoherently, until I managed to understand that you had escaped, she said: "I'm going, I can't make her come with me, she, too, has chosen you." It must have been very hard. And don't say that she asked for it. People don't always do what they should, or what they want to do, but they generally do what they are capable of doing. We're all somewhat egotistical and if we make sacrifices for someone it is almost always because we enjoy that sacrifice or because it pleases us or because the sacrifice is not that great. I probably should have said nothing. Who knows if with time you might have come to understand and forgive Rebecca without my needing to explain that there is plenty of blame for everyone. And, who knows if now you'll be able to pardon Leon and me.

Translated by Anne Fountain

THE LADY WITH THE POOCH
Jesús David Curbelo

A naked woman is a pretty common sight. But if she's leaning against a dog, a guy starts to take notice. Especially when it dawns on him, after he picks his jaw up off the floor, that the animal will play an important role in the drama that's about too unfold. And so it was: the fifth time I visited Astrid's home she received me in her birthday suit. After she spied me through the peep hole, she opened just the top half of the door and whispered, "Hurry. Get in here," I heard the latch click behind me, then came face to face with that marvel of a girl who, with a devilish look in her eye, was caressing her German shepherd's neck.

I met her at the writers' roundtable where I was jabbering away. She said to me, "You're Damaso, right? I'm Astrid."

"Nice to meet you," I murmured, as she held out her hand with long, purple nails.

Everything about her reminded me of a vampire's victim: tall, slim, dark circles under her eyes, mauve lipstick and a Modigliani neck ripe for sucking, biting, licking or any other lecherous verbs that came to mind. She was wearing shorts so short the threads hanging from their unraveling hem grazed the tops of her sculpted white thighs, against which stood out, like a tattoo, a thicket of ink-black locks that hung almost to her knees. A pink leotard covered her torso thrusting her large breasts forward; her sharply outlined nipples held me spellbound until she said:

"I'm a friend of Gabriel's. He's told me so much about you."

"Thanks, old buddy," I thought, reminded of how Gabriel sent to my office a pleiad of nymphs who fancied themselves poetesses, who shyly clutched their ubiquitous composition book—with a famous actor's picture on the cover—which contained the verses they thought were as good as Alejandra Pizarnik's. Their poems were almost always terrible and the authors were bonbons who melted into a pool of honey at the slightest innuendo. The story always ended the same way: they'd go to bed with me, for the moment spurning their boyfriends and lovers of their dreams, only to disappear later with lightning speed, disillusioned by my lack of enthusiasm for their talent.

"I write, too, y'know." Astrid continued with the next phase of the ritual I knew by heart.

"Well, if you like, I'll take a look at your work. Poems, right?" I asked, as I completed the third phase.

"Of course. Prose is a genre for older writers," Astrid answered, straying from the script.

"So, how old are you?" I queried offhandedly, trying to get back on track.

"Nineteen. Same as Rimbaud when he started to write." She strayed from the role of the sweet young thing with long hair, wearing the ubiquitous thick-soled tennis shoes.

"You've read Rimbaud, Astrid?" I quizzed her, having no choice but to improvise.

"No, but Gabriel talks about him all the time. He says Rimbaud and Whitman invented twentieth century poetry."

"Sure in a way," I parried vaguely. Trying to get back on track, I added, "Well, so where're those poems of your?" My curiosity always gets the better of me.

"Right here." She held out a stack of pages typed and paper-clipped in the upper left hand corner. "Don't go easy on me. I'm prepared for the worst."

In a blink of an eye, she turned her back with a *ciao* so quick it stopped me cold as I was devising ways to get her into bed, put her in this or that position, do this and that move that dazzled the girls every time. I almost didn't get to ask:

"Astrid, how can I see you again… to tell you my opinion?"

"Oh, sorry. Here's my address. But call before you come by, OK?"

And she was gone, leaving her calling card in my hand.

To my surprise, Astrid's poems were the best I'd read by a novice. Still, it was clear she didn't know one iota about literature. That I had to correct. I had to give her a form that would bring to the forefront her throbbing naiveté and the passion lying deep beneath her surface, like a mysterious current. I re-read her original poems, afraid of getting carried away, not by their literary merits but by the author's quivering tits that cried out from under the leotard for the master's touch. The poems withstood the test. They talked about love, as usual, but a love carved deep by larceny, a love whose wounds revealed to the world death, lies, loneliness, anguish, uncertainty and all the things (God love 'em) that impinge upon a poet's repose.

A week later I dialed Astrid's number. As soon as she said,

"Come on over," I flew to the door of her two-story cottage that had a garden, fence, garage and glass Venetian blinds. At the door awaited the sweet poet inquiring in English:

"*Well then…*"

"*Well your poems are…*" I replied in English. Then in Spanish, I enumerated the virtues and defects I'd seen and the easiest way they could be retooled.

"Perfect! Just what I need to get my book off the ground. Your advice is really terrific. Did you mark the poems or do I need to memorize what you're saying?"

I told her I'd made some marks, but if she liked we—the plural gave away my willingness to be transformed, unconditionally, into her assistant—could take her poems in hand until they were ready for publication.

She jumped at that. "You think they could be published? Where? Is there anything you can do?"

I said yes, convinced that *yes* was the *open sesame* to Astrid's legs. I put out of my mind the fact that I was sweating ink to get my own book into print and send it to any prize that came along, then endure that sinking feeling of waiting for a verdict, unfavorable most of the time when not shamelessly fixed to benefit someone's protégé.

We spent the afternoon sitting on the porch, crossing out a line here, searching for the exact idea there, just the right adjective, the superfluous word. It dawned on me that, for the first time, I was sinking my claws into someone else's poem, molding it as if it were my own. To be truthful, I hate the literary teaching profession. The way I see it, writing's a field where a person should learn what's possible in a fierce battle between language and plot. No one should to tell you that removing and adding commas and nouns will earn you the right to posterity. Yet, in the mix now was Astrid's body, the female mammalian smell that emanated from her armpits, from between her legs, from the air she moved through leaving behind the desirable perfume that rendered a rake like me conquered by the inescapable force of that pair of tits.

On my second visit she introduced me to her father: a laid-back guy in his forties, dressed to the nines. He didn't seem to mind his daughter's new friendship with a guy ten years her senior who he could plainly see was wooing her. Her mother, she explained, lived at the beach, where she'd worked in tourism for a

decade. She had divorced Astrid's dad because she'd had the hots
for some teenager. She'd replaced him with a string of other guys,
so many that Astrid didn't know who was the love of her mom's
life at the moment. They were cordial, nothing more. Despite her
mother's open-mindedness, Astrid detected a certain decadence
she didn't want to lower herself to — at this point she became
exasperated — she didn't like to ask for anyone's help. What's
more she didn't want me to push her into a particular focus for
her book. Her tirade was followed by my apology and a
conciliatory torrent of words about how, in the end, the essence of
the poems comes from your head and heart. I'm just a skilled
craftsman who can fine-tune your talent at this unavoidable stage
of apprenticeship. Astrid smiled, flattered by my little speech and
burst into a flood of reasons to justify our continuing.

On the third visit, I (we) came up with the title for her book.
We'd give it an English title — *Alice Has Gone*. The title was the
same as one of the poems in which Astrid confessed how she had
cast off infancy and lost her virginity and her spirit in two or three
run-ins she'd had with the wolf pack that was our world, where
everyone wanted to gobble her up by appealing to faith, reason,
justice or love. That day, she declared to me her need to get down
to business, step into the spotlight not as a lovely libertine but as a
role model for everyone else. Her father always tried to get her
involved in something useful, she said. He pushed her into
studying languages (English, French, Italian), shorthand, typing,
computers, any other field that would help her deal with modern
life.

"But being someone's secretary is not my life's dream. I want
to have my own secretary."

Although she sounded overly ambitious, I thought it didn't
hurt to have the illusion of transforming herself into an efficient
executive with a big paycheck, her own house, car and a bullet-
proof intimacy. Still, I argued, a Hollywood dream is hard to
achieve. There's always that person who spends her whole life
pursuing status, only to realize in the end that this was not her
true path, that she had cast aside a much more clear-cut path when
there was still time.

"Cheap philosophy," she snapped. "You have to be the best at
what you do. That's the only way to get where you want to go."

And at that point, I saw that Astrid was also determined to be
a winner, one of those people who don't back down, but who leap

the imaginary bar of fulfillment a couple of inches higher than her sisters. Instead of scaring me off, that discovery turned me into a very nice, very adolescent guy. The only thing that occurred to me to do was smile and succumb to the spiderweb that was enfolding me.

I didn't see her for several months. She disappeared the way she arrived: unceremoniously. I didn't even get a good-bye note. How was it possible that I could miss her so much after such a short time? I'd gotten so used to having her around. I thought about her non-stop: Astrid at breakfast, midmorning on a boring day at work, during lunch gulped down on the run, in the afternoons as I corrected the manuscript of some erotic novel. My fantasies killed any desire I might have had to be satisfied in my ramshackle marriage, so I took refuge at night in front of the TV. It protected my wife and me from conversations that invariably ended in a fight. The trick of masturbating in the bath like some pimply-faced kid wasn't enough to exorcise my bad mood. Over and over I constructed and deconstructed situations where we would reach an agreement, we'd kiss and have sex for hours in the weirdest places. Then we'd start all over again. I'd analyze our dates searching for the moment when I should have said what I didn't or couldn't have known to say. Now I was trying to fix that moment in a vicious cycle that left me exhausted and spent. "Maybe she didn't like me. Maybe she just used me to put her book together and she figured out she had to flirt with me. Maybe she knows I'm a sucker for her type." I tortured myself with fruitless comparisons to the sexy stars she'd mentioned in passing—Kevin Costner, Rob Lowe, Brad Pitt or that Mexican soap opera star, Cesar Evora. I kept getting tangled up in brain-teasers and tongue-twisters that shattered my track record as a professional seducer.

"Hey, Damaso. Long time no see." I snapped out of my daydream, aware that someone was calling me from the other side of the street. When I turned around: Astrid.

"Hi," was all I managed.

"I need you," she said as she kissed me on the cheek. And she added, "There's a prize that's perfect for my book. Could you help me with a re-write?"

"Sure," I answered, forgetting all about my plans to get

revenge, to put distance between us when she turned up, to show her I wasn't the kind of guy you can use. I said I'd check my calendar because I was loaded down with work. She said it's not much, just a minor revision. Of course, I didn't hesitate for a second: when should we meet — not letting her get a word in edgewise — how about tonight? She said, looking down, doubtful, her house was out, they're having a party. I said I'll pick you up, let's go somewhere. Then I added, inspired, how about a restaurant? She said great and mentioned an expensive seafood place. Then, half repentant, I put on my *ay mi madre* face and made the excuse that it's hard to get a reservation. Astrid came back with don't worry, thank God Dad has a friend there, *Oh* and I'll pay, I know it's really expensive.

I started to protest politely but got nowhere. The next thing I knew, I was hanging around the door of that place, waiting for her in the half light. The book as just a pretext. I knocked back a couple of drinks and she explained that she'd spent the tourist season with her mother, we started to chat. Then we careened off course into the emotional realm when I recklessly proposed a flexible, unconventional relationship based on passion, not affection.

"Hey!" she laughed. "That wasn't so hard, was it? I thought you were shy. Not you! *Bam*! You say it all in one breath, then sit there waiting for my answer."

"Almost all," I countered, with a lack of tact I cynically call sincerity. "I'm married."

"I know, I don't care. I'm gonna be with you, not her."

With that, she sealed the pact, but the traditional kiss didn't materialize until much, much later, when I hinted, 'We can go to a place I know of close by. My hideaway. It's quiet and discrete."

"Sounds good," she murmured. Off we went to Abel's mother's apartment. His mother, who was in no hurry to return from the States, had bequeathed that hideaway to her son and me for our extramarital shenanigans. There Astrid played the role of the good girl who dwells in a romance novel but who lets herself be swept away in the whirlwind of my lasciviousness. As we caressed each other with lips, tongues, teeth, hands, thighs, and arms, she stripped, with a talent for undressing while making it seem like I'd undressed her. In my initial ecstasy provoked by the abundant foliage of her pubic down, I spread her across the bed face up and ran my mouth over her entire geography, delighting in valleys and crevices, hills and lagoons with the skill of a surveyor taking great pains not to miss an inch of ground. When my tongue had circumvented her armpits, butt, and inside her thighs and was poised to penetrate her savagely, ready to deposit the power of my language and the fertility of my saliva, Astrid lightly grasped me by the hair and panted, "No, please, I don't like that." Although her rejection inhibited me for a moment, I opted to slide on top of her and bury my sex in a humidity that eagerly swallowed it all, wrung it, rubbed it, squeezed it and made it eject its sap amid a gyration of sighs, words, sweat, sodomizing fingers, bits and rasping breaths of pleasure.

Astrid granted me a half truce during which she described traumas, cited a list of the men she'd been with and confessed that no other human had ever given her such pleasure the first time. That triggered her attack on me at all four points of the compass in a rare blend of candor and debasement. My blood heated to the temperature of that crater where I hurled myself again and again until, just barely conscious, I saw it was time to quit being joined like Siamese twins, shower, get dressed, take my captive home, promising to come by the next morning, and make it home before my wife finished her shift at the hospital.

Every since I was little, I've been afraid of dogs. All dogs. Even the ones barking behind a window. Or the ones that would make mincemeat of you on a public street if they weren't under their master's control. That's why I froze, in the middle of Astrid's living room, when she urged me to pet that monster named Herod.

"Thanks, but he's not my type. I prefer you naked."

"Well, get used to him. Herod's my protector at times like these."

"When the villain tries to get you into the sack?"

"No. When my dad and step mom take the kids to the beach for a week and leave me all alone so I can invite the villain over and prove Herod's an angel." She savored each letter with the pleasure that only someone who offers and reclaims Paradise can.

Without further ado, she sat astride the animal's head and rubbed her crotch against his snout. Then she sprawled out on the couch and let that creature's tongue go in search of her scent, familiar after God knows how many scenes like that. Astrid stroked his ribs with a growing frenzy, while her right foot slid voluptuously down his belly till it perched on the red appendix of his sex. Despite my disgust I had an unstoppable erection. Astrid grabbed my waist with her right hand, drew me to her and took my member in the blink of an eye. I became one of the legs in that unholy triangle in which the dog launched his sperm to the ceiling and mine went into Astrid's mouth. She seemed to levitate amid Herod's licks, my pelvic thrusts and her own hands, which were stimulating her nipples and ass.

"Now that's sucking! Everything else is just talk," Astrid pronounced, lying limp. Not wasting any time, she led us (the dog and me) up the stairs to the bedroom, urging me to strip along the way. There, as if by accident, a gigantic bed was placed in front of an even more gigantic mirror that reflected our images contorting in the preamble to sexual frenzy. Astrid climbed on top of me and busied herself with spreading the fluids of her vagina over every nook and cranny of me. Then she begged, "Take me from behind, *papi.*" Trying to contribute even a tiny kernel of my imagination, I picked up a deodorant bottle off her dressing table and stuck it through her vulva, while I pried open her tight anal sphincter with spit and perseverance. At that moment Herod, doubtless drawn by the girl's aroma, greedily licked my back, butt, balls, and finally even my ass, giving me a huge charge that accelerated my movements inside Astrid. Possessed from the front with the improvised dildo and from the rear by my phallus, she lost control of her undulations and a pre-conscious mechanism took over, purely and physically instinctive, born of the pristine nucleus from which spring pleasure and agony, thirst and hurricanes, fever and the oasis of spying ourselves again in the mirror: two sinners and a beast roasting in ecstasy in some dark caldron in Hell.

That morning we leapt the barrier and set off to try out infinite combinations (the dog here, there, in this, in that, with this in his paw and that in our mouth), baptize objects (perfume bottles, douche bag, cucumbers, bananas, bottle necks), founders of a cabal. Our need sharpened to come up with bolder and bolder variations until, on the eve of her family's return, Astrid posed a panic-stricken question:

"What'll we do afterwards?"

"I don't know. I guess we'll keep on like this," I answered, not understanding the question.

"I'm talking about a different *afterwards*. What we have'll end one fine day. Where'm I gonna find a guy as crazy as you, who'll share me with Herod?"

From that day on, the lady with the pooch became a drug. I found any excuse to be away from home to chase after them and fornicate with them: in her father's cottage, Abel's apartment or dimly lit alleys where we fearlessly took chances, protected by the ferocious-looking German shepherd.

My home life became even more vapid. Over and over, I shrunk from contact with my wife in favor of my exotic fantasies. No matter how much she improvised to give me pleasure, she couldn't come anywhere close to the multitude of sensations, whims, and dark appetites the dog and the girl aroused. That finally did in my marriage. The angry looks, shouts, vile word, and insults we traded became common knowledge in the neighborhood along with the jarring clatter of broken plates, the crash of pots and pans against the wall and even a few reciprocated slaps. One day I left that hell hole for good after I broke the tape player to smithereens, insulted my wife in a way I could never take back and finally hit her square in the face with a fresh tortilla that went flying out the frying pan despite my effort to control myself.

The situation was no better at my mother's house. Mom has the terrible habit of treating me like a baby at the tit. *Where're you going? Who're you going out with? When're you coming back?* are her favorite questions. On top of that, she constantly quizzes me about the state of my finances. She figures out that I have no cash and pulls it out of the air to smooth over my bad temper when she gets so overprotective. Even so, my diabolical side always wins out and I opt to fight back against maternal love by drinking so much it frees me from her sermons. I counter her accusations of abuse and insolence with such furor and violence that I get my point across. To top it off, the rum was flowing freely. Astrid's father supported his family by making and selling a bootleg whiskey popularly known as "train spark." He fermented molasses from the sugar mills in water, then boiled it in enormous pressure cookers. The vapor flowed out of the cooker through valves, wound along serpentine paths, and was cooled under the tank's spout, then finally filtered drop by drop, through a funnel containing activated charcoal and other chemical devices. The result was a hellacious alcohol that shredded your liver and left the taste of guilt and misery in your mouth and on your soul.

We went through Astrid's poetry manuscript so many times we nearly set a record. We typed it up and she went in person to turn it in at the contest headquarters. The prize consisted of three hundred pesos and publication. The bloom of skepticism was on her face, but when all was said and done, I knew she had faith in my expertise in fine-tuning books and secretly aspired to make off with the reward. Then it happened: I was invited to be a judge. I turned it down. The envoy insisted. He pointed out my professional success, my reputation for being incorruptible and the need to choose each judge carefully so the verdict wouldn't be in doubt and wouldn't affect the prestige of the sponsoring institution. I accepted reluctantly, not wanting to offend such an effusive admirer and the organization he represented. Astrid jumped for joy when she found out. After mulling it over, she said:

"You'll know what to do. No matter what happens, I trust you."

The following week I received the package of twenty-three manuscripts. After the first reading, I eliminated thirteen whose authors didn't have a clue about what poetry was. After the next reading only six survived, including Astrid's. The other five remaining contestants fell into two categories: two were friends and three I didn't know. With so much on the line, I set out to probe the second of the trio of judges (I couldn't count on the third judge since severe aesthetic differences separated us and had turned him into my enemy). He said what I wanted to hear. He proposed nearly the same finalists. "The book by the girl is very picturesque but it lacks something," he pronounced. My risky second attempt drifted into a long discussion sweetened by two bottles of liquor that contributed beyond measure to finding the missing "something." I praised *Alice Has Gone* to high heavens. It was easy. In a way, I was merely speaking well of myself. Three days later we got together with the remaining judge and crushed him with solid arguments outlined by my new-found comrade-in-arms (I intervened only when necessary). The ruling was unanimous in favor of Astrid's poetry collection.

On awards' night, my friends left the hall without saying good-bye. Gabriel glared at me and made a gesture that meant "this time you've gone too far." My fellow judges frowned in disgust when they saw how I had manipulated the judging to give the award to my lover. My reputation and the respect people had for me went to hell. Now I was just one more of those immoral people like all the rest. But I didn't care. In the crowd, struggling to keep a grip on Herod's leash, Astrid smiled, promising me glory.

"I'm leaving, Damaso. I can't stand this city or the people a minute longer." Astrid declared, two weeks later, during a late breakfast at Abel's mother's house.

"What? Where're you going?" I inquired a bit harshly.

"You think you control me?" She looked at me mockingly. "I guess I can go wherever I want, whenever I want."

"What I meant was, why're you leaving now," I replied, as I tried to calm down and study her, "when things are going so well between us?"

"Going so well?" she grumbled. "Your teeny weenie salary as a literary editor barely covers your smokes. Your wife no longer supports you so you can write and your mother's getting tired of taking care of you. As for me, I don't work and I can't support you. Daddy, who always sees the big picture, has started to ask questions…"

"OK, but…" I stammered, completely stymied.

"*But* nothing. We can't go on like this. We're both adults. You know what they say, 'where there's money, there's freedom.' If Daddy and your mom pay for everything, they'd make our life hell with all their conditions. I can't handle that. Mom got me a job as a tour guide. I have an interview tomorrow with the head of the agency."

"Astrid!"

"*Astrid* what? Someone's got to hustle up some cash, right? Doesn't look like it's gonna be you. On top of that, you're not writing a fucking line."

"I thought that…"

"That you were gonna live on credit? No, *papi*. You need to be someone's boy toy. My boy toy, that is. This little shit-eating girl is gonna get down to business and see if she can save some money. Maybe you'll want to marry her…" she paused to gauge the effect of her tirade and, a bit let down, continued. "You need to get your act together, stop chasing after culture and go into tourism, like me. With the languages you know and your looks, Mom could find something for you in no time. Housing wouldn't be a problem. After all the nice things I've said about you, she thinks you're a good guy."

Without knowing it, Astrid dashed our relationship to the ground. That argument was a repeat of the one I endured from my wife. Always the same opinions, the same answers, the same quarrels. True, breaking up was not a good plan, but not as bad as battling stupid tourists who thought I was some servile native willing to put up with any humiliation just to plunder the meager sum they had scraped together after months of sacrifice so they could go on a giddy spree in the Caribbean. I said flat-out *no*, let's find a third option and offered several plans, trying in vain to come up with a solution.

"I'm sorry, Damaso. My mind's made up." Seeing me turn away at that, she softened a bit. "This isn't the end of the world. I'll come see you on the weekends. Or you can come to Mom's place. She won't mind if we stay there a couple of nights."

Off she went. In a few days she called me at work but I wasn't there. In her message she said they'd hired her on the spot and left a number where I could get in touch with her. She reminded me to come see her that weekend. I didn't leave the office for the next three afternoons, a slave to the phone, lifting up the receiver with the childish hope of hearing Astrid's voice telling me that it was a disaster and that she'd be back in the city any time now. Friday morning I made up my mind. I wouldn't go to the beach. I had to show that chick I was no sap ready to jump at her whim. Surely first thing on Monday Astrid would call, asking for forgiveness or at least demanding an explanation.

That didn't happen. She never called again. I never could get in touch with her at the number she left. "Who's calling?" asked that voice all receptionists have. I got one story after another, about how she's on the yacht with some Italians, in the hotel with some Canadians, or playing badminton with some newly arrived Germans. I had no luck contacting her through her father. He suggested I talk to his ex-wife. Maybe I could get a line on Astrid's whereabouts from her. Nothing. Her mother never answered my SOS. I sent two or three feverish letters that went unanswered. I went crazy. My alcohol consumption and absences from work doubled. Without Astrid the world was shit.

Then the roof caved in: my wife filed for a divorce, I got fired, Abel and Gabriel refused to listen to my laments and told me how stupid I'd been, my mother cut back on my financial aid and I discovered that Astrid had taken Herod with her. So I made a plan: with what little money I had left, I bought a German shepherd puppy and tried to train him in fellatio and licking. No use. My phobic terror of dogs got in the way of any interaction with the animal. I tried in vain to persuade the most depraved of my ex-loves: those who could wouldn't and those who would were busy. I also dared to propose the experiment to the many faceless girls I went to bed with to console myself. Chaos. Soon after I'd sold the dog for half what he cost me and redoubled my efforts to drink myself to death, Astrid's only letter arrived.

Dear Damaso:

Life is unsettlingly complex. And one must take advantage of one's opportunities. As you can see, I'm writing from Düsseldorf. I've been living here for a month. When you kept me waiting for so long, it was hard to forgive you and even harder to get a grip on my affection for you. Then I met Jorgen. He's a rich industrialist's son and he fell madly and sincerely in love with me. Just like in Pretty Woman, you must be thinking. That's one way to look at it. Rest assured, he was the only one and I didn't beg him to take me to Europe. Since we met, he has proposed to me. His parents, who came to Cuba for a vacation, love me. At first I considered turning him down, but I realized that one doesn't get too many chances in life. One must seize them before it's too late. You said that yourself, right? So I accepted Jorgen as my husband and overnight became a young society lady. Prostitute? You could say that, although to my way of thinking, a very high class one. Perhaps we women were put on this earth to find a husband who'll support us and plant the seed of a strong, outstanding offspring. I believe that's the reason for adultery, prostitution and many of the wars past and future: the search for balance between love and happiness. In a way, I love Jorgen and I'm happy with him. I'm gong to try to return the huge favor he did me when he ushered me into his world. You were very important to me, but in the end you were unattainable. We weren't going anywhere. You don't inspire confidence for two reasons: you love yourself too much and you can't guarantee your own well-being. That's not a put down, just a eulogy. Protect your freedom from other women who, like me, will pass through your life and will be dazzled.

Kisses, good luck and don't waste your talent.

PS I forgot to ask three things of you: understand me, take care of Alice Has Gone and look after Herod, my other great loss. He loves you (in his own way, of course).

Astrid

Inside the envelope was a picture of her in winter clothes with a blond guy, handsome as Prince Charming, and a black Doberman with excellent markings. On the back it said: *Jorgen couldn't resist my admiration for dogs so he gave me this one. His name is Pilate. How's that for coming full circle?*

It took a long time to recover from the alcoholic crisis I'd slipped into. I rejected all company except for the bottle and, at first, Herod, whom I'd collected from Astrid's mother's house like the spoils of a lost war. But it didn't work. Without the girl's scent, the animal was incapable of giving pleasure. Instead he would growl, offended at my tentative attempts to go near him. We felt the same distress, lovers abandoned by the bitch in heat who has quit wagging her tail in front of our muzzle, wafting the aroma of her sex. Two males cut to shreds by the absence of the same female couldn't live together. I swapped Herod for six bottles of vodka. I submerged the zoophilous chapter of my life in the amnesia of a drunken binge that lasted nearly a year, if you add up all the drinks I imbibed, the scenes I caused, the hangovers, the vague and traumatic sexual episodes with women each more despicable than the one before, the fears, the blaming, the police stations, the loss of jobs and getting drunk all over again to erase the mishaps that were multiplying. Then someone handed me a lovely copy of *Alice Has Gone*.

Astrid decided, who knows when, to dedicate her book to me. The dedication read "To Damaso, his book," Of course it was. Why didn't I see that from the start? I was the writer. Astrid Torres Peralta was only a pseudonym for my female side that was returning to me after flirting with a handful of promiscuous readers. That saved me. I figured it was my duty to extract my sullied soul by writing a torrent of poems that would restore my image—in my eyes and in everyone else's. I wasn't going to let myself be done in by an apocryphal spirit, by someone who existed just to inspire me to write that poem. She'd played the part of an innocent lamb eager to hook up with the hungry wolf who didn't hesitate to tattoo her innocence with a series of degradations. Sure I'd made her swoon, but she abandoned me in a blink of an eye, refusing to be trapped in any prison except one of her own making.

Through fiction, I conjured up the truth of such a ridiculous time and prepared for the moment—not long in coming—when I started to write *Alice Comes Back*. In it I'd see Astrid get out of a tourist Jeep, walk over, greet me with a barely perceptible wink and not even have the decency to ask about Herod. Really it wouldn't be necessary. The lamb of my vision would be leading her new toy, the dog Pilate, by the leash; with the other hand, a devilish look in her eye, she'd be caressing the arm of her latest shepherd, the German.

Translated by Pamela Carmell

HOW MUCH I LOVE YOU
Jesús David Curbelo

For Tula, her story

Marcial Méndez was obsessed with two things: women and synonyms. When it came to women, things always went badly for him. Synonyms cost him friendships, jobs and all kinds of opportunities in life. In a conversation, he'd quit listening to what people were saying and get waylaid by some colorful word and by hunting for equivalents. At that moment nothing else on the face of this earth mattered. One synonym called up another, then another, until Marcial's head was spinning with so many words. Finally the people he was talking to threw up their hands. That happened with women, too. Once their initial enchantment with his striking good looks and his flowery, gushing eloquence had worn off, they were turned off by his distraction or his mania to stitch together concepts, phrases, and paragraphs all centered on a particular idea.

In those days, only Lucía had endured his verbal onslaught. Now here he was on this balmy afternoon, a perfect chance to reflect as he adjusted his step to the pace of his thoughts, tightening his grip on the metal strap, looking at the ground, sighing, going over and over those days. He'd forgotten that some palm reader, soothsayer, witch, sorceress, fortune teller, oracle or daughter of an African witch doctor had predicted a horrible, lunatic end to his love for Lucía.

He met her, such an enchantress, temptress, in the hustle and bustle of people lined up in front of the movie theatre. Her slender, delicate figure caught his eye as she touched her body, pretending to hunt for something that bothered her. She's careful and discrete, he thought, embarrassed to scratch in public, so her hands steal over arms as if stroking velvet. But he'd been watching her for a while and knew for sure she was scratching, rubbing, poking, chafing, scraping away at her skin.

He sidled up to her and whispered in her ear something banal to get the ball rolling. Something is really bugging you. Mosquitoes, I guess, she conceded. He blamed such an unbearable riot of mosquitoes on the rain, the puddles, the trees in the park nearby and the tangle of bushes in need of pruning, along with local health conditions and the shortage of pesticides. She agreed with him. He paid for their tickets and took her lightly by the elbow, certain his luck was changing.

It was. They were born to see that movie together where the leading man is chased through the jungle and has to survive swamps, wild animals, raging rivers, cannibals and a string of other dangers to marry the heroine and return to his ranch and live happily ever after. Marcial felt her twist and turn nervously in her seat. It must be the suspense, he told himself, but after a while all her moving around, her restlessness, her agitation grew worse and he started to lose his cool.

Something wrong? he asked. She blamed the mosquitoes again despite the air conditioning and he, bold and audacious, didn't wait for a better sign. He got all cutesy, reciting that ditty his schoolmates made him read in their gross-out autograph session so long ago. Before he could get to the last verse, the audience yelled for him to shut up and he was forced to swallow his words which got all balled up in his throat:

Iwouldliketobeamosquitoandgetinsideyourmosquitonetandtell youinalowvoicehowmuchiloveyou.

She got the idea and laughed, amused. He rubbed his hands together. He'd scored, closed the deal, sealed the pact; he could kiss those lonely Saturday nights good-bye. No more hanging around watching girls or being the third wheel with friends who dragged him along to bars and stadiums. Lucía was still restless and Marcial Méndez suggested, irresistibly, Let's take a walk when we get out of here. We could get a drink, talk for a while, maybe get some dinner.

She agreed, and Marcial, ready to shoulder the expense, also shouldered her little bugs. The mosquito in the movie became an ant in the bar, a fly in the street and a butterfly in the restaurant. She allowed him to walk her home—he only had to ask once— where it was more of the same, mixed with hope. A beetle, a cricket, a spider, a fly, a lightning bug, or some other kind of insect, predator or vermin that drove her to shrug, gnaw on herself, dig into every square inch of her body. When she couldn't stand it any longer, she excused herself, went to the restroom, turned her clothes and underwear inside out, then returned, all smiles saying it was just my imagination. Then she realized it was nearly her bedtime and Marcial Méndez hadn't managed to get more than a few measly kisses.

He looked at her legs, thighs, hips, eyes, lips and convinced himself that the heavenly girl Mann had imagined couldn't have been shaped any other way. Lucía was a princess. There was even a pea under her mattress. He figured that out in no time at that crummy hotel they'd checked into, seeking privacy. Give it a rest, Lucía, protested Marcial Méndez in the middle of a fit of scratch me here and check me out there. You're too old for Hans Christian Andersen fairy tales. Then moved to tears by all that scratching, she defended herself, saying I warned you, Marcial. I can't sleep or relax or even concentrate anywhere but in my own bed. He took that to be a good sign as he was leaving in the morning without having made love, dead tired from the fruitless search for fleas, bedbugs, lice and chiggers.

Every weekend it was the same absurd, tragic, hellish scene until he saw no alternative: Marcial Méndez got married and settled into Lucía's room, her bed, her sheets, her pillow: An extremely tidy oasis where she was isolated from invasions of arthropods and coleopterans. But he harbored doubts. Could this have been a stratagem, a plan, a ruse, a dirty trick to lure an unwary man into the ordeal of matrimony? Looking into Lucía's sweet suffering face and seeing the unceasing fury of her hands searching all over her body for the lone bug that got away, Marcial was persuaded that there was no deception. He took pride in her nakedness and her immodesty, and in the fact that they could alleviate the fatiguing search each time they reached the pinnacle of love making.

Admittedly, between his job, visits to in-laws and parents, and a couple of flings on the side that the very handsome Marcial Méndez allowed himself out of spite or out of the pleasure of being even more frustrated, his time at Lucía's side was limited to taking her to bed and molding their flesh in the act of surrendering, offering, relinquishing themselves to a whirlwind that exorcised her itching and left her in a state of grace until dawn. Most of the time. One night Marcial awoke with a start to feel Lucía's legs locked around his, twitching uncontrollably. A rictus of pain slashed across her face. Fearing a bad dream, Marcial brought her back to her senses. But it was worse. Check here, in my groin, I think there's a bug in there doing cartwheels. Crabs. He was horrified remembering his latest deceptions, frauds, adulteries, about how some unscrupulous beauty must have infected him with filthy, sucking lice that had turned up in his wife's crotch. He dreaded a fight that would take him back to those lonely Saturday nights, something he couldn't tolerate.

There's nothing wrong with you, nothing, he shouted, hysterical, trying to reassure himself that no critter was prowling around Lucía's pubic down. But she was in serious anguish. Know what? she confided. Lately I feel things crawling all over my skin. It's always been like that, he argued, as long as I've known you. I'll bet you're allergic. No, no, she broke in. This time it's different, it feels like they're inside me, floating around in my blood. In the next several days, he was afraid, ready to bolt, but he concealed it, joked around, pampered her, gave advice, kisses, and caresses. Asleep in his arms, Lucía was once again the heavenly girl, the princess from a distant land plagued by the pea. He kept recalling she'd been the girl of his dreams, the one he fell in love with. For her he was ready to take the biggest step of all, do the moral thing and create a family, something that usually did in other couples. He went even farther: he controlled his mania to eye the chicks, to propose weird rendezvous in some dark place, an elevator, a bus, a train or packed theater. Out in public he investigated her pelvic triangle, her buttocks, the small of her back, the swell of her breasts, as if finding his way back to Paradise depended on it. For her he even renounced synonyms and aspired to dumb down his language to a very basic level of communication, so she'd be happy and not overwhelmed in her affliction.

Still he worried when he saw her suffering and suggested that it might be bad circulation. That gave her hope, so they went to the doctor and inquired about the most effective cure. That wasn't it. They ruled out scabies, psoriasis, pitinasis and skin cancer; her blood sugar, platelets, her hemoglobin and the entire lymphatic system were normal; no parasite roamed around in her belly. Psychiatric tests yielded nothing out of the ordinary. But what had been uneasiness changed to desperation, frenzy and was never under control again. At all hours, night or day, he found her crazily raking her skin section by section, with a chilling, vehement, insane desire. He stopped having guests over, taking walks, going to social gatherings, because his private Lucía was revealing without shame all aspects of her mania. She talked about pruritis, rashes, bites, chafing and tingling and nothing else, at all hours of the day and night. Marcial Méndez feared her wild eyes, her unstoppable hands, her howls of fear and the negative side effects of taking the sedatives, drugs and potions they prescribed for her to drink, smear on, smell, put under the bed, around the patio or behind the door. He confessed to himself that he was powerless to live alongside this monster. He overcame the thought of being judged too self-centered, too cowardly and weak to confront life's difficulties and got up the courage to speak his mind. But he never had to go through with it. Wise nature played her part: Lucía died one morning in the middle of a microorganism attack. With hardly a fuss, her heart stopped beating. Too much excitement, the surprised doctor diagnosed. Marcial Méndez, a victim of mixed feelings, half sorrow, half stupor, sighed with relief.

Now, here he was on this balmy afternoon, a perfect chance to reflect. He adjusted his pace to the train of his thoughts, tightening his grip on the metal strap around the hearse. He sighed again, wondering whether, now that Lucía's lovely body was underground, she would have to endure the impertinence of earth worms, tape worms, cockroaches, mice and bacteria, whether such darkness would be enough to keep them from plaguing her forever. Without realizing, he let go of the galvanized ring on the side of the hearse and tried to wipe away the prickling feeling descending his forehead. There was nothing there, not even sweat. He looked up and saw that the chauffeur was driving with one hand, engrossed in a battle with some invisible presence in his hair. The mourner on his left was unbuttoning his shirt to dig immodestly in his armpits. The guy on the other side did the same. And then another guy. Then a woman. He looked back to the end of the line, refusing to believe what he saw: hundreds of faces with the same dazed look, brushing off their mourning coats, hats, skirts, ears, glasses, teeth. A strange laugh came to his lips. He stifled it in light of the solemn ceremony, although he had to admit how funny that pathetic coincidence was. It was the nightmare that completed his destiny. He tried to banish it from his thoughts along with the compelling desire to rub, scrape, scratch, brush himself off—and the urge to laugh. He couldn't help thinking that those bugs would get inside him and writhe around, frolic around, all the way up to his eyes. He let a belly laugh slip out, felt it change to tears, flight of fantasy, itches. And he let it all wash over him.

Translated by Pamela Carmell

NOTES ON THE WRITERS AND TRANSLATORS

THE WRITERS

Raúl Aguiar, born in Havana in 1962, is the author of the novels *La hora fastasma de cada cual* (Ediciones Unión, 1995) and *La estrella bocarriba* [The star face up] (Letras Cubanas, 2001), the novela *Mata* (Letras Cubanas, 1995), the story collection *Daleth* (Ediciones Extramuros 1996), and other stories anthologized in Cuba and abroad. His story "Figuras" won Cuba's 2003 Iberoamerican Short Story Prize. He graduated from the University of Havana with a degree in geography, and teaches writing at the Onelia Jorge Cardoso Center in Havana.

Alejandro Aguilar (Camagüey, 1958), although trained as a historian, has worked mainly in the performing arts, as a lecturer at U.S. universities, and as a training developer in the software industry. He is the author of three novels (*La desobediencia* [Disobedience], *Casa de cambio* [Bureau of exchange] – honorable mention for the Italo Calvino Prize, 1997– both published in Puerto Rico and mainland U.S.; and *Razones para llamar a Sandra* – finalist in the Casa de las Américas Prize for Fiction, 2001) – and two collections of short stories: *Paisaje de arcilla* [Clay landscape] and *Figuras tendidas* [Stretched out figures], which won the Manuel Cofiño Prize in 1999.

Nancy Alonso was born in Havana and graduated from the University of Havana with a degree in Biology in 1972. She was a professor and researcher at the Havana Institute of Medical Science for more than twenty years and served in Ethiopia as a Physiology professor at Jimma´s Institute of Health Sciences from 1989 to 1991. She has published two books of short stories: *Tirar la primera piedra*, [Casting the First Stone] which won Honorable Mention in the 1995 David Competition of the Cuban National Union of Writers and Artists (UNEAC) and *Cerrado por reparación*, [Closed for Repairs] winner of the prize for Women's Narrative "Alba de Céspedes" in 2002. Her stories have appeared in the anthologies *Estatuas de sal* [Pillars of Salt] (Ediciones UNIÓN, La Habana, 1996), *Rumba senza palme né caresse* (Besa, Nardó, 1996), *Cubana* (Beacon Press, Boston, 1998) *Habaneras* (Txalaparta, País Vasco, 2000), *Making a Scene*

(Mango, London, 2002), *Open your Eyes and Soar* (White Pine Press, Buffalo, New York, 2003), and *Mi sagrada familia* [My Sacred Family] (Editorial Oriente, Santiago de Cuba, 2004), among others. She is a member of UNEAC and is currently preparing two books of short stories.

Aida Bahr (Havana, 1958) has recently completed a novel, *Las voces y los ecos* [Voices and echoes], and is at work on another one. She is director of a publishing house in Santiago, Cuba, Ediciones Oriente, and editor of their magazine. Her work has appeared in many anthologies in Spanish and in translation into other languages. She is the author of several collections of stories, including *Hay un gato en la ventana* [There's a cat in the window] (1984), *Ellas de noche* [Women at night] (1989), *Espejísmos* [Mirror images] (1998), and several screenplays.

Marilyn Bobes (Havana, 1955) is a short story writer, poet and journalist. She studied history at the University of Havana, and worked as a journalist for the Latin American press agency, Prensa Latina, and for the magazine *Revolución y Cultura*. In 1979 she received the David Award for Poetry for her book *La aguja en el pajar* [The needle in the haystack]. For her fiction, she has received an Edmundo Valadés award (Mexico, 1993) and second place in the Magda Portal competition (Peru, 1994). Her books include *Hallar el modo* (poetry, 1989), and *Alguien tiene que llorar* [Somebody has to cry], (from which the story included here is taken) winner of the Casa de las Américas prize in 1995, and *Alguien tiene que llorar también* (2001). She was a co-editor of the anthology of Cuban women's stories *Estatuas de sal* [Pillars of salt] (1996). Her novel, *Fiebre invernal* [Winter Fever], won the 2005 Casa de las Américas Prize.

Jesús David Curbelo (Camagüey, 1965) has published many volumes of poetry as well as collections of short stories (*Cuentos para adúlteros* [Stories for Adulterers] in 1995 and *Tres tristes triángulos* [Three Sad Triangles] in 2000) as well as novels: *Inferno* in 1999 and *Diario de un poeta recién cazado* [Diary of a Newly Caught Poet) in 1999. The many prizes he has won include the David Prize for Poetry in 1991 and the José Soler Puig Award for fiction in 1998.

Eduardo del Llano (Moscow, 1962) has lived in Havana since 1964, and has a degree in Art History from the University of Havana. A writer of fiction, poetry, essays and film scripts, he has published collections of poetry (*Nostalgia de la babosa*, 1993), six novels (some in collaboration with others), the most recent of which are *La clessidra di Nicanor* (1997), *Obstáculo* (1997) and *Tres* (2002). His eight collections of short stories iclude *Criminales* (1994), *El beso y el plan* (1997), *Cabeza de ratón* 1998 and *Los viajes de Nicanor* (2000). He has taught Latin American art, photography and film studies at the University of Havana and elsewhere, has won many prizes and awards, and has participated in many international film festivals.

Adelaida Fernández de Juan (Havana, 1961) is a physician specializing in internal medicine, and author of many short stories, including those published in the volumes *Dolly y otros cuentos africanos* (1994) about her experiences in Zambia 1988-90. It appeared in English as *Dolly and Other African Tales.* Her second story collection, *Oh vida* [Oh life] (1998) won the National Short Story Prize of the Cuban National Union of Writers and Artists. Her story "El beso" [The kiss] received Honorable Mention in the 2004 Julio Cortázar Short Story Competition. *La hija de Darío* [Darió's Daughter], her third book of stories, won the 2004 Alejo Carpentier Prize. *Nadie es profeta* [No one is a Prophet], her first novel, was published in 2006.

Mylene Fernández Pintado (Havana, 1963) is a practicing lawyer who represents the Instituto Cubano del Arte e Industria Cinematográficos (ICAIC). Her stories have won prizes in the *La Gaceta de Cuba* competitions, in the Spanish 1998 III Premio de NH de Relatos awards, and the Cuban National Union of Writers and Artists' Premio David in Cuba for her collection of short stories, *Anhedonia* (1999). Her novel *El otro lado del espejo* [The Other Side of the Mirror] has just been published. Her work has appeared in many anthologies in Spanish, and in translation.

Francisco García González (Havana, 1963) has a degree in History from Havana University. He is a writer, editor, and screenwriter. His short story collections include *Juegos permitidos* [Games Allowed] (1994), *Color local* [Local Color] (1999) and *¿Qué quieren las mujeres?* [What Do Women Want?]

(2003). He has also published a historical essay, *Presidio Modelo, temas escondidos* [Model Prison, Hidden Agendas] in 2002, and *Historia sexual de la nación* in 2006. His stories have appeared in anthologies in Cuba, Spain, and the U.S. He won Cuba's Hemingway Short Story Prize in 1999, and has served as editor of the cultural journal *Habáname.* His articles have appeared in periodicals in Cuba, Mexico, Chile and the U.S. He is the author of many film scripts.

Alexis Sebastián García Somodevilla (Havana, 1964) won the Caimán Barbudo prize in 1989, for his collection of short stories, *El deshollinador* [The Chimney Sweep], published in Cienfuegos in 2000. His collection *Senderos virtuales* [Virtual paths] was published in 2002. He is the Librarian of the Archivo Provincial Histórico of Cienfuegos.

María Elena Llana (b. 1936), journalist and poet as well as a short story writer, is the author of *La reja* [The Gate] (1965), *Casas del Vedado* [Vedado Homes] (1983) winner of that year's Critics' Prize, and *Castillos de naipes* [Houses of Cards] (1998), which includes "The Rooms." Her latest two collections, *Ronda en el malecón* [Loitering on the Malecón] and *Apenas murmullos* [Barely Murmurs], which includes "A Five-Hundred Year Old Rum," were published in 2004.

Ronaldo Menéndez Plasencia was born in Havana, Cuba in 1970. His stories have appeared in numerous anthologies in Cuba including *Los últimos serán los primeros, Anuario UNEAC 1994, Fábula de ángeles,* and *El ánfora del diablo,* among others. He is the author of four books: *Alguien se va lamiendo todo,* winner of the Premio David (Ediciones Union,1996); *El derecho al pataleo de los ahorcados,* winner of the Premio Casa de las Américas (Lengua de Trapo, 1998); *La piel de Inessa,* winner of the Premio Lengua de trapo de Narrativa (Lengua de Trapo, 1999); and *De modo que esto es la muerte* (Lengua de Trapo, 2002).

Miguel Mejides (Camagüey, 1950) won the David prize for his 1977 book *Tiempo de hombres* [Time of Men], the 1981 UNEAC Rodríguez prize for *El jardín de las flores silvestres* [The Wildflower Garden] and the Juan Rulfo short story prize in 1994 for "Rumba-Palace," published in 1996. He has also published novels such as *La habitación terrestre* [Inhabiting the Earth] and *Perversiones en el Prado* [Perversions in the Prado].

Leonardo Padura Fuentes (Havana, 1955) essayist, journalist, and novelist is famous for his series of detective novels ("The Four Seasons") featuring the exploits of Mario Conde. He has received numerous national and international prizes and has published two books of stories: *Según los años pasan* [As the years go by] and *La puerta de Alcalá y otras cacerías* [The Alcalá Gate and other hunting scenes]. He has published books of interviews about salsa and baseball, as well as many critical essays. Recent works include: *Adiós Hemingway* [Goodbye Hemingway] (2001), *Culture and the Cuban Revolution* with John Kirk in 2001, and another Mario Conde novel, *La neblina del ayer* [The Mist of Yesterday] (2005). His works have been translated into numerous languages.

Senel Paz (Havana, 1950), one of Cuba's best-known writers, won the Juan Rulfo Prize for best short story in 1990. His prize-winning story, "El lobo, el bosque y el hombre nuevo" [The Wolf, the Forest, and the New Man], became an international success as the popular movie *Fresa y chocolate* [Strawberry and Chocolate], directed by Tomás Gutiérrez Alea. Paz was co-author of the *Fresa y chocolate* script and has continued scriptwriting in both Cuba and Spain. He has written a novel scheduled for release in early 2007.

Antonio José Ponte, poet, fiction writer and essayist. Two collections of his poems have been published: *Poesía (1982-1989)* (Ediciones Letras Cubanas, 1991) and *Asiento en las ruinas* (Ediciones Letras Cubanas, 1997). He has published five collections of essays. Two volumes of his short stories have been published in English translation: *In the Cold of the Malecón*, translated by Cola Franzen and Dick Cluster (City Lights, 2002) and *Tales From the Cuban Empire*, translated by Cola Franzen (City Lights, 2002). His first novel, *Contrabando de sombras* [Trafficking in Shadows] was published by Mondadori (Barcelona, 2002). He recently completed a second novel titled *La fiesta vigilada* [The Closely Watched Fiesta], to be published in Spain by Anagrama in 2007. He lives in Havana.

Ena Lucía Portela, born in Havana (1972) where she still lives, is a novelist and short story writer. She won the UNEAC National Novel Prize in 1997 forher first novel, *El pájaro: tinta china y pincel* [The bird: Chinese ink and pen], published in 1999, as was her collection of short stories, *Una extraña entre las piedras* [A strange woman among the stones]. She was the recipient of the Juan Rulfo Short Story Prize given by Radio France International in 1999 for her short story, "El viejo, el asesino y yo" ["The old man, the assassin and I"]. Her novel *La sombra del caminante* [The walker's shadow] was published in 2001, and a third novel, *Cien botellas en una pared* [One hundred bottles on a wall], won the Jaén Novel Prize in Spain in 2002.

José Antonio Quintana Veiga lives in Nueva Gerona on Cuba's Isle of Youth. He has published three books of short stories including *Precio de los zapatos* [The Price of Shoes] (Nueva Gerona, 2002) and the novel *Callejera*. His story "Mi amor y mi caña," included here, won the first honorable mention in the annual best short story contest of *La Gaceta de Cuba*, magazine of the National Union of Cuban Writers and Artists.

Karla Suárez was born in Havana in 1969, and presently resides in Paris, where she is a systems engineer, much of the year. Her collections of stories, *Espuma* [Foam], published in 1999, and *Carroza para actores* [Carriage for actors], which includes the stories included here, published in 2001, have won many awards. Her first novel, *Silencios* [Silences], received the Lengua de Trapo Fiction Prize in 1999, and has been translated into many languages, and her second novel, *La viajera* [The traveler] was published in 2005.

Anna Lidia Vega Serova was born in 1968 in St. Petersburg, Russia, daughter of a Cuban father and a Russian mother. She has lived in Havana since she was 20, and writes exclusively in Spanish. She is also a painter. She won the 1996 Special Prize of the Asociación Hermanos Saíz, and the 1997 Premio David for her collection of stories *Bad Painting* (1997). Her second volume of stories, *Catálogo de mascotas* [Catalog of mascots] was published in 1998, and the third, *Limpiando ventanas y espejos* [Cleaning windows and mirrors] in 2001. Her most recent book is a novel, *Noche de ronda* [Nightwatch], 2004.

Mirta Yañez (Havana, 1947), has written fiction, poetry, literary criticism, and children's books, and has taught Latin American literature at the University of Havana. In 1988 and 90 she won the Critics' Prize for the story collection *El Diablo son las cosas* [To the devil with it] and for the essay *La narrativa del romanticismo en Latinoamérica* [Romantic narrative in Latin America]. Other books she has published include *Las visitas y otros poemas* [The visits and other poems] (1986), *Una memoria de elefante* [An elephant's memory] (1991). She is the co-editor of the anthology of Cuban women's stories *Estatuas de sal* [Pillars of salt] published in 1996, and the editor of *Cubana: Contemporary Fiction by Cuban Women* (1998).

THE TRANSLATORS

Mary G. Berg's recent translations from Spanish include editions (*Open Your Eyes and Soar: Cuban Women Writing Now* (2003), novels: *I've Forgotten Your Name* (2004) by Martha Rivera (Dominican Republic); *River of Sorrows* (2000) by Libertad Demitrópulos (Argentina); and *Ximena at the Crossroads* (1998) by Laura Riesco (Peru), as well as stories, women's travel accounts, literary criticism, and collections of poetry, most recently *Quincunx* and *The Book of Giulio Camillo* by Carlota Caulfield (Cuba) and *Antonio Machado's The Landscape of Castile* (with Dennis Maloney). She teaches at Harvard Extension and is a Resident Scholar at the Women's Studies Research Center at Brandeis University, where she writes about Latin American writers, including Clorinda Matto de Turner, Juana Manuela Gorriti, Soledad Acosta de Samper, and contemporary Cubans.

Pamela Carmell teaches Spanish in St. Louis. She has translated Luisa Valenzuela, Manuel Puig, Gloria Fuertes, and Delmira Agustini, among others. Her translations have appeared in numerous journals and anthologies. Her translation of Antonio Larreta's novel, *The Last Portrait of the Duchess of Alba* was a Book of the Month Club selection. Her translation of poems by Belkis Cuza Male, *Woman on the Front Lines*, received the Witter Bynner Prize. She is co-translator of *With Eyes and Soul*, poems by Nancy Morejón, published by White Pine Press in 2004. Carmell's translation of *The Last Cato*, the best-selling novel in Spain by Matilde Asensi, was published by Rayo/Harper Collins in 2006. She is at work on the translation of José Lezama Lima's *Oppiano Licario*, forthcoming from Dalkey Archive Press.

Dick Cluster's translations of Cuban fiction include *Cubana: Contemporary Ficton by Cuban Women* (Beacon, 1998, ed. Mirta Yáñez, tr. with Cindy Schuster); Pedro de Jesús, *Frigid Tales* (City Lights, 2002); Alejandro Hernández Diaz, *The Cuban Mile* (Latin American Literary Review Press, 1998); Antonio José Ponte, *In the Cold of the Malecón and Other Stories* (City Lights, 2000, tr. with Cola Franzen); Leonardo Padura, *Mascaras* (selection, Whereabouts Press, 2002); and Abel Prieto, The *Flight of the Cat* (Random House Mondadori, 2005). He is also the author of the novels *Return to Sender* (Dutton, 1988), *Repulse Monkey* (Dutton, 1989), and *Obligations of the Bone* (St. Martins, 1992), and, with Rafael Hernández, of History of Havana (Palgrave MacMillan, November 2006), a popular social history of the Cuban capital.

Cristina de la Torre has translated novels by Rosa Montero (Spain), Carmen Riera (Spain) and Nora Strejilevich (Argentina) as well as numerous short stories, many of them by authors from Cuba where she was born. She has received translation fellowships from NEH, the Howard Foundation, and the Banff International Centre for Translation. De la Torre lives in Atlanta and teaches Spanish and literary translation at Emory University.

Anne (Anita) Fountain was born in Buenos Aires and earned graduate degrees at Indiana University and Columbia University. She teaches Latin American literature and culture and coordinates Latin American Studies at San José State University. Her recent publications include: *José Martí and U.S. Writers* (2003) and *Versos Sencillos: A Dual Language Edition* (2005). Her translations of Martí's poetry have also appeared in: *The New Anthology of American Poetry (Vol. I: Traditions and Revolutions, Beginnings to 1900* (2003); *A History of Modern Latin America* (2nd edition) (2005); and *Bomb Magazine*, summer

2004. Her translation of Nancy Alonso's *Cerrado por Reparación* [Closed for Repairs] is forthcoming from Curbstone Press.

Cola Franzen's recent publications include *Horses in the Air and Other Poems* by Jorge Guillén (City Lights, 1999), bilingual, winner of the Harold Morton Landon Translation Prize awarded by the Academy of American Poets; *All Night Movie*, novel by Alicia Borinsky, translated with the author (Northwestern UP, 2002), and two volumes of work by Saúl Yurkievich: *Background Noise/ Ruido de fondo*, poems, and *In the Image and Likeness*, prose pieces (Catbird Press, 2003). In 2004 she received the Gregory Kolovakis Award from PEN American Center. She lives in Cambridge, Massachusetts.

Louise Popkin's translations of Latin American poetry, drama and fiction have appeared in literary journals such as *Beacons, Kenyon Review, Triquarterly* and *Mid-American Review* and in anthologies of literature in translation. Authors whose work she has translated include Claribel Alegría (Nicaragua), Ricardo Elizondo and Héctor Manjarrez (Mexico), Margarita Niemayer and Sonia González Valdenegro (Chile), Mempo Giardinelli and Juan Gelman (Argentina), Mario Benedetti, Teresa Porzcekanski, Leo Masliah, Idea Vilariño, Amanda Berenguer, Eduardo Galeano, Hugo Achugar, Hiber Conteris and Mauricio Rosencof (Uruguay). Her most recent publication is a translation of Rosencof's *The Letters that Never Came* (U. of New Mexico Press, 2004). She divides her times between Montevideo, Uruguay, and the Boston area, where she teaches Spanish at Harvard Extension.

Barbara D. Riess has translated the Chicano novels *Puppet* (University of New Mexico Press, 2000) and *Sanctuaries of the Heart* (University of Arizona Press, 2004) by Margarita Cota-Cárdenas. She was the translation editor for *Postmodernity in the Periphery: Latin America Writes Back. An Interdisciplinary Cultural Focus.* (Emil Volek, ed. Routledge Press, 2002) and contributed to *Spain: A Traveler's Literary Companion.* (Peter Bush, Lisa Dillman, eds. Whereabouts Press, 2003). She received her PhD in Latin American Literature and Translation from Arizona State University in 1999 and is currently an Assistant Professor of Spanish at Allegheny College. Presently, she is working on a manuscript on Cuban women's short fiction during the revolution and a collection of short stories by María Elena Llana in translation tentatively titled *Havana's Survivors: Those that Neither Left nor Stayed Behind.*

Guatemalan-born **David Unger** has just completed a new novel, *In My Eyes, You Are Beautiful.* He is the author of *Life in the Damn Tropics* (Syracuse University Press, 2002, Wisconsin University Press, 2004, [*Vivir en el maldito trópico* : Random House Mondadori, Mexico, 2004; Recorded Books 2005; Locus Publishing, Taiwan, 2006 and Yingpan Brother Publishing, China, 2007]). He has translated eleven books, among them Teresa Cárdenas's *Letters to My Mother* (Groundwood Books, 2006), Rigoberta Menchú's *The Honey Jar* (Groundwood Books, 2006) and *The Girl from Chimel* (Groundwood Books, 2005), Ana María Machado's *Me in the Middle* (Groundwood Press, 2002), Silvia Molina's *The Love You Promised Me* (Curbstone Press,1999, Sor Juana Inés de la Cruz Prize and shortlisted for the 2001 IMPAC Prize); *The Popol Vuh* (Groundwood Press, 1999); Elena Garro's *First Love* (Curbstone Press); Bárbara Jacobs' *The Dead Leaves* (Curbstone Press); and Nicanor Parra's *Antipoems: New and Selected* (New Directions).